D1248466

Everybody Loves Somebody Sometime

(Especially Himself)

Other Books by Arthur Marx

The Ordeal of Willie Brown
Life with Groucho
Not as a Crocodile
Son of Groucho

Broadway Plays

The Impossible Years
Minnie's Boys

The Story of DEAN MARTIN and JERRY LEWIS

Everybody Loves Somebody Sometime

(Especially Himself)

ARTHUR MARX

HAWTHORN BOOKS, INC.
Publishers/NEW YORK

To
Lois,
Andy,
Steve,
Perry,
Elsie,
and
Groucho

Library of Congress Catalog Card Number: 73-14235

ISBN: 0-8015-2430-X

First Printing, July 1974
Second Printing, August 1974
Third Printing, November 1974

Contents

Acknowledgments

My thanks to the following people, who so graciously granted me in-depth
interviews:

Goodman Ace
Joey Adams
Steve Allen
Herbie Baker
Seymour Bernes
Norman Blackburn
Joe Bleeden
Buddy Bregman
Judy Briskin
Jay Burton
Rita Chandler
Herman Citron
Freddy Fields
Gloria Franks
Norman Frisch
Jerry Gershwin
Ernest Glucksman
Hal Goodman
Ed Hartman
Al Gordon
Abel Green
Cy Howard
Charlie Isaacs
Sheldon Keller
Donald Kreiss
Norman Lear

Sheldon Leonard
Jacques Leslie
Dino Martin, Jr.
Elizabeth Martin
Jeanne Martin
Don McGuire
Al Melnick
Bill Miller
Lou Perry
Artie Phillips
Milton Pickman
Marshall Robbins
Walter Seltzer
Marie Shear
George Sidney
Ed Simmons
Louis Sobol
Dick Stabile
Ben Starr
Joe Sully
Norman Taurog
Alexander Tucker
Hal Wallis
Harry Warren
Julie Wilson
Bud Yorkin

Everybody Loves Somebody Sometime
(Especially Himself)

♩Introduction

In 1956, when it became fact and not just gossip column rumor that Dean Martin and Jerry Lewis were breaking up as a team, comedian Lou Costello published an open letter in the Hollywood trade papers begging the comics to forget their petty differences and go back together again.

They owed it to their fans, wrote Costello. In deference to the millions who had helped them make millions, he advised Martin and Lewis to sacrifice their egos, just as he and his own partner, Bud Abbott, had learned to sacrifice theirs.

Almost before the ink was dry on the *Hollywood Reporter* and *Daily Variety*, Abbott and Costello had a bitter fight of their own and broke up, with Costello going off to New York to be a regular on a weekly TV variety show Steve Allen was hosting and Abbott, ailing from the shock of the split, checking into a hospital for treatment.

That story illustrates better than most the tenuous relationship of most show business partnerships. If two partners aren't willing to sublimate their own egos, give in on important business decisions, and make great compromises in their respective life-styles, they are going to spend a great deal of time arguing, their work will suffer, and eventually they will break up.

The fate of most show business partnerships is just another bleak page in the history of man's inability to get along with his fellow men—even at the expense of his own career, his own pocketbook.

Gilbert and Sullivan, Gallagher and Shean, Kaufman and Hart, Clark and McCullough, the Marx Brothers, Wheeler and Woolsey, Abbott and Costello, Marge and Gower Champion, Nichols and May, and Lerner

3

and Loewe all scored their initial triumphs as partnerships, only to dissolve the winning combinations at the pinnacles of their careers.

The pattern seems to hold true no matter how successful the team may be or what its money-making potential is for the future. At the time Martin and Lewis decided to get a divorce from each other, the combination hadn't even begun to tap its money-making potential.

In the ten years since they had first teamed up in a second-rate nightclub in Atlantic City, the value of their act had skyrocketed from a modest $600 a week to a position in the entertainment industry where the combination was worth, in terms of raw box office gross, $20 million annually from films, nightclub engagements, records, and their weekly NBC television show.

Breaking up such a successful combination didn't make any sense, which is why most of Martin and Lewis's friends, relatives, agents, and business advisers opposed the move. But who ever said that performers with colossal egos to feed always acted sensibly? Once they made up their minds to split, all of their agents and all that money couldn't put Martin and Lewis back together again.

So, regardless of the consequences, the dissolution was to be made permanent following the pair's final two weeks at New York's Copacabana in July 1956.

Martin and Lewis's final show together—July 24, 1956—was a sad affair for the many friends, fans, and the merely curious who jammed the Copa to pay their last respects to the team and, not incidentally, to watch Lewis bury Martin.

In a business where nothing is ever certain except that the "box office" is usually lousy the week before Christmas, there was one thing most of the Broadway wise guys were willing to make book on: Jerry, a born clown in the mold of Charlie Chaplin, would go on to bigger and more spectacular comedic accomplishments, while Dino, who at best was nothing more than a pallid imitation of Perry Como and Bing Crosby, would unquestionably be consigned to a life of crooning in second-rate nightclubs, until booze, dames, and his obvious lack of big-time charisma would sink him in the quagmire of show business oblivion.

Martin and Lewis had never been better than on their final night together at the Copa, where, it seemed, every celebrity in Manhattan had gathered to see the swan song of a great act.

They pulled out every schtick in their comedy bag for the star-studded audience—from squirting seltzer down Milton Berle's shirt front to cutting off Monte Proser's necktie.

The sophisticated café society crowd wouldn't let them quit. When finally there wasn't another laugh to be milked, the twosome sang a chorus of "Pardners" (from the Lewis and Martin film of the same name), joined hands for a last bow, and then hugged each other awkwardly.

Suddenly, out of the crowd stepped old Mr. Show Business himself—Jackie Gleason—lachrymose from the sentimentality of the occasion and also seven or eight highballs. Jumping onto the stage, he grabbed a mike, wiped away a tear the size of a Blarney stone from his eye, and said, "Folks, this can't be allowed to happen."

The audience roared its approval. Martin and Lewis smiled wearily and shook their heads negatively. This was it. Finis.

Many in the audience actually wept—but mostly for their beloved Dino and what was to become of him. Nobody was worried about Jerry Lewis. At thirty, he was still young enough to make a new start. He had more *chutzpah* than Howard Cosell. And he was a "big talent."

1

By the Sea, By the Sea, By the Beautiful Sea

The late Sophie Tucker, a show business legend in her own time, was strolling along the boardwalk in Atlantic City, New Jersey, one muggy July afternoon in the mid-1940s when she spotted a crowd gathering at a point along the beach. They were watching the waterlogged form of a skinny youth being hauled from the surf by a handsome, Italian-looking man, who apparently was the victim's friend.

As the spectators closed in, a lifeguard brushed the rescuer away and started applying artificial respiration to the half-drowned youth. After a few suspenseful moments, the victim suddenly sat up, winked at the throng, and exclaimed, "If you think I'm dying now, come and see us entertain tonight at the Club 500."

Then, to the bewilderment of his audience, he leaped to his feet and ran down the beach with his Italian cohort.

The date was July 25, 1946—almost a year since nuclear explosions over Nagasaki and Hiroshima had rocked the globe and brought a surprising but welcome end to World War II. Harry Truman was president. Douglas MacArthur and Dwight Eisenhower were heroes, and "To Each His Own" was number one on "The Hit Parade."

The American people, after four years of wartime austerity—gas rationing, tire rationing, food rationing, wage and price controls, and casualty lists—were ready for a good laugh. And the two con artists Sophie Tucker had seen tricking the public on the beach were standing in life's wings, waiting to supply it, if only they could trap a few people into the Club 500.

Their names, which will come as no surprise to anyone who picks up this book, were Dean Martin and Jerry Lewis. But, at the time, they were completely unknown to everyone except their wives, girl friends, mothers, and possibly their agents.

Both were young—Martin was twenty-nine, and Lewis barely twenty; both had been doing "singles" and getting absolutely nowhere until fate teamed them up in Atlantic City; and both were totally unprepared for the lightning that was about to strike and make them not only wealthy men but show business legends in their own right.

Certainly nothing in either of their backgrounds augured any future theatrical stardom—Martin's early life, in particular.

But to coin a phrase (with a little help from that old hack William Shakespeare): "Some people are born stars, some achieve stardom, and some have stardom thrust upon them."

In Martin and Lewis's case, it was probably a little of all three, but with the emphasis on the latter.

2

I Don't Want to Set the World on Fire

Looking backward, the secret of Dean Martin's extraordinary success has always seemed to be "complete indifference" when opportunity comes knocking—whether the person doing the knocking is the president of NBC with a million-dollar job offer or a beautiful girl who'd like to become his wife.

At every important juncture in Martin's life, he has tried to turn his back on what would seem to others to be a "once in a lifetime" opportunity to be touched by the man with the golden scepter, only to have fate quickly interfere and reject his rebuff.

Only a man with tremendous self-confidence, probably the result of inherited wealth and a degree from Harvard, could get away with such an attitude. Dean Martin had none of that going for him in the beginning. In fact, Dean Martin isn't even his real name.

Martin was born Dino Paul Crocetti on June 17, 1917, in Steubenville, Ohio. He was the second son of an Italian immigrant couple—Guy Crocetti, a barber by trade, and his wife Angela. Martin's brother Bill was born in 1914 and, until his death in 1963, managed Dino's business affairs.

Guy Crocetti had emigrated to America from Italy at the beginning of World War I and had chosen Steubenville as a place to settle his family on the recommendation of his two brothers, who had already preceded him to this vice-ridden city on the banks of the Ohio River.

At the time, Steubenville had a population of about 20,000—a large proportion of whom were Italian, Irish, and Swedish immigrants who had been attracted there because of the town's proximity to the Weirton and the Wheeling steel mills directly across the Ohio River in West Virginia.

The steel mills needed cheap unskilled labor and Steubenville's immigrant masses could supply it.

In addition to being the source of cheap labor, Steubenville also supplied the nation with croupiers and stickmen. Steubenville was a wide-open town during the years when young Dino was growing up. Prostitution and gambling were rampant. Gamblers referred to it as "Little Chicago." In Steubenville, a person bent on sinful pleasures could find a whorehouse or a gambling joint as easily as he could a drugstore. About the only place in Steubenville where a person couldn't place a bet was the barber shop where Guy Crocetti worked.

Guy Crocetti was as honest as he was the perfect prototype of the Italian immigrant barber who plied his trade in small-town USA in the first quarter of the twentieth century.

He was about average height, slightly built, with a long thin face, shiny black curly hair, a large Roman nose, a fastidious-looking hairline mustache, and eyes the color of ripe olives that gazed sadly out at the world from under an awning of shaggy eyebrows.

Compared with Steubenville's main occupations—gambling and bootlegging—barbering seemed like a nonprofit business. A shave and a haircut cost only twenty-five cents in those days. But everything else was cheaper too, and it was possible for a barber to clip out a modest living if he stuck to his chair ten hours a day and worked all day Saturdays too.

"Pop worked hard—too hard," recalls Martin, with a faraway look in his sad dark eyes. "It eventually killed him." (This is one reason why Martin, who has been referred to as the "world's champion hedonist," refuses to put work before pleasure today.)

"But we Crocettis had everything we wanted. I had a bicycle. He had a little house, a car, and good food. As a cook, my mother was the greatest. Her specialties were spaghetti and meat balls, veal and peppers, or sausages and peppers."

It was peasant fare, but Mama Crocetti's cooking obviously agreed with the young Dino.

By the time he was fourteen years old, he had grown into a six-foot 146-pounder with wavy black hair and a husky figure. The only flaw in his looks was a large aquiline Italian nose, which, by its owner's own admission, had no indentation where the bridge met his forehead.

Although it's apparent that Martin didn't exactly lead the classic Dickensonian childhood of deprivation we've all grown to accept as standard from every entertainer who has made good, the neighborhood in which he grew up was a hard-boiled one, and the tough kids he bummed around with at Wells High School didn't exactly stimulate an intellectual appetite. Five of his buddies later wound up in the penitentiary. "And," avers Dino, "folks around Steubenville were laying five to one I'd eventually join them."

As a student, Martin couldn't settle down. He didn't care for reading, and he privately confesses today that the only book he ever read in his entire life was *Black Beauty*. He couldn't tolerate the discipline and rigid hours of the classroom.

According to an ex-schoolmate of his at Grant Junior High, Dino was always "clowning around in class. He'd entertain us by cutting up, wisecracking with all the girls and leaping over desks like a high jumper.

"I remember one time he was up on one of the desks doing a jig, and a teacher came by and caught his whole act. She sternly ordered the class to settle down and hauled Dino up to the front of the room to give him a reprimand, but they both burst out laughing instead. The teacher couldn't help herself. Even the teachers liked him. He had them howling with laughter when he started cracking his off-the-cuff classroom jokes.

"Dino had an eye for pretty girls then, too. There was always a smile on his face and a joke on his mind, and the girls would follow him around the schoolyard, giggling. He's kept his same boyhood charm all these years. It's helped make him the lovable entertainer he is today."

In those days Dino had no particular goal in sight, when and if he ever got sprung from Wells High School. Certainly, entering show business had never crossed his mind, although it's been rumored, apocryphal or not, that he did engage in a little barbershop-quartet singing in his father's tonsorial parlor from time to time.

Strange as it may seem to anyone who has watched Dino perform with the bevy of curvaceous beauties on his TV show, he didn't work very assiduously at girl chasing in his youth. Mostly, this stemmed from his having little money to spend on girls and none of the polish he has since acquired. In fact, despite his outward bravado and irrepressible clowning, he was extremely lacking in self-confidence, almost bashful if one can believe it.

"If you want to know the truth, I was ashamed of the way I spoke," revealed Dino in a magazine interview. "My English was lousy. I couldn't hold a conversation."

As a result, he preferred the company of his own sex. With men he didn't have to apologize for his uncouth tongue and rough manners. Moreover, he could engage in outdoor sports with men. He was a natural athlete and loved basketball and football. Girls were for sissies.

When he was in the tenth grade, Dino decided he'd had his fill of learning (if you can call doing a jig on a school desk "learning"). One night at the dinner table, Dino announced to his father, "Pop, I want to quit school."

"Why?" asked Papa Crocetti. "You think you know more than the teacher?"

"Yes," said Dino with a grin. "Besides, I want to make some money."

"Okay, if it will make you happy," replied Papa Crocetti, "go to work."

According to Martin, his folks were the kind of parents kids dream about. "All my mother and father wanted was for every Crocetti to be happy." He emphasizes this in order to put an end to all those stories that his father was such a poor provider that Dino had to quit high school to peddle papers to help support the family.

There wasn't much work around in 1931, however, for a fourteen-year-old son of an Italian immigrant who hadn't even finished high school. In 1931, Herbert Hoover was still president, and the United States was wallowing in the throes of its worst depression. Millions were unemployed, and former Wall Street financiers were selling apples for a nickel apiece on street corners.

Young Dino was one of the lucky ones. His father's brother, Uncle Joe, was a milkman, and he hired Dino as his assistant. But this job only lasted a few weeks. Dino, in his teen-aged exuberance, used to gallop up the house stoops to make his deliveries, often bumping his load of milk bottles on the brick steps and breaking them open. When Dino's losses from breakage due to his carelessness started cutting into Uncle Joe's profits, the old man had to fire him.

Dino's next job was at a filling station, pumping gas. But when that didn't work out either, Dino's older brother Bill wangled him a job bundling hot coils at the Weirton steel mill in West Virginia. Dino and his coworker would stand in front of a wooden platform approximately half a block long. Hot coils of steel wire would be lowered to the platforms, cooling as they came down from water being splashed on them. At a certain point, Dino would bang the end of a coil with a sledge hammer. Then he'd pull a lever, and the coil would be tilted into a box car.

That employment lasted until a four-ton coil of hot steel dropped from a crane one day, narrowly missing Dino and almost snuffing out his life. "Hey, a guy could get killed that way," exclaimed Dino, and promptly tendered his resignation to the foreman. There had to be a safer way of earning a living than working in a steel mill. (Even in a depression, a certain pattern in Dino's work philosophy was developing—no job was worth keeping if it endangered him, physically or emotionally.)

There followed a period of unemployment, during which Dino continued his association with the gang of tough kids he knew in high school. He shot pool in the local billiard parlor, played basketball in Coleman's Gym, and swam in the Ohio River. Otherwise, he did nothing to indicate he'd ever wind up a millionaire, with his own helicopter to fly him from his $300,000 estate in Bel Air to his $700,000 ranch in San Fernando Valley.

As he outgrew the awkward age—at one point, he claims to have been so clumsy that he broke his collarbone on a tackling dummy—Dino became friendly with a small-time fight manager named Tony Romano. Told by Tony that there was good money in fighting and also that he had the physique for it, he started taking boxing lessons at the gym where the local fighters worked out. When he could handle his dukes with the necessary expertise, Dino joined the ranks of the amateur boxers who fought in small clubs in that area. He weighed 146, and fought as a welterweight.

Under Tony's guidance, Dino fought thirty bouts as a welterweight in West Virginia, Ohio, and western Pennsylvania. He won twenty-four of them, but the victory spoils to an amateur were usually just a two- or five-dollar drugstore watch. "My manager and I would sell it and split the loot," recalls Martin.

Dino finally worked himself up to the plateau where he was a semipro making ten dollars a bout—"which was enough to buy my dad a fountain pen or my Mom a box of candy."

Dino's fighting career ended the night one of his opponents threw a powerful right cross and flattened his already misshapen nose. When he realized that at ten dollars a match he couldn't even afford to have his nose repaired correctly, he says, "I blew the racket."

When he was sixteen, Dino got a job delivering bootleg whisky in Steubenville and Canonsburg, Pennsylvania, unbeknownst to Mr. and Mrs. Crocetti. Dino worked with two of his cronies. "The three of us delivered the stuff in a coupe after dark. Boy, was that hooch bad! We could have run the car on it, and saved gas."

When his mother and father discovered that Dino had a job in one of the rackets, they made him quit. To assuage them, Dino got a clerk's job at an establishment known as the Rex Cigar Store. Little did Mr. and Mrs. Crocetti realize that the cigar store was a front for one of the biggest gambling joints in Steubenville.

At Rex's, Dino's main job was selling punchboard chances over the counter. But when he had two or three hours off, he'd go into the back room, watch the big boys at play, and fool around with the chips until he learned how to handle them. A quick study in everything but school, Dino soon learned how to operate the roulette wheel, how to shoot craps, and how to deal blackjack. When he began to beat the house at its own game, the management made him a croupier in self-defense.

Because Angela Crocetti was a conscientious mother, with a strong sense of morals, it was inevitable that she'd eventually learn that the

Rex Cigar Store did not trade solely in tobacco. One night when Dino came home from work, she decided to confront him with her suspicions.

Angela was a plumpish woman, with a face that might have been created by Modigliani. She had friendly black eyes to match her hair and a large Italian nose that made it easy to understand how her son Dino acquired his.

"You're a gambler?" she asked Dino as he walked in the door.

"No, Mom, not a gambler. I'm a stickman."

"But they gamble in that place where you work," said Mrs. Crocetti. "I heard that from Mrs. Lamberti in the butcher shop."

"Mom," explained Dino patiently. "You remember that Cary Grant movie about Monte Carlo we all went to see?"

"I remember, son."

"And the man with the stick, in the nice-looking tuxedo, who stood behind the table?" continued Dino. "He didn't gamble. He just worked there."

"You're the man with the stick?"

"That's right, Mom."

Angela Crocetti smiled forgivingly. "Well, then it's fine, Dino."

Dino's salary for working the chips and the dice tables was eight dollars a day. With tips, and on a good night (meaning one during which they didn't get raided), he could earn up to twenty dollars.

"I also did a little knocking down," confesses Dino with a sly grin. "During the course of a day, I could steal maybe as much as five silver dollars."

Sometimes he'd palm them; on other occasions he'd work with a friend, who'd stand alongside him and pretend to be one of the players.

"You can't do that at Las Vegas without having the pit boss, who's keeping an eye on everybody, say, 'Naughty, naughty,' " points out Dino today, "but back in Steubenville I could take ten and hand it to the guy who was helping me without getting caught."

To this day, Martin is a skillful manipulator of a deck of cards. Often he amuses his friends and children with feats like dealing himself four aces while everybody else gets the kind of poker hands you wouldn't dare open with, even if the stakes were only milk-bottle tops.

Dino's card-handling ability and his skill at palming silver dollars combine to make him one of the best amateur magicians in show business today.

At Las Vegas, when he's killing time between shows at whatever hotel is paying him $50,000 a week to entertain the suckers, Dino will frequently take a turn as dealer at one of the blackjack tables. If one of his opponents happens to be a bountifully blessed young girl, she can be fairly certain he'll deal her the kind of hand that will enable her to beat the house.

To return to Steubenville's answer to Horatio Alger, Dino was soon making himself $125 a week between his legitimate salary as a stickman and what he was able to "knock down." With his earnings, Dino was able to help his father pay off the mortgage on his house and also send his brother Bill back to college.

But Dino had one legitimate talent. He could sing. He'd never had any voice training, of course. In fact, to this day—and even though his records have sold in the millions—he can't read a note of music. He has to learn every song by ear, and, if ever he learns it wrong, according to Lee Gillette of Capitol Records, "he has a rough time changing."

On one of his biggest sellers, Carmen Lombardo's "Napoli," Dino learned the melody wrong, and no amount of rehearsing could change it. As a result, Gillette had to write Lombardo after the recording session and explain to the composer that what was on the record was "Dean's version" and he'd have to settle for that. Lombardo did, and "Napoli" was a tremendous hit.

Dino, however, had no illusions about becoming a recording artist when he used to lie in a hot bath in his Steubenville days and imitate the current crooning sensation, Bing Crosby.

"I copied his style a hundred percent," confesses Dino. "I wasn't alone. Frank Sinatra and Perry Como did too. They'll tell you they did, if you ask them."

From the start Dino knew he didn't have a "big voice," just a nice and easy style.

"The thing is, not to seem to try too hard," he explains. "If I'm relaxed, I can relax an audience. That's one of the secrets of being an entertainer." It's certainly one of the secrets of Dean Martin's success.

While he was working at the Rex Cigar Store, Dino frequently attended dances and parties at roadhouses like Reed's Mill and Walker's Nightclub. Usually there'd be a four- or five-piece combo at these places, and Dino's friends, aware that their Italian cohort had a pleasant baritone voice, would often urge him to get up and sing.

Being an obliging sort of fellow, Dino would stand in front of the band and do his imitation of Crosby, only he didn't label it that. The patrons of Reed's Mill and Walker's Nightclub loved it. So did the hoodlums who ran the gambling houses.

One night, a Columbus, Ohio, bandleader named Ernie McKay was playing at Walker's. At his friends' urging, Dino got up and did his usual stint with the band. McKay was so impressed that he offered the youngster a job as singer with his combo at fifty dollars a week.

"I'm not really a singer," replied Dino with genuine modesty. "It's just that my pals make me sing."

"I like your style," insisted McKay. "I want you with my band."

Dino shrugged. "Why should I work for fifty dollars a week when I'm making a hundred and a quarter?" And he walked back to his table, unconcerned.

His pals at the table thought he was making a mistake. "Dino, tell the guy yes," insisted Izzy McGregor, a freckle-faced Scottish lad who worked in the casino with him.

"Are you crazy or something?" exclaimed Dino. "I steal that much a week."

The subject was dropped, at Dino's insistence.

But fate was watching out for Dean Martin, just as it would continue to watch out for him at every important juncture in his life. Or, in the words of an old Jewish philosopher, "If you have luck, you don't have to be smart."

When word got back to the three small-time hoods who ran the Rex Cigar Store that their young protégé had turned down an opportunity to sing with a name band, the men were disappointed. Especially upset was Tony Tarantino, a dapper-looking Damon Runyonish character, who was the boss of the triumvirate.

Promptly after the gaming room closed that night, Tony gathered his two subordinates, Lighthorse Harry Barbra and Dom Gilbertoni, around one of the green-topped poker tables and outlined to them exactly how he felt. In a nutshell, he said that no graduate of his establishment had ever had a chance to get into show business before, and he didn't think it behooved Dino to blow an opportunity to become famous—and in the process splash a little glamour on the men who helped put his foot on the first rung of the ladder of success.

"Dino is a good kid," he concluded. "He's the only one of us who's got a chance to get away from here and make something of himself."

"But if the kid don't wanna sing, he don't wanna sing," pointed out Lighthorse Harry.

"If he don't want to sing, we'll make him sing," stated Tony. "After all, this is America, the land of opportunity."

"And the land of the free," echoed Dom Gilbertoni.

"All who agree," said Tony, "do so in the usual manner."

The others agreed in the usual manner, by knocking their automatics on the green felt tabletop.

A course of action was decided on. When Dino reported for work the next morning, no one spoke to him. The silent treatment continued for a couple of weeks, with Dino growing more and more depressed.

Finally, he came to the group and said, "Okay, guys, what do you want me to do?"

"Take the singing job," advised Tony.

The next day, Dino joined McKay's band in Columbus, Ohio. He was billed, somewhat fraudulently, as "Dino Martini—Nino Martini's cousin." Nino Martini was a popular tenor and recording artist of the period.

A week later, Dino was back at the gambling house, asking for his old job. Tony gave it to him, but again none of his pals spoke to Dino.

A few more days passed, and Tony finally took pity on him.

"Okay, why'd you quit?" asked Tony.

"I can't live on fifty bucks a week."

"All right, then," said Tony. "You go back, and we'll get up a pool and send you an extra hundred dollars a week."

Their offer was not without strings, however. In return for making up the difference, they all took "pieces" of Dino's future. Dino accepted Tony's deal and promptly returned to Columbus.

This arrangement, which smacked of something out of *Guys and Dolls*, went on for a year and a half, with hardened characters of the Rex Cigar Store contributing their own ill-gotten gains so that at least one of them could have a shot at getting out of "the rackets."

It was to be a long time, however, before their investment paid off.

Dino was with McKay only a few months when Sammy Watkins, a Cleveland bandleader, heard him sing and offered him a job with his organization, at a fifty-dollar-a-week raise.

With the lack of business acumen typical of the manner in which he was to handle his affairs most of his life, Dino quickly signed a contract with Watkins, without bothering to read the fine print. The fine print (not usual in band agreements then) gave Watkins not only a hold on Dino's services but a 10 percent agent's fee that would continue for seven years—regardless of the identity of Dino's employer.

This habit of signing papers that any sharpie pushed in front of him was to come back and plague Dino not too many years later. But at the time all Dino could see was the raise in his weekly income.

In Cleveland, two things happened in the twenty-three-year-old crooner's life: He changed his name from Dino Martini to Dean Martin, and he met Elizabeth McDonald.

Elizabeth, or Betty as she was known to her friends and family, was born in Morton, Pennsylvania, a small town outside of Philadelphia, in 1921. Betty's father was an executive in the Schenley liquor company.

When Betty was seven, her father moved the family to Swarthmore, Pennsylvania, home of Swarthmore College. There Betty, the youngest of three daughters, grew up to be a vivacious teen-aged brunette.

"My sisters both graduated from Smith with honors and got their master's degrees. I was the dummy of the family," explains Betty. "My dad always wanted a son, but he gave up when I came along and concentrated on making me a tomboy."

Although she looked like anything but a tomboy, with a tall, well-proportioned figure, sparkling dark eyes, long flowing black hair, and beautiful even white teeth that contributed to an engaging Irish smile, she turned out to be an accomplished sportswoman. She was particularly expert at lacrosse, and graduated from high school with three athletic scholarships—to Strasburg, Temple, and Swarthmore.

Betty chose Swarthmore because she knew it would please her parents to go for her college degree in their home town.

There were problems, however, right from the start. Because of her athletic prowess, Betty was treated as something of a celebrity on the campus.

"I spent all my time signing autographs and competing in my various sports," says Betty today, "and I forgot all about the fact that I was supposed to be there to get an education."

The dean, however, didn't forget, and, one day during Betty's first semester, he summoned the young Irish girl to his office. "I thought he was going to chew me out for not studying and skipping some classes," Betty remembers. "But instead he didn't say a word. He just handed me a slip of paper saying I was out—permanently. I didn't know how to tell my father, but of course I had to. He could see how upset I was. Well, he was leaving for Cleveland, Ohio, on business, so he told mother, 'I'm going to take Betty with me to take her mind off things.'

"We stayed at the Hollenden Hotel. The first night we went downstairs, and there was Dino singing in the dinner club with the Sammy Watkins Band. Dean kept looking over at us and talking to the trombone player. I learned later that the trombonist had said, 'Don't you know who that is? That's Governor Lausche and his daughter! Come on, I'll introduce you.' Well, Dean was afraid to take him up on it, I guess, because he knew his friend really had no idea who we were."

While Betty and her father were in Cleveland, Schenley informed Mr. McDonald that he was going to be transferred to the shores of Lake Erie permanently. Betty and her father stayed in Cleveland to look for a house, while the rest of the McDonalds remained behind in Swarthmore to prepare themselves for moving day.

During this period, Dino kept following Betty around the Hollenden Hotel. Betty was actually flattered that the personable Italian singer was so enamored of her, but one day she pretended to be angry, wheeled on him, and told him to stop annoying her. Sensing that she didn't mean it, Dino asked her for a date instead. Of course, she accepted.

They fell in love on their first date.

After the McDonalds moved to Cleveland, Betty dated Dean for three months. At that point, an unwanted separation seemed imminent. The Sammy Watkins Band was about to take to the road for a series of one-night stands, and, in those days, good Catholic girls from nice families didn't go on trips with young men who weren't their husbands.

Since Dean didn't want to leave the attractive brunette behind, marriage seemed the only solution. But before he would propose officially, he first had to take Betty back to Steubenville to get the approval of the people he respected most—not his parents, "but the guys who worked at the Rex Cigar Store," recalls Betty with good humor.

"That was the first place he took me when we arrived in his home town —the Rex Cigar Store. He had to get their opinion of me. I guess I passed their inspection because that night he proposed. I met his parents too, and they were adorable. We were great friends from that moment on. Mama Crocetti even made my wedding dress."

Before there could be a wedding, however, Dean and Betty first had to get special dispensation from the Catholic church. In those days, Catholic weddings required the posting of the banns at least six weeks before the ceremony.

Because the Sammy Watkins Band was about to leave town, Betty's priest gave the young couple permission to marry immediately, and the ceremony was held the following day—October 2, 1940—in Cleveland's St. Ann's Church, with not only the Crocetti and McDonald families present but also the entire Sammy Watkins Band.

The next day Dean and Betty left for Louisville, Kentucky, in the bus with the other musicians of the Watkins organization.

From that time on, until she gave birth to their first son, Craig, in June 1942, Betty accompanied Dean and the band on most of their road trips. But once the Martins started to acquire a family, it became difficult for Betty to be on the go so much. Consequently, she stayed home and was separated from Dean a good deal during the ensuing years of their marriage.

Of the four children the couple eventually had together, Dean could only be present at the birth of Craig; and according to Betty, who remembers that day fondly, her big strong Dean fainted in the taxicab when he was taking her to St. John's Hospital.

In the following two and a half years, Betty gave birth to two more children—Claudia, on March 16, 1944, and Gail, on April 11, 1945. Recalling that period, Betty laughingly states, "Dean used to say 'I'm afraid to send her a telegram for fear she'll get pregnant.'"

Except for their obvious compatibility in bed, Dean and Betty seemed to have little else in common. Betty was shy, hated large parties, and was a conscientious mother. Dean was gregarious, loved drinking and staying out late, and wasn't much of a homebody, even when he was in town.

Although she may not have realized it in the first flush of her marriage to Dean, circumstances would soon be forcing Betty to spend more and more of her nights in lonely solitude, without her man, for several reasons.

In the first place, Dean is basically a "man's man" and always has been. From his early youth, he has usually preferred the company of other men, except when he wants sexual gratification. Second, he's a gambler. And last of all, the business he was embarked upon—singing with a band—made unusual demands on a person's time.

When it wasn't on the road, the Sammy Watkins Band usually played at the Hollenden Hotel in Cleveland. But dance bands worked late hours, and often Dino didn't get home to Betty until two or three in the morning. Sometimes, when he wasn't feeling sleepy, Dino would stop somewhere on the way back to their small apartment and play cards with a friend.

One night, after he had been with Watkins for two years, Dino lingered in his dressing room after his singing chores to play a game of gin with Merle Jacobs, the Music Corporation of America (MCA) agent who did the booking for Watkins's band.

Between hands, Jacobs said to Dino, "Why don't you quit Watkins and do a single? I can get him to let you go."

"Who'd want me?" asked Dino.

Jacobs explained that a fellow countryman of Dino's—a skinny young Italian-American boy named Frank Sinatra—had just scored a fantastic success at the Riobamba in New York City, and, as a result, all the nightclub booking agents were "beating the bushes for Italian baritones."

"You're a good bet for nightclubs too," added Jacobs. "Maybe I can even get you into the Riobamba."

Dino told him to take a shot at it and went back to dealing the cards.

A few weeks later, in the fall of 1943, Irving Zussman, a tall, handsome, dark-haired man who handled public relations for the Riobamba, was sitting in his office at the nightclub feeling slightly suicidal. The reason was that Frank Sinatra, who'd been packing the customers into the place for the last ten weeks, had just signed a movie contract and was leaving for Hollywood that afternoon.

Zussman was the one who had talked Arthur Jarwood, the nightclub's owner, into "taking a chance" on Sinatra after the Copa and La Martinique had turned him down. The feeling around Manhattan had been that Sinatra could only appeal to bobby-soxers. Sinatra proved that everybody but Zussman was wrong—so wrong that now New York was losing the thin singer for good, and Zussman had no star to fill his place. Suddenly Arthur Jarwood burst into the office, all excited.

"I just found another singer for us who might be a real surprise," exclaimed Jarwood. "Merle Jacobs brought him over."

"Yeah, who?" asked Zussman, brightening.

"Some guy named Dean something-or-other. He's a complete unknown and he looks very funny, because he's got the biggest schnozzola I ever saw outside of Durante's. But he sings just like Crosby."

The Dean something-or-other who sang just like Crosby was, of course, Dean Martin.

For his New York debut, Dean rented a place in the London Terrace Apartments, a group of posh buildings in lower Manhattan, and brought Betty, who was pregnant again, and Craig on to share it with him. The rent was high—about $200 a month—but his future looked good. He was going to be making $400 a week at the Riobamba.

Dino followed Sinatra into the Riobamba in September and was only one of several acts on a bill of nonentities.

Variety covered Dino's opening, and this is what the so-called bible of show business had to say in its September 29, 1943, issue:

DEAN MARTIN
Songs
8 Mins.
Riobamba, N.Y.

Cleveland's entry in the swoonstakes is Dean Martin, a thin-visaged dark-haired baritone who's making his New York debut with this date. The New York competition is apt to be a little too tough.

Martin, seemingly, would be lost without that mike. He's lacking in personality, looks ill-fitting in that dinner jacket and, at best, has just a fair voice that suggests it would have little resonance without the p.a. system.

With *Variety*'s review being the kindest Dean Martin received in the New York press, it wasn't surprising that New Yorkers weren't exactly knocking down the doors of the Riobamba to get in to see him perform. Seven weeks later, the Italian Crosby from Steubenville was out of work again.

MCA came up with a few other short-lived jobs for Dino following his Riobamba stint, but because of his lackluster showing at the Cuban nitery, everybody was convinced he wasn't another Sinatra, and consequently his periods of unemployment grew even longer than his proboscis. Things finally became so tough for Dino that he and Betty had to vacate their London Terrace apartment, because they couldn't come up with the rent money, and move into cheaper quarters. They owed so much back rent, however, that the management of the London Terrace Apartments put a thirty-dollar-a-week lien on Dino's future earnings until the debt was paid off.

In February, Dino sent Betty and Craig back to Ridley Park, Pennsylvania (a suburb of Philadelphia), so she could be with her parents when she had her second baby, Claudia. Betty's parents had moved back to Philadelphia after a short stay in Cleveland.

At the time of Claudia's arrival, March 16, Dean was playing Montreal and didn't come home.

Following that, Betty and her two children remained with her parents for long periods of time while Dino kicked around the Eastern seaboard, living and singing in second-rate nightclubs and hotels. To fill in when he couldn't get crooning dates, Dino would occasionally be forced to abandon singing altogether and accept employment as a dealer in the gambling houses in the small towns on the road.

Weeks passed, and it became apparent to the cold-blooded men who ran MCA that Dean Martin wasn't the kind of client who could keep them in Brooks Brothers suits and lavish offices furnished with expensive antiques.

Not only wasn't Dino very much in demand, but when MCA did get him employment, he usually neglected to pay their commissions because he owed money to so many other people in town and was being hounded by creditors. Dino's income—mostly in the $200-a-week-or-less bracket—could in no way keep up with his passion for booze, broads, and the Belmont Racetrack, to say nothing of other games of chance.

About the only person on the Broadway scene who sensed that Dino had any kind of theatrical future was an independent talent agent named Lou Perry, a slightly built, dapper-dressing man of Italian descent, with thin lips, a full head of sleekly combed black hair, and a good gift of agent's gab.

Operating from a small, sparsely furnished office on Broadway, directly across the street from the old Capitol Theater, Perry specialized in handling "young talent," the kind the larger agents couldn't be bothered with. He got them jobs in the smaller theaters and nightclubs, wet-nursed their budding careers, and even lent them money between jobs when necessity required it. Then, like so many of his unfortunate ilk, he generally lost them to the larger agents the moment they shot into any kind of prominence. One of the "nobodys" Lou Perry was handling at the time, but who quickly went to another agency as soon as he became important, was a young comedian named Irving Kniberg. Today he's known as Alan King.

Dino Martin came to Lou Perry's attention through Arthur Jarwood, proprietor of the Riobamba. Jarwood introduced them while Dino was still singing there. But at the time Dino was tied to MCA, which seemed bent on keeping him.

After months of not getting paid their commissions, however, MCA was willing to sell Dean Martin to the highest and only bidder, Lou Perry, who bought his contract from MCA for $200 plus the $345 in back commissions Dino owed them.

Perry soon discovered that he had taken on quite a load. In addition to being jobless, hopelessly in debt, and completely irresponsible as a family man, Dino had no place to live when he was in New York City. Finally Perry took pity on Dino and invited him to share his room in the Bryant Hotel at Fifty-fourth Street and Broadway—not exactly a chic neighborhood. Because he was in such desperate financial straits, Dino accepted Perry's generous offer.

The Bryant Hotel catered to actors and other show business types who weren't in the upper tax brackets. Perry's quarters consisted of one room with a double bed.

For the three years Dino was his houseguest, Perry insists that his client didn't pay a "nickel for rent," nor did he ever repay him when he finally did move out. Furthermore, Perry takes credit for picking up the tab for all of Dino's food, laundry, and tailoring bills and for lending him money to send to Betty to help meet some of the costs of having and raising the new baby.

To further complicate Perry's existence, Betty would sometimes come into Manhattan from Philadelphia on weekends and share the one room with her husband and his benefactor. On these occasions, Perry would be very accommodating. He'd let Dino and Betty have the double bed and he'd discreetly disappear somewhere. Fortunately for Lou Perry, who wasn't fond of being evicted from his own bed, Betty Martin spent more time with her parents in Pennsylvania during that period than she did with Dino at the Bryant Hotel.

"It was a rotten time for me," recalls Betty today, "because each time I went home the girls I grew up with, who were all married with their own homes, would make remarks about Dean being out of work again. The leader of the snide remarks was my mother. I never to this day told Dean how hard that time was for me. He was having a rough time also trying to get a start. When Thomas Wolfe said 'You can't go home again,' it was obvious he was never married to Dean Martin. I went home 200 times. After wearing out that welcome, I took my kids and went to stay with Dean's parents in Steubenville. That's where Gail was born in April, 1945."

Aside from supplying Dean with free room and board, other services that weren't specifically spelled out in their management contract but that Perry willingly performed for his client included helping Dino dodge the numerous process servers who were after him, paying some of Dino's debts when the pressure couldn't be removed by fast talk or nimble foot-work, and acting as his first golfing companion.

Dino had been introduced to the game of golf on a trip to Montreal, where Perry had booked him into a cheap nightclub. Upon his return, he enthusiastically reported to Perry, "Hey, guess what I did in Montreal?" Perry was afraid to guess; it might cost him money. He was relieved to learn that the news Dino was so anxious to impart was only that he had played golf for the first time and had fallen in love with the game.

After that, Perry used to take Dino out to a public course in Oceanside, Long Island.

Although a natural in any sport he decides to take up (today he shoots in the low seventies and sometimes plays for $5,000 a round), Dino was a real hacker when he was first introduced to the game, and it's a tribute to Lou Perry's patience that he'd play on the same course with him.

Lou Perry was less patient, however, about Dino's looks. Although Dino could sing like Crosby, there was a growing feeling around Manhat-tan that one of the things that was holding him back in show business was his nose, which was still long, sharp, and hooked (as a result of that blow in the ring).

Dino, too, was dissatisfied with the shape of his nose; in fact, he was extremely self-conscious about it. Unfortunately, plastic surgery took money. That, in contrast to his nose, was in very short supply.

A chance meeting with a couple of his old friends from Steubenville— who were now bookies around Times Square—was instrumental in trans-forming Dino into a sex symbol. When one of the bookies inquired as to how their old stickman from the Rex Cigar Store was making out in show business, Dino confessed, "All right, but I could be doing better if I had 500 bucks for a nose job."

After considerable persuasion, Dino got them to agree to lend him the necessary $500, provided he could find someone to guarantee payment. The "boys" were well enough acquainted with Dino's fiscal irresponsibil-ity to know that his signature alone wasn't worth the paper on which it was written.

So once again Lou Perry was summoned to come to Dino's rescue. In a four-man parley in the privacy of his room in the Bryant, Perry agreed to guarantee payment "or they could take back the new nose."

Dino promptly hired one of New York's better plastic surgeons and checked into a hospital. When he was released and the bandages were removed a week later, Dino no longer resembled Pinocchio; he was almost handsome. With a few strokes of his scalpel, the surgeon had accomplished what God had found impossible, inspiring one Broadway wise guy to remark, "What God could do if he only had money!"

Following Martin and Lewis's initial success as a team, there were many stories making the rounds, most of them apocryphal, concerning where Dino got the money for the operation. And when he became rich and famous, he was sued right and left by hoods and other more respectable people—all of them claiming to have lent him the money for the corrective surgery in return for "pieces" of his future.

One of the claimants was the late Angel Lopez, who owned the Havana-Madrid on Broadway and Fifty-first Street, where Dino and Jerry had both worked as "singles" before meeting each other and forming an act.

New York publicity man Irving Zussman, who was a partner of Lopez's at the time, remembers seeing a note for $1,000 that Dino had signed in exchange for a loan from Lopez. According to Zussman, Dino never repaid the money, and Lopez never pressed him for it.

How could so many people not accustomed to lying claim to own a share of that now famous schnozzola?

Zussman, who today is still one of Broadway's top publicists, offers what is probably the most logical explanation: "Dino must have used the needed nose job as a money-borrowing device and hit a number of people for a few thousand each." One thing no one can argue about: Dino's career did take a slight turn upward after his operation. Whether this was directly attributable to the resculpturing of his nose or simply that the wartime manpower shortage was being felt in the entertainment industry —at one point, the pickings for Uncle Sam were so slim that even Rudy Vallee was accepted for military service—no one can be sure.

Whatever the reason, by 1945 Dino was being booked regularly into midtown places like La Martinique, Leon and Eddie's, the Havana-Madrid, the Glass Hat, and also out-of-town spots like the Chez Paree in Chicago, the Conga Monga in Montreal, and the Latin Quarter in Camden, New Jersey—at salaries ranging from $300 to $800 a week. Marriage and fatherhood, welcome or not, were proving to be a blessing to Dino in one important aspect anyway; they were keeping him out of the wartime draft and available for work.

After the Martins' first daughter, Claudia, was born, Betty's conjugal weekends with Dino in Perry's hotel room became more sporadic than ever. If Dino wanted to see her, it was up to him to do the traveling— either to the home of her parents in Philadelphia or to his own parents' place in Steubenville, where she sometimes stayed.

This Dino wasn't inclined to do. He had his own interests in the big city. Between his singing career, his penchant for gambling, and the many girls-about-Broadway who were after his body now that he had the profile of a leading man, Dino had little time left for being a family man.

Even a letter from Betty to Dean around the Christmas holidays in 1945 could not shake him from his hedonistic existence. The letter, scribbled in pencil on a piece of pulpy unlined paper obviously torn from a dime-store stationery pad, began by stating "how sorry" Betty was that Dean wouldn't be home for Christmas and ended with a plea for him "to at least send $100" so she could buy Christmas presents for the children and both sets of grandparents.

Dino, however, wasn't completely without a heart. Betty recalls that Dino sent her "about thirty dollars," which was all he could afford. Although his income was increasing, the bill collectors were still hounding him.

For a time, there was such a shortage of cash in Dino's wallet that he and Sonny King, another ex-pug turned crooner, were forced to scrounge for money by staging boxing matches in Perry's hotel room and charging fifty cents admission to anyone who wanted to watch. In addition to the admission paid, there was a lot of betting action between the participants and the various Damon Runyon characters who attended the bouts.

The nickels and dimes that Dino wound up with were pathetically small compensation for an afternoon of exposing his expensively sculptured nose to Sonny King's right hooks. And after one bout in which Dino took a direct hit on the nose, splattering blood all over his face, Lou Perry had to call a halt to any future fisticuffs.

It was around this period in Dino's life that the movie industry first showed an interest in his dubious talents.

Milton Pickman, a scout for Columbia Pictures, caught Dean Martin's act while he was performing at Loew's State and recommended him for a test to his boss, Harry Cohn.

The test, which included two other hopefuls, Blossom Plumb and Ruth Sitarr, was shot at Fox's Tenth Avenue studios (where all the major movie companies rented space for their eastern screen tests), and the results were immediately shipped to Columbia czar Harry Cohn at his Gower Avenue fortress in Hollywood.

A movie career, with a long-term contract and a steady weekly salary, seemed to be the only solution to Dino's rapidly worsening monetary troubles. But, early in February 1946, Pickman received the following letter:

Dear Milton:
    We have just seen the Dean Martin, Blossom Plumb and Ruth Sitarr tests. They are a complete waste of time and money.

Dean Martin may have some ability in a night club, but he cannot talk at all.

Yours

Harry Cohn

Dino had barely recovered from that disappointment when Joe Pasternak, the producer of many of MGM's better musicals, popped into Leon and Eddie's one night—"Celebrity Night"—when Dino was doing his big number, "San Fernando Valley," for the crowd of celebrities who thronged there once a week to case the new talent.

Pasternak liked Dino's voice and decided he wanted him for the picture he was preparing, *Till the Clouds Roll By*.

Before MGM would sign Dean Martin, however, Joe Schenck, the company's production head, insisted on seeing a screen test of the young Italian. So George Sidney, one of Hollywood's leading directors of that period, was immediately dispatched to Fox's Tenth Avenue to record Dino on film.

Sidney photographed Dean singing "San Fernando Valley" and then, to show his bosses that the Italian was more than one dimensional, had him strip down to his waist and do a little shadow boxing. This was to demonstrate his muscular physique, something Sinatra didn't have.

Pasternak was delighted with the test and signed Dean to an MGM contract calling for a starting salary of $300 a week, with many escalations at option times. Of course, the whole deal hinged on Joe Schenck's ultimate approval and signature, but that was considered a mere formality.

Dino, naturally, was on Cloud Nine, buying drinks for all the boys and girls at the Havana-Madrid, where he was currently appearing, as he waited out the next few suspenseful weeks for Schenck to make his movie career official.

Then came Schenck's reply to Pasternak:

We already have Tony Martin under contract. Why do we want another Italian singer?

Joe Schenck

It proved to be one of the big breaks of Dean Martin's career that Joe Schenck wasn't aware that Tony Martin was a Jew, not an Italian. For if MGM had seen fit to sign Dean Martin to a $300-a-week stock contract, chances are he'd have been lost amidst all that talent on the Culver City lot (Judy Garland, Frank Sinatra, Clark Gable, Gene Kelly, Robert Taylor, Mickey Rooney, Elizabeth Taylor, Deborah Kerr, Spencer Tracy, and Katharine Hepburn—to name just a few), he'd have been dropped at the first option time, and he'd never have met Jerry Lewis.

3

The Marriage of Figaro

In contrast to Dean Martin, who is a "loner" and admits it categorically, Jerry Lewis, once he became a star, could never feel at ease unless he was surrounded by a large retinue of friends, employees, and stooges.

"I rarely had less than thirty or forty people in my house," Lewis recalled recently. "And wherever I went, it was always with a crowd. Several times in New York I went hungry rather than face going into a restaurant by myself."

This quirk of having to travel in platoons is not atypical of other great entertainers in our society; Jackie Gleason, Al Jolson, Milton Berle, and Frank Sinatra, when they were riding high, all had to have their armies of cronies with them everywhere they went.

A fear of being alone, plus almost a psychotic need to be constantly reassured of greatness, unquestionably accounts for much of their crowd mania.

With Lewis, it was his whole motivating force. Few people ever had greater cause to fear being alone or more of a need to be reassured that he wasn't totally worthless than did Jerry Lewis as a child.

Lewis was born in Newark, New Jersey, on March 16, 1926. His real name is Joseph Levitch, and he is the only son of Danny and Rea Levitch, a couple of borscht-circuit entertainers who performed under the name of Lewis because they believed it would help their careers. The change in name didn't help Danny and Rea, for, despite years of struggling, they never quite made it out of the borscht circuit.

Jerry's mother Rea was a typical Jewish balabosta type—short, dark,

and very possessive of her boy "Joey." She sang and played the piano—
sometimes for radio station WOR—and wrote music arrangements for her
husband.

Except for being somewhat shorter than his son, Danny in his youth
was a dead ringer for the Jerry Lewis audiences know today. Danny sang
and did imitations—mostly of Al Jolson. According to Jerry, his father
was "a wonderful mimic" and "a big talent." Despite this fact, his bookings were confined mostly to the smaller resort hotels in the Catskills and
around New Jersey and to some of the unimportant burlesque houses in
greater New York City. He never earned much money, but he was a hard
worker and a conscientious provider.

"If he made sixty dollars, he sent forty-five dollars to my mother," states
Jerry. "They were poor and couldn't help leaving me alone. But I'm
supersensitive, and it killed me."

Joey's formative years smacked more of Tiny Tim's than anything you'd
see in a Warner Brothers musical. While his parents traveled the hotel
and small-time theater circuits in the winter months, little Joey was
boarded out with his Grandma Sarah (on his mother's side), various
aunts, uncles, and cousins, and just about anyone else who would take in
the undernourished-looking waif for a few weeks or months. He never had
a room of his own until years later, when he was self-supporting and living
away from home.

When no relatives would accept him, Danny and Rea would be forced
to drag little Joey along on their show business hegiras.

Joey liked life on the road better than being left behind in Irvington,
New Jersey, where the Lewises had a tiny clapboard house, but it was a
helterskelter existence at best.

He was continually on the move, having his schooling interrupted,
being locked in dressing rooms while his parents were on the stage, living
in the cheapest accommodations in hotels, trying to make contact with
strange children, and never being able to develop lasting friendships or
interests. It's little wonder that, as an adult, he wound up with a series of
nervous disorders—frequent colds, sinus attacks, hay fever, mastoiditis,
hives, extreme depressions, loss of appetite due to tension, and even a
mild heart attack.

Joey was a sickly child at birth, and when he was two years old, he
was afflicted with a spine condition that might have left him crippled for
life had it not been for his Grandma Sarah in whose care he was left most
of the time when his parents were away.

Grandma Sarah first noticed the trouble, took him to a doctor, and saw
to it that little Joey got the proper medical treatment and therapy. His

recovery was complete, but his Tiny Tim days left an imprint on his mind that no doubt partially motivated his decision years later to devote his time so unsparingly to raising funds to fight muscular dystrophy.

After he could run and play again, Joey started doing crazy things around the house to make people laugh.

"I used to climb the pipes in the kitchen and dangle like a monkey— just to attract attention," remembers Jerry. "Some of my relatives said I needed a keeper."

After being alone with his grandmother so much, little Joey was convinced that Grandma Sarah was the only one who really loved him, who understood his loneliness. When he was afraid at night, she would let him lie on the floor next to her sewing machine, with his head cushioned on scraps of cloth she had cut. The mature Jerry Lewis can still remember how reassuring it was to wake up and see Grandma Sarah's foot going up and down on the sewing machine pedal.

He felt she was the only one in the family who thought he was anything. In times of great self-doubt, he would say to her, "The trouble with me is that I'm nothing."

She would stroke his head and say, "You're a human being, aren't you?"

"Yes, but I want to be *something*," he would answer.

Grandma Sarah understood what little Joey meant, for there was good communication between the two—something he didn't have with his parents.

Then one day the old lady got sick, an ambulance pulled up in front of the house, and two white-coated men carried her out on a stretcher and drove her away to the hospital in Irvington, New Jersey. Both of Joey's parents were very mysterious and silent about what was wrong with Grandma Sarah.

The hospital was on top of a large hill. The Lewises' cottage was at the bottom of it. According to Jerry, "All the kids in the neighborhood knew that when we looked up and saw a blue light on the third floor of the hospital, someone was being operated on in the operating room."

The same night the ambulance took Grandma Sarah away, little Joey sat alone in an empty house and watched the blue light go on. Hours later the blue light suddenly went out. Joey rushed to the phone and called the hospital.

"Could you please tell me the condition of my grandmother, Mrs. Rothberg?" Joey asked.

"Your grandmother just expired, sir," replied the operator.

"I don't know what that means?" asked Joey. "Does it mean she's all right?"

"I'm sorry, son," said the operator, "but your grandmother just passed away."

Stunned, Joey couldn't hang up the phone for several minutes. He felt so alone that he couldn't force himself to break the contact with the hospital where his grandmother was.

For a year following his grandmother's death, Joey went to live with an aunt and uncle in Albany, but for eight months he could hardly eat or sleep.

Joey had another traumatic experience when he was back living with his mother and father again. Home alone one night when the two of them were out working separate jobs, Joey got terribly scared. Finally, he couldn't stand his aloneness anymore and went out to try to find his mother. He knew she was working somewhere in downtown Irvington, so he walked a mile through the dark streets looking for her.

He came to a building where there were double swinging saloon doors at the entrance and the sounds of much revelry emanating from inside. Believing he recognized his mother's piano playing but afraid to enter the place, Joey peeked in through a green-painted window, the upper half of which was open.

What he saw was a murky-looking room, containing a long bar, disreputable-appearing customers lined up at it, and his mother working as a cocktail pianist and accepting tips from a bunch of drunken strangers. Jerry was so ashamed of what his mother was doing for a living that he ran back home to the empty house, preferring to be scared rather than to watch her degrade herself.

That experience left its mark on the impressionable young Joey too. Today he can't stand to see a drunk "without wanting to throw up." He still finds it difficult to go into a bar and have a drink; in fact, he has little taste for liquor at all.

The summer was Joey's favorite time of the year, for it was then he was able to join his parents, whom he loved dearly, for a full three months and not have to worry about school or being dumped in some unwilling relative's flat.

In the summertime, Danny and Rea worked the Catskill Mountain resorts that catered to the middle- and lower-middle-class Jewish trade. They were the kind of hotels where, according to comedian George Jessel, "There was so much sour cream in the dining rooms a person could go snow-blind."

Even though Danny never made the big time, Joey idolized his father and remembers wanting to be like him at a very early age. In fact, he was only four years old when he decided he wanted to follow in his father's footsteps. He remembers the occasion well.

His mother and father were playing the President Hotel in Swan Lake, New York. One night before the show, Joey persuaded his father to let him sing "Brother, Can You Spare a Dime" for the captive audience.

Joey had an extremely high-pitched, squeaky voice, and the musicians in the small orchestra didn't know how to transpose what was written on the sheet music to his key. So Joey had to sing "Brother, Can You Spare a Dime" almost a full octave minus one note above the orchestra.

When some members of the audience started to giggle, Joey struggled so hard to get back on key that he broke up all the guests in the room. Instead of being embarrassed, Joey enjoyed the sound of the laughter. (As he would later recall, "Not every kid would have liked being laughed *at*, but I was a strange child.")

From that night on, Jerry was always after Danny to let him do his "Brother, Can You Spare a Dime" bit for the hotel guests. When Danny refused, Jerry would secretly go through the audience before the start of every show, and beg the guests to yell for him and applaud wildly.

A true stage mother, Rea Lewis *kvelled* proudly whenever her little *Bubeleh* performed as a child. But in the beginning, Danny did everything possible to discourage Joey from a show business career.

"It's a lousy life," he used to tell his son.

"Why?" asked Joey. "*You* like it."

"You want your son to wind up sleeping in living rooms like you have to?" pointed out Danny. "Forget it. Get an education."

But the nomadic existence they led made getting an education virtually impossible. Joey was smart and got good marks when he stayed in one class long enough to recognize the teacher and become familiar with the work. But how could even a smart kid develop good learning habits when he was constantly being yanked from one school and dropped into another to accommodate his mother's and father's theatrical schedule?

One year, when Joey was in the fifth grade, his parents took him with them while they played an engagement at a hotel in Lakewood, New Jersey. As a result, Joey missed two months of school and some very important work. When he returned, he wasn't able to catch up with the rest of the class, no matter how hard he studied. At the end of the term, all the kids in the fifth grade stood up and marched down the hall to the sixth-grade classroom—that is, all except Joey, who didn't get promoted.

As the others filed out, he was left sitting at his desk in the fifth-grade classroom, very much *alone*. As Joey sat by himself in the empty classroom, he was plagued by the same feeling of hopeless terror that he had experienced the night his Grandma Sarah died. From that moment on, Jerry abandoned any pretense of ever becoming a scholar, or even an average student.

To cover his humiliation at being left back and also because his frail, knock-kneed physique was often the butt of the other kids' jibes, Joey developed various defense mechanisms in school. He found that by affecting funny faces, like that of a baboon or a mongoloid idiot, or by using his squeaky voice when answering a question or just acting extra clumsy and purposely tripping and doing pratfalls he could make the other students laugh. This behavior earned him nicknames like "Ug" for "Ugly" and "Id" for "Idiot," but Joey didn't care because he discovered that by making his schoolmates laugh, he was also tricking them into liking him a little more.

So while the other children were enlarging their brainpower, Joey was developing his repertoire of clownish mannerisms. His classroom deportment didn't exactly earn him the title of Teacher's Pet, but it did come in handy when he was trying to establish himself as a nightclub comedian. It also explains the childishness of some of his comedy routines today and why his comedy has such a large appeal for young people. It was originally fashioned for them, and he never changed the formula.

The Chaplinesque pathos that Jerry Lewis sometimes manages to inject into a characterization in his better films, such as in *That's My Boy*, is no doubt highly derivative of the loneliness and neglect he frequently experienced as an only child of peripatetic parents.

His bar mitzvah, for example, which every Jewish boy looks forward to as a time of great familial celebration and feasting, was a complete disappointment to the thirteen-year-old Joey.

Jerry recalls a perfunctory ceremony in a "bleak barn" of a synagogue. No other relatives or people attended, and Danny and Rea barely made it there themselves. They had been across the river in Manhattan auditioning for a job and rushed into the synagogue at the last minute—just in time to hear the last of Joey's traditional "Today I Am a Man" speech made to an empty house and then sit down with him and the rabbi at a little table and partake of a glass of cheap wine and a piece of cake. Following that, Danny and Rea rushed off again to perform at radio station WOR.

At Irvington High, Joey went out for cheerleader and made it. Students remember him as being one of the wackiest cheerleaders in the institution's existence. Frequently, the football team couldn't compete with Joey's antics on the sidelines for the audience's attention. If the visiting team scored a touchdown, he'd throw a tantrum on the grass and scream and kick. On other occasions, he'd purposely step into a bucket of water and pretend to struggle to extricate his foot. One day, he kicked so hard that the bucket sailed off his shoe and landed upside down on the coach's head. That ended his career as a cheerleader.

To earn spending money, Joey frequently took part-time jobs after school. His first employment was as a counterman at a drugstore in

Irvington. This job lasted until the night he jokingly jabbed through a toasting English muffin with such enthusiasm that the fork touched an electric outlet and short-circuited the entire store, causing some fifty customers to flee to the street without paying their checks.

For a while after that, he worked as a shipping clerk in a hat factory, but his heart was in show business.

Finally, at fourteen, he landed a job ushering at the Paramount Theater in New York.

It was during his Paramount ushering days that his determination to become a performer was really solidified. He recalls today that he actually could get "a high on" just by standing in the back of the theater and watching the pit rise up with the orchestra riding on it at the beginning of the stage show.

He'd stand in the aisle in back of the house and dream of the day when Henny Youngman or Milton Berle would break his leg and Mr. Weitman, the manager, would be desperate for a replacement. At which point in his daydream of glory, Joey would run up to him and cry out, "Sir, I can do it—I've watched his routine and I can do it word for word if you'll only give me a chance."

"I guess I'll have to," the manager would reply. "Now get up there on the stage and give it all you've got."

And Joey would do just that and be a big hit.

But Henny Youngman never broke his leg, and Jerry had to wait ten more years to play the Paramount.

While Joey was daydreaming about becoming a star, his father and mother were hired to be regular entertainers at Brown's Hotel in Loch Sheldrake, New York, in the summertime and at the Hotel Arthur in Lakewood, New Jersey, a winter resort. This coincided with the ending of Joey's formal education.

In the middle of his first year in high school, in his manual training class, he ruined a saw by trying to cut through a board that had a nail embedded in it. This act of unpremeditated mayhem on public school property caused the manual training teacher to exclaim to the rest of the class, "All Jews are stupid." In a rare display of courage, the unmuscular Joey punched the teacher in the jaw, knocking out one of his teeth, and was promptly expelled from Irvington High.

Joey immediately applied for, and got, a full-time job as a busboy at Brown's Hotel and the Hotel Arthur, where, coincidentally, his father sang and his mother played the piano. That was the move that unofficially launched him on a show business career.

In his off hours, Joey, then fifteen years old, began fooling around with a record act, a routine he first saw performed by Reginald Gardiner, the English comedian.

When Joey thought he had the act down pat, he tried it out on the guests at Brown's. While a phonograph offstage played the records of operatic and popular singers, Joey, attired in ridiculous costumes, mouthed the words and clowned for the audience, as if he actually were singing the numbers. For example, he did Igor Gorin singing *Figaro* and *Il Trovatore*, wearing a fright wig made of a mop and a tattered frock coat.

It was pure burlesque, but the routine got such yaks from the guests that even Danny Lewis had to admit that little Joey had talent and ought to be encouraged.

One of the staunchest supporters of Joey's act was Irving Kaye, a middle-aged ex-comedian who was down on his luck and temporarily working as a bellhop at Brown's. Kaye was a short man, with a stomach that couldn't be contained just by force; it hung over his belt. He was also nearly bald, with just a fringe of hair on the outer perimeter of his skull, and he was continually chomping on a foul-smelling cigar.

Kaye thought Joey had what it took to be a success in the big time, and after catching his record act in the dining room one night, he offered to help him get some professional theater bookings.

This enraged the usually kindhearted Mr. Brown. Good busboys were hard to find in that war year of 1942, and he was worried that if Joey became too interested in show business, he would neglect his chores in the dining room and might even quit altogether.

The matter came to a head when Irving Kaye actually got the youngster a booking at a small theater in Hoboken, New Jersey, for seven dollars a night.

"Vot's the matter?" fumed Brown when he heard of Joey's intention to take the night off to go to Hoboken. "All this isn't good enough for you?" And he indicated a mountain of dirty dishes Joey was supposed to wash.

"The kid's got talent," insisted Kaye. "You want to hold him back?"

Furious, Brown turned to Joey and screamed, "Young man, either you busboy with Brown's or you sing *Figaro* in Hoboken! But not both."

Faced with such a choice, Joey chose Hoboken, and Brown not only fired him but Irving Kaye as well.

The loss of their jobs turned out well for both Joey and Kaye. Joey's act was received with the same enthusiasm in Hoboken as it was at Brown's. And thus encouraged to commit himself to show business as a career, Joey then hired the mature Kaye as his traveling companion and road manager, a position Kaye still holds with Jerry Lewis today.

One of the first things Joey did after he decided to make show business his career was to take his father's name of Lewis and change his first name to Jerry. Why?

"I thought it over," recalls Jerry, "and I said to myself, 'How can anybody called Levitch get laughs?' So I changed it to Jerry Lewis."

His first booking as Jerry Lewis was in a seedy burlesque house called the Palace Theater in Buffalo, New York. The strippers all looked like rejects from a two-dollar brothel, and the male customers appeared to be more interested in being sexually stimulated while watching nude girls gyrating on the stage than in laughing at any alleged comedy the management was foisting on them.

As soon as the inexperienced Jerry Lewis walked out on the stage and started to imitate Igor Gorin, the sex-starved crowd of derelicts in the audience began to holler, "Bring on the babes!"

Jerry actually burst into tears and fled to his dresssing room to pack. Later, as he was sneaking out the stage entrance, Jerry was intercepted by a white-haired bulbous-nosed man in a baggy-pants outfit who introduced himself as Max Coleman. Max was a veteran burlesque comedian and an acquaintance of Jerry's father.

"Aren't you Danny Lewis's son?" he asked Jerry.

"Yeah."

"You're not acting like it," Max told him. "In this business, when you've got a bad audience, you gotta work harder. You don't quit."

Jerry took his advice and unpacked his suitcase. When he went out for the next show, Coleman sat in the audience and got the laughs started. This built up Jerry's confidence, and for the rest of the week he managed to struggle through his record act without getting booed off the stage.

It wasn't easy to survive in the highly competitive world of New York show business with just a record act, however, and although Kaye was having some success booking his young protégé into small out-of-the-way theaters for very little money, Jerry's future didn't look too promising for the big time.

Danny Lewis felt that what his son needed was a first-class agent. But because record acts seemed to be a dime a dozen, none of the regular agents wanted to handle Danny's son.

Hoping to meet someone of influence, Danny and Rea got into the habit of schlepping little Joey to Lindy's Restaurant every night after the theater.

Lindy's, at Forty-ninth Street and Broadway, was the favorite corned beef and sturgeon–dispensing emporium for the show business crowd. Al Jolson, the Marx Brothers, Jackie Gleason, Milton Berle, Eddie Cantor, Tallulah Bankhead, Abe Lastfogel (head of the powerful William Morris Theatrical Agency), and practically every other person who meant anything in the world of show business used to meet at Lindy's to slake their kosher appetites when they were in town.

Unfortunately for Danny and Rea Lewis, the prices at Lindy's reflected the wealth of most of its celebrated patrons. They could not afford to eat at Lindy's, nor were they important enough to get a table even if they could afford the tab. So the three Lewises would stand on the sidewalk near the main entrance, looking hopefully at every celebrity who entered or departed from Lindy's through the revolving door.

Whenever she did recognize someone, Rea would nudge Jerry in the ribs and say, "Make a funny face, dear—here comes Abe Lastfogel," or "There's Milton Berle—make like an idiot and talk funny."

Danny and Rea's stage-parental perseverance finally paid off in a small way. One night while the Lewises were standing in front of Lindy's with their noses pressed against the window pane, Abbey Greshler—one of the sharpest independent agents in New York—recognized Danny and Rea and invited them and their son into Lindy's for a cup of coffee and "a piece of Danish."

Greshler was then—and still is—a thin sickly-looking individual, with eyes that are sunken-in (like a skull's) and a complexion the color of unbaked pastry dough with lots of flour on it. His complexion is so sallow, in fact, that a stranger, upon seeing him for the first time, once remarked, "How long has that man been dead?"

While the Lewises and Greshler were gorging themselves with kosher goodies at a back table, Danny was able to talk the agent into taking a look at Jerry's act the next time he performed and giving him "an honest opinion." Jerry's next booking, a few days hence, was a split week, at seven dollars a night, at the Ritz Theater on Staten Island. Greshler felt sorry for the Lewises and agreed to make the trip, provided Danny paid the nickel for the ferryboat fare.

Knowing Greshler was in the audience, Jerry performed more nervously that night than usual. Greshler remembers that he wasn't exactly overwhelmed by the boy's *Figaro* bit; however, he recalls recognizing instantly that "the kid had a genius for mugging."

After the performance, Greshler went backstage and told Jerry that he thought he had a lot of talent, but if he hoped to make any real money, he'd have to do something besides pantomiming to an operatic recording.

"What do you want me to do? asked Jerry nervously.

"You'll have to start talking," pointed out Greshler. "Can't you talk?"

Jerry confessed that he was scared to death to open his mouth in front of an audience. He was afraid they'd laugh at his high squeaky voice. That's why he hid behind the protection of the *Figaro* record.

"Well, if you'd just do some emcee work as well as your record specialty, I've got a better chance of getting you jobs in the clubs," was Greshler's final take-it-or-leave-it assessment.

Since it was now a question of either conquering his fear of speaking in front of an audience or returning to being a busboy at Brown's, Jerry agreed to use his own voice as well as the record's.

"Good," said the fast-thinking Greshler. "I've got a job for you next week at the Gaiety Theater in Montreal. They want someone to emcee the whole bill."

"The whole bill?" Jerry practically fainted at the thought.

Despite his fear, Jerry showed up at the theater in Montreal. But, a few minutes before he was scheduled to go out on the stage, he panicked and placed a frantic telephone call to Greshler.

"I can't do it," he told Greshler hysterically. "I'm afraid to be an emcee. I'll just do my record act."

"If you don't do it," threatened Greshler, "I'll cancel you out right now. And you'll have to look for a new agent."

Afraid to face an irate stage mother if he failed, Jerry pulled himself together and managed to get through not only that night's performance but the entire Montreal stand. His introductions, however, were straighter than Ed Sullivan's.

Despite Jerry's ineptness as an emcee, Greshler was able to book him into some of the smaller cafés around New York after his Montreal stint and also into a few of the larger movie theaters in other states.

In 1944, when Jerry Lewis was still only seventeen, Greshler booked him into the Downtown Theater in Detroit, Michigan. His job was to fill in with his solo act during intermission for sixty dollars a week.

On the same bill was Ted Fio-Rito's orchestra—which was featuring a stunning, dark-haired girl vocalist named Patti Palmer. Patti had a good figure and a pleasing contralto voice, and when she stood in front of the band and belted out a sexy lyric, it mattered not to Jerry that she was already in her twenties while he was only a teen-ager.

It was love at first sight for Jerry, who was still a virgin and also in need of someone to mother him. Or perhaps he simply has an affinity for Italians. As he was to learn on subsequent meetings with Patti, her real name was Esther Caloniko, she had been born in Cambria, Wyoming, where her father, an Italian immigrant, had worked as a coal miner. Her mother was also a native-born Italian. Patti's parents had been divorced when she was a child, and she and Mrs. Caloniko had moved to Detroit where her mother worked on the assembly line in an automobile factory.

Jerry was on the same bill with Patti for a few weeks, however, before she took him seriously as a suitor. Perhaps the young comic was too immature for her Neapolitan tastes, although by the age of seventeen he was already well over six feet tall, with a clean-cut, Ivy-league appearance, complete with crew haircut and features that some people considered handsome.

To make Patti notice him, Jerry frequently resorted to the sophomoric tricks of his cheerleader days at Irvington High. Specifically, Jerry would hang around in the wings backstage, and when Patti would finish her stint in front of the band and be returning to her dressing room, he'd leap out at her from dark corners with mad grimaces or he'd try to emulate Count Dracula and grab the startled Patti by the neck and pretend to sink his teeth into her flesh so he could suck the blood.

All this was to impress Patti, who was understandably skeptical of his ability to support a family as a professional comedian.

When the older girl still refused to date him, Jerry would place frantic phone calls to Patti at all times of the day and night. For example, she'd just be getting to sleep in her hotel room at 2:00 in the morning when the ringing phone would jar her back into consciousness. The caller would be Jerry, and he'd say something like, "The potion is mixed. Say you'll marry me or in two minutes I'm a dead man!"

If Jerry couldn't get Patti's attention in a restaurant where they'd be having breakfast, but at separate tables, a favorite ploy of his was to dump a bowl of oatmeal over his head.

"Now why did you put oatmeal on your head?" Patti remembers one waitress asking Jerry.

"Because I didn't have Cream of Wheat," answered Jerry, affecting his favorite mongoloid expression.

On one occasion, Patti entered her dressing room to make a quick costume change and found Jerry hiding behind the door.

"What are you doing there?" she demanded angrily.

"Peeking," he answered, giggling bashfully. Even though she was half undressed at the time, Patti couldn't remain angry. In fact, his answer broke Patti up.

Another tactic of Jerry's was to run down the theater aisle during the show, make a Douglas Fairbanks leap onto the stage where Patti was singing, and throw himself on his knees at her feet. There he'd fawningly kiss the hem of her skirt as he proclaimed his love for her.

Finally, Jerry's behavior around the theater, both on and off the stage, grew so erratic that Ted Fio-Rito complained to the manager.

"I've been around a lot of actors all my life," he said, "but this kid worries me. I think he's light in the head."

He may have been light in the head, but he had a one-track mind when he knew what he wanted.

One night, when Patti returned to her dressing room, she found a pair of pink baby shoes dangling from her mirror and, attached to them, a note that read, "I haven't a buck, but what do you say we get married and fill these?"

When Ted Fio-Rito heard that Patti was actually considering the young comic's unorthodox proposal of marriage, he dropped into her dressing room for a father-daughter chat. He pointed out that there was a chance the band might get a motion picture contract—and the deal included Patti—but only if she promised never to see "that nut with the record act" again. He was taking her mind off her career.

"I can't *ever* see him?" exclaimed the disappointed Patti.

"Well, maybe in a straitjacket on visitor's day."

"But I love him," pleaded Patti.

"Look, honey, it'll never work out," said Fio-Rito, getting close to the real reason he objected to the union. "He's Jewish, you're Roman Catholic. The two don't mix."

Hoping God would be more understanding, Patti continued seeing Jerry, even though she had to quit Ted Fio-Rito's band in order to enjoy that pleasure.

But jobs for competent vocalists were plentiful, and soon she was singing with Jimmy Dorsey's orchestra. The Jimmy Dorsey Band was one of the most popular "swing" groups in America at the time, and it just so happened that they frequently appeared at Bill Miller's Riviera at Fort Lee, New Jersey, not far from where the Lewises lived.

Until Jerry was eighteen, he and Patti were only able to see each other when they happened to be playing the same towns or when their professional paths converged for a few hours between trains or buses. But as soon as Jerry reached the age of consent, he and Patti decided to get married.

Before they could marry, however, Patti's mother insisted on meeting the prospective bridegroom.

Concerned that he might not make the right impression if he played the role in the accustomed way—with the bride's parents doing the quizzing —Jerry decided beforehand that the best defense was a good offense.

He arrived at Mrs. Caloniko's modest apartment soberly dressed and carrying a small black notebook. Almost before the puzzled Italian lady could welcome him into her living room. Jerry sat down, placed the notebook on his knee, and started to put her through an exhaustive interrogation.

Maintaining a completely deadpan expression and jotting down her answers as carefully as an insurance investigator, Jerry asked where Mrs. Caloniko was born, the name of the priest who married her, the number of persons in her family, her income, her record as a citizen ("How many times have you been arrested?"), her drinking habits, her church attendance habits, and finally how many children she thought her daughter could give him?

After taking several pages of notes, Jerry intoned very gravely, "I see," clapped the notebook shut, and rose to his feet. "Thank you," he said. "You'll be hearing from me." And he departed.

After her suitor had gone, Patti asked her mother what she thought of Jerry. "I think he's upset," answered Mrs. Caloniko without hesitation.

Her mother's negative attitude notwithstanding, Patti officially accepted Jerry's proposal,—provided she be allowed to keep her job with Dorsey's band. Jerry was not wildly enthusiastic about Patti mixing marriage and a career. But on the money he was making with his record act, Jerry could hardly say no to her request, especially if the two of them were to continue eating. So he acquiesced, and in October 1944 he and Patti eloped to New York and were married by a justice of the peace.

The reason for the elopement was to avoid family conflict. Patti's mother was, of course, Catholic; Danny and Rea were strictly kosher. As a result, the wise young couple (or were they simply scared?) decided that a nonreligious ceremony was the only possible way they could prevent both sets of in-laws from feeling that they were favoring one faith over the other.

In addition to the religious aspect, Rea Lewis wasn't exactly overjoyed at the prospect of losing her one and only "little Joey" to any girl, let alone to a *shiksa*. To mollify Rea, Patti and Jerry returned to Newark a few weeks after their elopement and were wed a second time in an orthodox Jewish ceremony in the same temple where Jerry had had his bar mitzvah.

The solemn ceremony was conducted under the traditional velvet canopy, with the elder Lewises looking on proudly. Deadly serious, wearing a white yarmulke and a blue serge suit, Jerry Lewis was determined that nothing would spoil this occasion for the mother and father he loved so well.

Everything went off as smoothly as a first-class production of *Fiddler on the Roof*—until it came time for the young bridegroom to crush the symbolic glass wine goblet with his foot.

Whether the rabbi was buying an extra-strong grade of goblet or Jerry Lewis needed to put on weight, no one to this day is quite sure. All anyone can recall is that Jerry was unable to crush the glass. First he trod lightly on it. Then he stamped hard on it with his heel. Finally, in an act of sheer desperation, he leaped high into the air and came down on the goblet with both feet, repeating this action over and over again with no better results—as the canopy overhead swayed dangerously.

Since it was now a question of which would collapse first—the goblet, the canopy, or the bridegroom—the rabbi called the wedding a draw, and Jerry and Patti stole away to their first home—a fifty-dollar-a-month walk-up flat in Newark, New Jersey.

It wasn't many months after the two of them had set up housekeeping that Patti discovered she was pregnant. Evidently, Jerry hadn't been kid-

ding when he had threatened to fill those pink booties that Patti had
found hanging from her dressing room mirror back in Detroit.

Whatever Jerry's prior feelings about wives not mixing marriage and
careers had been, this latest development in their romance definitely
precluded Patti continuing to sing with Dorsey's band. Unless a girl were
Kate Smith, she couldn't possibly get away with standing in front of an
audience with a stomach the size of an inflated balloon and singing, "I
Won't Sit Under the Apple Tree with Anyone Else but You."

With Patti personally sidelined, it was going to be strictly up to the
eighteen-year-old Jerry to keep the two of them from starving. And
Jerry, even with Greshler handling him, was doing little more than that,
although by mid-1944 he was being employed fairly regularly as an
emcee in some of the smaller midtown cafés, such as La Martinique and
the Glass Hat, which was in the Hotel Belmont Plaza, at Forty-ninth
Street and Lexington Avenue. But this seemed more a result of the wartime manpower shortage than a tribute to Greshler's agenting or Jerry's
talent as an emcee who featured a record act. As an emcee, he was still
about as funny as Lawrence Welk, and when he introduced an act, he
stammered worse than a bashful student making his first speech in the
school auditorium.

According to Abbey Greshler, pontificating in his plush Sunset Strip
offices today, the consensus in 1944 about Jerry Lewis's performing was
that "he was a no-talent bum and I should stop him. But he had something crazy in his face, the way he moved, and I had faith in him."

Only Greshler could see it. The first time Jerry played the Glass Hat in
1944, the manager of that establishment grabbed Greshler immediately
after his client finished performing and demanded, "What's with this
lousy kid? Don't he tell any gags or stories? You sold him to me as an
emcee, not an undertaker!"

Luckily for Jerry's career, there was a war on, and even untalented
emcees were hard to find.

Jerry's salary, when he did work, was usually around eighty dollars a
week. Out of that, he had to pay a 10 percent commission to Greshler,
his income tax, and his traveling expenses, when he was lucky enough to
obtain a booking in another town. What remained was hardly enough to
support a growing family—even uncomfortably—much less sock anything
away to cover the medical costs of the Lewises' impending blessed event.

When Patti was pregnant with Gary, the Lewises could afford only one
maternity dress. By the time Gary was born, Patti had washed it so many
times that it was shiny; there was no nap to the fabric anymore.

To cover her threadbare rags, Jerry, in a burst of extravagance, bought
Patti a used fur coat—of dyed squirrel. It was hardly the thing to wear to
the Waldorf Basement, where Jerry was doing his record act, but Patti

thought it was the most elegant thing she'd ever seen. From the way she swept through the Waldorf Basement to her table, one would have thought she was modeling a $10,000 mink.

Then, just before reaching her table, Patti caught one of the chic café society matrons (who was clad in sable and diamonds) making a face as she went by in her dyed squirrel. Patti felt so humiliated that she could never bring herself to wear the coat again, no matter how cold the weather was. "Not because of the woman's snobbish attitude," recalls Patti, "but because it reflected on Jerry. It destroyed his gift."

Not only was the young and highly emotional expectant father a meager provider in those days, but he was totally irresponsible when it came to handling what little money he did make.

There was a time, for example, nearing the end of Patti's first pregnancy, when Jerry was out of work and all the two of them had in the bank was thirty dollars. Then, from left field, Greshler got Jerry a booking in a nightclub in Montreal. Ordinarily, this would have been considered a stroke of good fortune, but Jerry didn't like to travel without Patti, and this trip she would have to stay home because she was having a rough pregnancy.

"I'm not going," exclaimed Jerry to the ailing Patti. "I can't leave you alone."

"But you have to work," insisted Patti. "We need the money."

Jerry was ambivalent about leaving her alone, right up to a few hours before departure. Then inspiration born of desperation hit him, and he dashed out of the apartment without explanation. A short while later, he rushed back with a small furry object in his hand.

"Here's someone to keep an eye on things," said Jerry, shoving the ball of fur into his wife's arms.

It was a six-week-old cocker spaniel, on which he'd squandered more than half of their thirty-dollar nest egg.

4

My Buddy

Despite being destined to flunk his first movie exams, Dean Martin had established something of a reputation for himself as a crooner by the time his and Jerry Lewis's professional paths initially converged in 1945, when both men were booked into the Glass Hat simultaneously.

Jerry was the emcee, with his same old record act, but Dino was the featured singer, commanding a respectable salary of $500 a week plus the closing spot on the bill.

Crooners, in those tumultuous sentiment-ridden terminal years of World War II, were suddenly very much in demand, and even Dino was making big money for those days. Just prior to their meeting at the Glass Hat, Dino had pulled down $650 a week at Loew's State. Following that appearance, Lou Perry had gotten him $900 a week in Chicago, where his bouncy style of singing and breezy banter delighted audiences and brought in overflow crowds. Booked for two weeks, the popular Dino was held over for fourteen and was suddenly considered a name attraction not only on the shores of Lake Michigan but at Manhattan's Glass Hat as well.

Jerry, however, was lucky to be making $100 a week, and he was still no name at all, except when the proprietor of a café where he was bombing called him one—usually something uncomplimentary.

The first time Dean Martin and Jerry Lewis became aware of each other's existence was in 1944, when a mutual friend introduced them on the corner of Forty-ninth Street and Broadway.

Dean looked like a typical Broadway sharpie, with slightly greasy hair and a loud pin-striped suit, which was his idea of a classy outfit in those days. Jerry, at seventeen, looked as if he were barely old enough to have had a bar mitzvah, with a high pompadour hairstyle and a conservative, ill-fitting, ready-to-wear suit that featured padded shoulders covering his tall gangling body.

The two young men shook hands, exchanged show business small talk briefly, and then went their separate ways.

Jerry's first impression of Dean was that he was "conceited, snooty, and standoffish." Dean thought Jerry was "a young wise guy."

They retained these opinions of each other until the two of them met again in the middle of 1945, when they just happened to find themselves appearing together on the same bill at the Glass Hat. The intimacy forced on them from being on the same bill caused Dean and Jerry to alter their earlier and hastily formed opinions of each other, and they became friends.

According to Betty Martin—who was in New York at the time, visiting Dean with their two children, Craig and Claudia, who were three and one, respectively—it happened this way:

Betty and Dean and their two kids shared one room on the second floor of the Belmont Plaza Hotel, directly across the hall from where Jerry Lewis was staying alone. Jerry had left Patti back home in Newark to take care of their new baby, Gary, who'd been born on July 31 of that year. One day when Dean and Betty wanted to go shopping without dragging their two small children along, Jerry offered to be their baby-sitter. The Martins quickly accepted, and during the rest of the engagement Jerry became their regular baby-sitter.

Jerry was a lonely young man in those days, with hardly any friends except Patti. His desire to have somebody to talk to when he was away from home on the road no doubt motivated his original offer to baby-sit for the Martins. Obviously he saw in it a chance to become friendly with a nice young couple, but especially Dean.

Even though Jerry's first impression of Dean was that he was "snooty and standoffish," Jerry secretly admired the Italian from the moment they first shook hands on Broadway. Dino, with his Italian joie de vivre and casual manner, seemed to be, at the age of twenty-eight, everything that the younger performer was not.

Whereas Jerry was a skinny weakling, who looked as if he needed a crash course from Charles Atlas, Dino was the strong, handsome, and virile type, who could handle himself in any situation. He wasn't afraid of his employers, and he wasn't bashful about taking a poke at a heckler whose chatter became a little too obnoxious. Whereas Jerry was uptight in front of an audience, Dino wasn't afraid to kid the patrons. Moreover, he had such a relaxed easy way of delivering a song that it sometimes seemed as if he were falling asleep while still holding onto the mike.

Also Dean never seemed to take his singing very seriously. In fact, he frequently kidded around with the lyrics in such a way as to make the songs' composers wish he'd stop singing their creations.

"And now I'm going to sing, 'If I Had It to Do All Over Again, I'd Do It All Over You,' " was one of his standards. From there he might segue into a parody of "The Girl Next Door"—"The Girl Next Door's My Favorite Whore."

Real classy stuff, but the tourists and the drunks ate it up.

Jerry found it easy to admire a man with that kind of gall, and during their two-week engagement together at the Glass Hat, he started to resort to his old high school tactics to get the Italian Crosby to notice him. He began clowning around with Dino and kidding him about his lackadaisical style of singing and the loud sport clothes he wore. To his surprise, he found that Dino seemed to like him and would return the compliments by ribbing him back about his high squeaky voice, his butch haircut, and his tongue-tied approach to emceeing.

Dino even lent Jerry a few of his own "one-liners" to help spice up his introductions, but Jerry was so uptight about his ability as a monologuist that the audiences sensed it and refused to laugh.

Besides coaching him, Dino acted as Jerry's protector. Once a heckler in the audience called Jerry a knock-kneed ape. When the skinny tongue-tied Jerry couldn't get rid of the heckler himself, Dino came to his rescue and personally bounced the obnoxious guy from the club.

By the time the two of them finished their first engagement together at the Glass Hat, Jerry was beginning to regard Dino as the older brother he wished he'd had when he was a kid.

For a few months, their bookings kept Jerry and Dino apart. Then, in January 1946, their professional paths crossed again—this time at the Havana-Madrid. The Havana-Madrid was a rumba spot catering mostly to Spanish-speaking clientele. Desi Arnaz, Carmen Miranda, Carmen Amaya, and Xavier Cugat were patrons at the place when they were in town. Although Dino's only other tongue was Italian, he was a favorite at the Havana-Madrid and always did well there.

But Jerry Lewis's record act was a complete disaster at the Havana-Madrid. The customers flocked there either to dance the rumba or to be crooned to softly in their native tongue while they were getting crocked on margueritas. Many didn't understand English, and they didn't find it amusing at all when Jerry Lewis bounded out on the stage and started mouthing the lyrics of "The Beer Barrel Polka" to a recording of the Andrews Sisters and making funny faces as he imitated each of the sisters.

To this day, nobody can be sure why Jerry Lewis was booked into the Cuban nightspot, and Jerry, after laying an egg there for a couple of nights, was positive from the way Angel Lopez was scowling at him that it was only a question of time before he would be fired.

On the third night, Jerry took Lou Perry aside before the show started and asked Dean's manager if it would be all right if "I fool around on the floor with Dean after he does his full act?" For some reason, Perry liked Jerry. He checked with Dean, who said, "Sure, let the kid fool around."

Nobody knew what Jerry meant by "fooling around" until, during Dean's last number, he appeared among the tables dressed as a busboy, precariously balancing a large tray of dishes on one hand raised over his head. As he wove his way through the tables, he suddenly appeared to lose control of his heavy load, and the whole tray of dishes went crashing to the floor.

"Oh, sorry, kind sir," apologized Jerry, as Dino stopped his song in midlyric and fixed his twinkling black eyes on the mock busboy. "I hope I didn't interrupt anything."

"No, I was getting pretty tired of that song, anyway," responded the quick-thinking Dino.

The audience roared as Jerry got down on his knees and started picking up the broken crockery piece by piece, and Dino came down off the stage to help him. All the while, the two of them continued their ad libs.

At the next show, Jerry repeated the stunt, and the two of them expanded the bit by throwing in a few more lines and pieces of business. The Spanish-speaking patrons seemed to understand slapstick, and the laughs were good. By the end of the engagement, even Angel Lopez was looking at Jerry with more-tolerant eyes. Jerry was so elated that he even asked Dino if he'd consider teaming up with him.

"What for?" asked Dino.

"Audiences love us," replied Jerry. "I'll bet we could make a lot of money together."

But Dino shrugged off Jerry's offer. He liked Jerry, as one would tolerate a pesty kid brother, but he had been a "loner" since 1943, and although he never admitted it, he was probably slightly resentful of the younger man's steady intrusion into his act. One engagement was enough. He didn't need a partner who did slapstick. He had sex appeal.

So, once again, Dino spat in fate's eye, only to have fate ignore the insult.

Until the summer of 1946, Dino and Jerry played many of the same nightclubs on the East Coast, but always on different dates. Jerry continued to admire Dino, but from afar.

When he knew that Dino would be following him into a club in a strange town, Jerry would often leave written messages behind in the dressing room for him—messages tipping him off on everything from where to find the best Italian restaurant to how to handle the local audiences.

Dino got in the habit of returning the favor by scribbling messages of his own and pasting them to the mirror when he knew Jerry would be following him into town.

Their missives, while admittedly not on the same literary level as George Bernard Shaw's letters to Ellen Terry, are, nevertheless, fairly eloquent proof of the affection that was already blossoming between Dino and Jerry.

"Hello, Jerk. Played to eleven people here last night. Was I a smash!"

"Hear you laid an egg in Newark. Why don't you tape your stuff so folks won't have to watch you?"

"Idiot, that big blond's name is Myrna—but you can't date her. She loves me."

At that time in his life, Jerry wasn't doing any more than admiring the good-looking girls he met along the nightclub circuit. He had a wife whom he adored and a one-year-old son, and he intended to keep both of them. Patti felt the same love for her "little idiot" and tried to be with him as much as possible. But on his salary there was no money to spare for nurses or baby-sitters, and much of the time she was trapped in their apartment while he was out trying to make audiences laugh.

Besides, she had almost died giving birth to Gary, and that experience had left her weak and ill during the first half of 1946. This alone precluded her from doing much nightclubbing with Jerry.

As for Dino and Betty, their marriage was having a different kind of trouble—incompatibility. Despite several years of exposure to life in the big city, Betty was still basically a shy country girl who hated nightclubs and was turned off by the noisy extroverted show people and half-drunk customers who infested them.

As a result, Betty was rarely seen with Dino. She either stayed at home with the children in their New York apartment or else took them to Philadelphia on protracted visits to see her parents.

Her frequent prolonged absences gave Dino the complete freedom he enjoyed when it came to other women. This arrangement suited him fine despite the rather large family he was swiftly acquiring with Betty.

Betty may not have come around often, but when she did, she always seemed to be pregnant. "She should have had a zipper on her stomach," one friend from that period recalls. In 1945, Betty gave birth to Gail. That made a total of three children in the brief span between 1942 and 1945. And one more, Deana, was still to come before the Martins officially separated in 1948.

So whether Dean and Betty were seen together very much or not, it's obvious they *were* together at least four times during their marriage.

Whether Dino and Betty's prolific output was intentional or merely the result of being either "Catholic or careless," to borrow Clare Boothe Luce's classic line, Dino has never revealed. Knowing Dino's other habits, it was probably the latter.

A devout Catholic Dino has never been, according to those closest to him. "He's a respecter of religion, and he probably believes in God," states Ernie Glucksman, who produced Martin and Lewis's first network television show, "The Colgate Comedy Hour," and was with them constantly in their early years as a team.

Although Dino may believe in God, there seems little evidence that he's a practicing Catholic who goes to church on Sunday mornings. The only practicing he's ever seen doing on Sunday mornings is on the first tee at the Bel Air Country Club.

His second wife, Jeanne Martin, states it even more emphatically. "Oh, he's religious," she says, "but religion had nothing to do with all those kids. He was just very young and uneducated and probably hadn't even heard of contraceptives."

Whatever the reason, history records that Dean Martin was in the process of acquiring a rather cumbersome family by the time he and Jerry Lewis were treading the same nightclub boards.

There were no nightclub boards to be trod for Dean Martin, however, for the week beginning July 20, 1946. Summertime was usually slow in show business, and, for the first time in many weeks, Dino was out of a job—just lying around Lou Perry's hotel room, waiting for his agent to come up with something. His debts were now compounding at a frightening rate, and the future looked bleak.

By a strange reversal of events, Jerry Lewis *was* working that week— at the Club 500 in Atlantic City, where he had been hired to do his record act.

Catering strictly to the summer tourist trade, the Club 500, which fronted on the boardwalk, was a barn of a place, garishly decorated, with mirrored pillars and the usual postage-stamp-size tables, and, like most of the other joints along the boardwalk, it featured gambling entre nous in the back room.

The Club 500 was owned by Skinny D'Amato, who looked as if he had just stepped out of a George Raft gangster film of the mid-1930s. Thin and dark-visaged, D'Amato was a dapper dresser who leaned to loud striped suits with wide lapels, two-tone shoes, and lots of jewelry.

The man who "fronted" for D'Amato, and who also booked all the talent, was Irving Wolf. Wolf had never seen Jerry Lewis's act before booking him into the Club 500. He had taken him strictly on the strength of Abbey Greshler's statement that "the kid would kill the people."

After seeing Jerry perform at the first show, D'Amato wanted to kill

Wolf who, in turn, wanted to kill Greshler. Jerry's record act had laid such a gigantic egg that you could make an omelet out of it large enough to feed everyone in Atlantic City.

About 9:45 that same night, the phone in Lou Perry's hotel room rang. The caller turned out to be Jerry Lewis. He was phoning from the Emerald Apartments, where he had paid his rent in advance for a week, and he was in tears.

"I opened here, and they canceled me after the first performance," he sobbed. "They say I'm stinking up the joint and I can't go on any more."

The distraught Jerry pleaded with Perry to think of something to save his job. "Patti's sick, and I'm desperate for the $175 a week they promised me. If I go home without it, she'll probably divorce me."

"Why are you calling me?" asked Perry. "Why don't you talk to Abbey Greshler? He's your agent."

"Because they told me if Abbey Greshler ever shows his face in Atlantic City again, they'll stick him in cement and throw him in the ocean," said Jerry.

Feeling sorry for Lewis, even though he didn't have much faith in his ability as a comedian, Perry calmed him down by saying he'd try to think of something and hung up, with the promise that he'd call him back as soon as he had worked out a plan.

The plan had already begun to flower in his mind. Remembering that the Club 500 had been interested in using Dean Martin but had always refused to meet his price, Perry phoned Irving Wolf and presented him with a proposition. He could have the services of Dean Martin starting Saturday, and for only $500 a week, provided he kept Jerry Lewis on the bill and didn't fire him.

"Absolutely not," countered Wolf. "That boy doesn't bring in customers. He chases them away with that corny record act."

"Don't let him do his record act," advised Perry. "Just keep him around until Dean gets down there. They do a very funny bit together."

"What kind of a bit?" asked Wolf, still chilly to the idea.

"He fools around in Dean's act."

"What kind of fooling around?"

"Never mind. Just take my word for it. The audience will love it."

Reluctantly Wolf agreed, and said Dino could open Saturday night.

Next Perry called Jerry back and told him the deal. "Just don't go near the club," he insisted. "Stay where you are until Dean gets there. You'll just do your busboy bit."

So Jerry Lewis, who was destined to become the "important half" of the team of Martin and Lewis in just a few short months, had to spend the rest of the week hiding out in a cheap apartment hotel while he waited anxiously for Dean Martin to show up in Atlantic City and save his job for him on Saturday—the same Saturday, July 25, 1946, that Sophie Tucker strolled along the boardwalk in front of the Club 500 and saw a handsome Italian youth rescuing a skinny and bedraggled Jewish-looking youth from the surf.

When the Last of the Red-Hot Mamas finally realized that the drowning she had just witnessed was only a crass publicity stunt, she burst into laughter—laughter that caused the flesh on her gargantuan frame to shake like a bowl of soft Jell-o.

Remembering that many years earlier W. C. Fields had also worked as a "drowner" along the same boardwalk to attract attention to the establishment where he was juggling, Miss Tucker took a chance on wasting a precious evening of her time and dropped into the Club 500 around 8:30 to see what the enterprising young con men had to offer.

Not entertainment, certainly. Judging from the first ten minutes the twosome were on the stage, it was evident to Sophie Tucker that Martin and Lewis didn't add up to *one* W. C. Fields. This was comedy? A half-assed Bing Crosby making double-entendre jokes to some of Tin Pan Alley's great standards and a moronic-looking kid in a crew haircut and a busboy's outfit stumbling around the room with a tray of dishes while his partner was crooning, finally dropping the tray on the floor.

For ten minutes, Sophie Tucker didn't crack a smile. Neither did anyone else—to Dino and Jerry's dismay and bewilderment. For some reason, the customers at the Club 500 weren't as easy to please as the ones at the Havana-Madrid. Certainly Irving Wolf was no pushover. He just stood in the wings, glaring vengefully at them.

"Lou Perry sold me you two as a comedy team," Wolf finally snarled at Dino and Jerry at a point in the show when the two young men had given up trying to be comedians entirely and were relying solely on Martin's crooning to keep the audience from walking out on them. "If you guys don't get funny soon, you're through."

In desperation, Jerry began interrupting Dino's songs with all kinds of crazy ad libs, which were absolutely apropos of nothing—cracks like "You know what, Dean? If I go out with girls, I *get* pimples"; and "You're not for real—you have talent—I just have nerve."

Following that, Jerry leaped to the drums and shouted to Dean in a lisping voice, "May I play the drums for you, dear thir?"

"Why not, baby?" answered the bemused Dino.

"Oh, thank you, kind thir," responded Jerry. "I am so unworthy of you."

At that point, he pulled a set of novelty-store comic teeth from his pocket, shoved them into his mouth, and started pounding on the drums until he had completely drowned out Dino's ballad.

As the customers began to chuckle, Jerry continued his assault on his straight man. Grabbing the orchestra leader's baton from him, Jerry started to lead the orchestra. Then, as Dino made another attempt to sing, Jerry turned off all the lights in the room, causing dining room employees to drop whole trays of dishes.

Encouraged by the audience's laughter, Jerry decided to resurrect his record act. Only it was better with Dino assisting him. Every time Jerry opened his mouth in broad imitation of Igor Gorin or the Andrews Sisters, Dino would pick up a bottle of seltzer and squirt it into Jerry's mouth, nearly drowning him. Jerry, in turn, grabbed a bunch of celery off a ringside table and hit Dino over the head with it.

"Be careful of my new nose," quipped Dino. "The doctor didn't guarantee it against celery."

When it became obvious from the yaks they were getting that the audience liked this sort of thing, Jerry strode to a ringside table, paused in front of a man partly preoccupied with eating a steak dinner, grabbed the plate, and smashed it to the floor, steak and all.

Taking a cue from Jerry, Dino grabbed a highball from a passing tray, took a sip of it, sputtered and coughed as if the drink were poisonous, then emptied the rest of the glass's contents into a customer's face.

The audience gasped, and for a split second there was total silence in the cavernous room. It was apparent from the murderous glances that Skinny D'Amato was shooting Martin and Lewis that if he ever got his hands on them, he would have them encased in cement and dropped into the Atlantic.

Suddenly Sophie Tucker, prominent at her ringside table, threw back her huge head and roared. This broke the tension, and the rest of the customers followed her example. Gales of laughter filled the Club 500, and some of the customers urged them on to further madness by shouting, "More, more."

As Jerry glanced nervously in D'Amato's direction, the proprietor relaxed his glare into a thin smile and nodded eagerly at the pair to "Keep it up."

From that moment on, the destruction that Martin and Lewis perpetrated in the name of comedy was cataclysmic. They grabbed trays from waiters, squirted soda down dowagers' blouses, flung steaks clear across the room, and bullied the customers into sitting on the floor and singing campfire songs and then into joining a conga line.

After the second show, which was equally as riotous, Sophie Tucker pushed her way through the crowd of admirers suddenly surrounding the newly born comedy team and announced to the throng that Martin and Lewis were "a combination of the Keystone Kops, the Marx Brothers, and Abbott and Costello." She predicted to the local press that they would leave their mark on show business for many years to come.

The next evening, customers were lined up clear around the block waiting to get into the Club 500 to see the team everyone was raving about. Large as the club was, Skinny D'Amato was forced to put on six shows a night, raise Martin and Lewis's salary to $750 and hold them over for six weeks.

Hard as it was for Dino and Jerry to believe, it had actually happened: Out of the ruins of Skinny D'Amato's broken crockery a real crowd-pleasing comedy act had arisen. Not only had it arisen, but it was on its way to such sudden stardom that neither the Martins nor the Lewises were quite prepared for it.

5

Hitch Your Wagon

Another person who was caught by surprise was Lou Perry. The first inkling he had of the exciting happenings in Atlantic City was the Monday morning after their opening, when he received a phone call from Irving Wolf telling him what a hit the boys were and tipping him off that Abbey Greshler had somehow got wind of Martin and Lewis's smash opening and had been there since Sunday making all kinds of overtures to Dean Martin. He advised Lou Perry to jump on the next train and get down to Atlantic City immediately if he didn't want to lose his client to Abbey Greshler.

Perry couldn't believe that Dean Martin would walk out on him after all he'd done for him. Besides, he had a management contract with Dino. Nevertheless, he took the next train out of New York, just to be on the safe side. Arriving at the Club 500 that afternoon, Lou Perry found that what Wolf had been telling him indeed seemed to be true.

Greshler, only too well aware of Dino's shaky financial situation, had already been on the scene for a day and a half, standing right alongside Dino at the crap tables most of that time, filling his ears with glowing talk about the high-paying jobs he could get him if only he'd stay teamed with Jerry Lewis and let *him* handle the two of them. Moreover, Greshler was offering to lend him money—not only for gambling but also to help get him out of hock.

How much did he need? $1,000? $2,000? $5,000? All Dino had to do was name the figure, and he could have it. Married to a wealthy wife by that time, Greshler could well afford to advance Dino any sum he needed. Dino settled for something in the $5,000–$10,000 bracket, claiming he could use the cash to pay off some of his debts and buy a house for his mother and father.

As further proof of the kind of service Dino could expect if he switched managers, Greshler was already talking about a booking for Martin and Lewis at the Latin Casino in Camden at $1,250 a week, beginning the day their engagement at the Club 500 ended.

Since Dean Martin has never been the kind of a fellow to let little things like loyalty and gratitude interfere with his own best interests, he played right along with Greshler's game, and almost before Lou Perry realized what was happening, he was Dean Martin's agent in name only.

Of course, he still had an actual contract with Dino. But like most documents to which Dino affixed his signature in those days, it was virtually worthless—as, indeed, are most management contracts if a client chooses to ignore them.

Perry found that out when he took his complaint to the American Guild of Variety Artists, which generally plays King Solomon in show business disputes. Twice a board of arbitration ruled that Lou Perry had the "sole and exclusive rights to manage Dean Martin," and twice Dean Martin ignored their decision. Perry hung in there for a few months, but because of a surprising and ironic reversal in the order of Martin's and Lewis's respective importance, Perry's role was to diminish significantly.

To Perry's surprise, once Martin and Lewis caught on, the person people talked about the most was Jerry Lewis. Because most laymen and critics are pitifully unaware of the importance of a great straight man, Jerry Lewis was considered the "really funny" member of the team—"the kid with the talent." His brand of comedy was more explosive, more frenetic, and hence more noticeable than was Dino's quiet and droll contribution.

As Jerry Lewis's importance to the act grew in people's minds, so did Greshler's influence in the business, because he was the agent handling the "talented half." If people wanted to make a deal for Martin and Lewis, they automatically went to the agent who handled Jerry Lewis— the same self-serving Jerry Lewis who had broken down over the phone to Lou Perry and cried real tears because he was about to lose his job and the same Jerry Lewis who, only a week later, phoned his own agent and alerted him to a situation that enabled Greshler to grab half a million dollars in potential commissions from the man who had helped Jerry, who wasn't even his client, get his first big break.

Well, who could blame Jerry if he was a bit anxious? At twenty, he was a baby, and he had a baby of his own and a sick wife to support. He also didn't have much of a future without Dean Martin. Jerry Lewis may have been a school dropout, but he was smart enough to be aware of Dean's importance to him even then. With him, he knew he could really go places. Without him, he was liable to be a busboy again for real. So he hitched his wagon to the star he was about to eclipse for the next ten years and sat back and left the driving to Abbey Greshler.

Dino—more from his laissez-faire attitude of taking life as it came and not trying to control his destiny than from any overt desire to hurt his former manager—seemed willing to turn things over to Abbey Greshler too.

Eventually, Lou Perry received an official letter of dismissal from Dean Martin. When this happened, he threw in his managerial towel and allowed Greshler to buy Dino's contract from him. "I believe he let it go for something like three or four thousand dollars," recalls Betty Martin today. "Dean really could have done something better for him than that if he really tried. I mean, after all that wonderful little man had done for him."

But Perry's pride wouldn't let him make more of an issue out of it. He felt that as long as the switch in agents would help Dean, he'd go along with it. It was a gesture that certainly proved Lou Perry had a heart of gold.

With Abbey Greshler at the main controls, the Martin and Lewis rocket to stardom took off from its Atlantic City pad in the last half of 1946 at a speed that's rarely been equaled before or since in show business.

In the year and a half following their emergence as a comedy team at the Club 500, Martin and Lewis scored stunning triumphs in theaters such as Loew's State and the Capitol and also in every major nightclub along the eastern seaboard, from Miami to Philadelphia, and as far west as the Chez Paree in Chicago.

After their stint in Atlantic City, Greshler booked them into the Latin Casino in Camden, New Jersey, at $1,250 a week.

For a brief time, Dino received the lion's share of the weekly take. But as soon as Lewis established himself as the powerhouse of the act, Dino voluntarily agreed to split everything fifty-fifty. In obeisance to Dino's age and vaster experience in the business, however, Jerry awarded him top billing.

In January 1947, after a long and successful stand in Camden, Martin and Lewis moved into Manhattan's famed movie showcase, Loew's State. There, playing on the same bill with *The Jolson Story*, starring Larry Parks, they played to capacity houses, and for the first time *Variety* had an opportunity to see them together on a regular proscenium theater stage:

This new act, composed of Dean Martin who at one time began making an impression on the crooner parade, and Jerry Lewis, a young comic, has a good future. Deriving maximum benefit from the fresh, clean, youthful appearance of the pair, the turn does a smart job of tickling customers' funny bones at the State, which is playing to capacity houses with *The Jolson Story*.

Though there's a pattern to the act, based on Martin's neat vocaling and Lewis's complete lack of inhibition, it seems to the customers to be almost completely ad lib. The two combine to work over "That Old Gang of Mine," Martin foiling for Lewis, decked out as a moronic bartender, do vocal takeoffs of various top stars, etc. All they do cannot be detailed, but virtually every bit of it is good for solid laughs. All in all, these two kids have themselves a fine act. There are rough edges, but they'll wear away and what's underneath will wear a good deal longer.

In March of the same year, they scored another smash at the Latin Casino in Philadelphia at $1,500 a week. This time they didn't have to take a back seat to a hit movie. They were the headliners and were billed as such.

Proving that the business they did on Manhattan's main stem was no fluke and that they didn't need the Jolson film to help them bring in business, in Philadelphia they broke a nine-year-old attendance record previously established by Ted Lewis and were held over for twelve weeks. Twelve weeks in Philadelphia—you'd have to be a smash in order to stand it there that long (or else be Mike Douglas).

While they were in Philly, Bill Miller signed them for $1,800 a week to headline at his place—Bill Miller's Riviera, right across the Hudson River from Manhattan, in Fort Lee, New Jersey. The Riviera seated over 1,000 people, but Martin and Lewis had no trouble filling it. In fact, they were such a smash that they spent the entire summer and part of the fall there. New Jersey couldn't seem to get enough of them.

Leaving the Riviera, they played seven record-breaking weeks at the Chez Paree in Chicago; then they moved to the Capitol on Broadway. Following those appearances, they were booked back into the Havana-Madrid, where Jerry had first started "fooling around" in Dean's act. Only now it wasn't for $200 a week; it was for $2,000. In addition, Angel Lopez would have to swallow the $1,000 loan he had once made to Dino. They settled down there for another long run.

Although the pay was good, there wasn't a great deal of status to playing places like the Havana-Madrid. There were dozens of small nightclubs like it around New York, all featuring saloon comics of the caliber of Jack E. Leonard, Morey Amsterdam, and Jerry Lester. But those clubs usually weren't springboards to careers in the movies or on radio, or even to the more sophisticated night spots like the Copacabana on Sixtieth Street and Ciro's in Hollywood. *Variety*, when it reviewed their act at the Havana-Madrid, indicated as much.

> Lewis tees off the fun with his synchronized mugging and motions to records of Danny Kaye's "Dinah," and Cyril Smith's "Sow Song." Guy's got stint down to perfection. Martin then warms up his pleasantly smooth baritone on a group of pops. Young crooner is greatly improved since opening at the club last winter. He still bounces around, jounces the mike and kids audience, but his completely relaxed manner builds up a nice intimacy with the crowd, and he gets plenty of applause.
>
> Rowdy action that pulls belly laughs, though, starts when Martin and Lewis team up to carry last twenty minutes together. The hoked-up gags and impressions probably wouldn't go in the more sedate niteries, but it's sock here.

With *Variety* putting such emphasis on the rowdiness of their act, Martin and Lewis might have been mired down in the small-saloon milieu forever if Abbey Greshler hadn't been such a good salesman.

When he first approached Monte Proser, who produced the shows at the fashionable Copacabana, with the suggestion that he put Martin and Lewis on, Proser turned a deaf ear to the idea. What did he need with two fellows whose main claim to fame seemed to be that they could break a little crockery and squirt seltzer in customers' faces? He was running a sophisticated big-time operation.

And he was right. The Copa wasn't just another saloon. It was the biggest place in Manhattan—not only in size but also in reputation. Its very name, in fact, was synonomous with glamour, sex, and uninhibited but very expensive merriment. Just say the name Copacabana, and the average person immediately conjured up visions of champagne corks popping and beautiful, bosomy, half-draped Copa Girls kicking, bumping, and grinding their way into sugar daddies' hearts.

"Forget *Variety*," pleaded Greshler. "Go see for yourself."

Mainly to get Greshler off his back, Proser finally dropped into the Havana-Madrid one night early in 1948 when Martin and Lewis were still playing there. What he saw made him laugh, and he promptly came up with an offer. He'd give them $1,500 a week.

"Only $1,500 a week!" exclaimed Jerry.

"We can make more than that at Loew's State," said Dino.

"That's all I can pay for a nonstarring act," explained Proser.

When Dino and Jerry learned that, in addition to having to take a cut in salary, they also wouldn't be headlining, they told Greshler to forget it. They'd rather go back to Philadelphia.

But Greshler took them aside and said, "Are you both crazy?"

He pointed out that the Copa was the showcase of the nightclub world and that if they were a hit there, they'd have it made. Furthermore, if they didn't take the job, they could start looking for a new manager.

Jerry and Dino decided to go along with Greshler and signed to play the Copa for two weeks, starting April 8, 1948.

An opening night at the Copa usually brought out the crème de la crème of café society and the Broadway crowd. Martin and Lewis's opening was no exception. Everyone who meant anything was there, from Earl Wilson to Walter Winchell, from Milton Berle to famed showman Billy Rose—but not to see Martin and Lewis. The main attraction was Vivian Blaine, the nasal-voiced comedienne who several years later was to score a fantastic success on Broadway in *Guys and Dolls*, singing "A Person Could Develop a Cold."

Except for Dean's and Jerry's wives, Abbey Greshler, and Rea and Danny Lewis, very few of the first nighters were even aware of Martin and Lewis's existence—such is the fame one achieves from appearing at places like the Havana-Madrid and the Club 500.

"Who the hell are Martin and Lewis, anyway?" one Broadway wise guy quipped shortly before the curtain went up on the first show. "Sounds like the guys who discovered the Northwest Passage."

By midnight, no one would ever mistake them for Lewis and Clark again.

Martin and Lewis exploded into full stardom that night, and on the way there they wreaked more havoc than a Japanese taxi driver.

Jerry opened the act in his usual way, by introducing his partner.

"And now I'd like you to meet Dean Martin—one of the greatest singers in the country. I don't know how he'll do in the city, but, anyway, here he is."

Although a mild joke by today's standards, the audience screamed, perhaps because his tall good-looking Italian straight man seemed the perfect foil. Dino smiled thinly at his partner's insult, and then sang a hit tune of the day, "Slow Boat to China," in his usual languorous imitation of Crosby. But the reaction of the women in the room wasn't the usual reaction. The girls screamed at every little lyrical nuance, and a few of the younger ones even swooned—much as they once did for Frank Sinatra.

Then Jerry, sporting a face like an orangutan and relying on a variety of voices (all screechy), bounded back on the stage. For forty minutes he did rubber-faced imitations, led the orchestra into noisy chaos, and belittled and heckled his straight man, Dino, who stood by taking the abuse good naturedly and patiently (at least on the surface).

When Dino sang, Jerry tried to sing too, only he brayed. He also performed a rubber-legged dance; littered the stage with sheet music, instruments, and musicians; tackled the bandleader; and punctuated all his activities with pratfalls.

Eventually, Dino worked his way back into the act, joining Jerry in their usual schtick of watering customers' cigars, turning off the lights, spilling trays of food, and staging short sprints with Jerry around the elegant premises. Before the show was over, Dino also managed to squeeze in a couple of choruses of "Prisoner of Love" and "San Fernando Valley."

But although it was evident that Dino exuded plenty of sex appeal, the dominant tone of Martin and Lewis's act was comedy—of a brand never before seen, at least not by most of the lay customers. Many of the professionals in the audience were privately claiming they'd seen it all before —in their own acts—and they accused Martin and Lewis of helping themselves generously to everyone else's material. (One newspaper critic, in fact, called Jerry Lewis "an unfunny Milton Berle.")

But the audience couldn't care less whose material they were using. Martin and Lewis stopped the show cold.

When the emcee stepped to the mike and announced, "And now the Copacabana presents its star attraction—Vivian Blaine," the crowd didn't hear him. They just kept hollering, "Bring back Martin and Lewis."

Eventually, the emcee quieted the crowd enough to bring on the headliner, but Vivian Blaine's act simply wasn't strong enough to follow the roughhouse comedy that preceded her.

Good trouper that she was, Miss Blaine struggled bravely through her act, but it was plain from her opening number that the audience wasn't in the mood for quiet comedy. When Vivian Blaine left the stage with no demand for an encore, ringsiders could see tears in her eyes.

Between shows, Jerry and Dino, their faces aglow with instant success, were sitting at a table with Betty, Patti, Danny and Rea Lewis, and Abbey Greshler, relaxing, drinking, and accepting congratulations from some of the celebrities in the room, when Juley Podell, who owned the Copa, beckoned from behind an artificial palm tree that he wanted to see them in private. He looked displeased.

"Boys," he began in his gravel voice, as he pulled them into his private office and shut the door, "I'm afraid I'm going to have to make some changes in the show."

For a few seconds, Dino and Jerry knew how Cinderella felt when the clock struck twelve and her carriage was about to be turned back into a pumpkin. Podell was probably going to fire them for upsetting his star.

Jerry gulped. "You want us to leave?"

"We have a contract," Dino reminded him.

"I'm tearing it up," said Podell, "and giving you a new one. From now on, you boys will headline, and Vivian Blaine will have second billing."

That good a trouper Vivian Blaine wasn't. She quit as soon as she was informed of the new arrangement, and Martin and Lewis had the Copa all to themselves.

In the euphoria of those events, Jerry Lewis had one ambition still unrealized. He wanted to meet Billy Rose, so, after the second show, he asked *The New York World-Telegram* columnist Jack O'Brian if he'd arrange an introduction. O'Brian gladly obliged and escorted the excited Jerry over to the ringside table where Rose had watched the show and introduced the two of them.

In the ensuing conversation, Rose was elaborate in his praise of Martin and Lewis, but he had one reservation. Fixing a flinty eye on the brash young comic, he said, "You're funny, but your material's not up to your abilities." Then he added, with complete sincerity, that there would be no holding them if they ever got really first-rate material.

To the shock of everyone around, Jerry reared back and said to the man who had made millions through his astuteness in show business, "Dean and I don't need material!"

It was to be a long time before Jerry Lewis would learn the meaning of humility—perhaps never.

6

Stairway to the Stars

Judging from the reaction around Manhattan to Martin and Lewis's opening at the Copa, the majority of people felt the way Jerry did. Even *Variety* was singing their praises with unqualified enthusiasm now:

> Dean Martin and Jerry Lewis really hit the big-time at their opening last Thursday at the Copa. Both have been around singly and jointly, recently at the Capitol on Broadway, but not until their Copa bow did they truly arrive as potential comedy stars. Here's a case of two being better than one; usually it's after a team splits up that one or another component steps out into real stardom (viz. Durante, Fay, et al.).
>
> Although subbilled to Vivian Blaine, attractive strawberry blond songstress who went from band singing to Twentieth Fox, and is now back in the saloons, Martin and Lewis are the real stars of the show—and will prove the draw. They work in yeoman fashion and permit one another enough latitude for individual scintillation. It's only after each makes impact on his own that whatever stepping on one-another's-laughs and lines occur. And then it doesn't matter. The audience has given both a neutral 100 percent vote for individual talent: Lewis for his comedy, and Martin for his vocalizations. Both are versatile in each other's specialties, plus everything else from legmania to knockabout acro-antics, and the blend goes together like Park and Tilford.
>
> Martin's balladeering, with mike, includes "Won't Be Satisfied," "Never Loved Anyone," "Oh, Marie" (in Italian), "Rock-a-bye Your Baby" (a la Jolson), and then Lewis comes back for his clown waiter business with the prop buck teeth and other hokum for "That Old Gang of Mine," the imitations, the pigeon English twists on the lan-

guage, and the rest of it. Lewis's marathon around the room; the knockabout comedy, etc., sell like new cars without bonuses.

Walter Winchell wrote, "Martin and Lewis are the best two-man comedy team since Gallagher and Shean."

Earl Wilson wrote, "Martin and Lewis have emerged as the new Olsen and Johnson."

Life said, "The new comedy team at the Copa are a howling success."

Time wrote, "Lewis is a natural wack. And an antidote to the team's craziness is Martin's singing. In the antidote is the team's future."

The New York Times had this to say:

> Dean Martin is a personable baritone of Latin caste who sometimes manages to get off a complete romantic song in a husky, casual style often likened to Bing Crosby. Equally often, however, he is verbally or acoustically shanghaied into serving as a hapless foil for the strident and nonsensical but compelling antics of Lewis, who makes his actual age of twenty seem alternately much too young and much too old for his nonstop defiance of realities.

Other critics compared Martin and Lewis with Laurel and Hardy, Abbott and Costello, Weber and Fields, Smith and Dale, and just about every other pair of comics who ever stepped on a stage.

Bill Davidson wrote in *Collier's*:

> They are closest, perhaps, to the Marx Brothers of the early days, with Lewis, in his more explosive moments, approaching the wild ad-lib exuberance of Groucho and Harpo combined; and Martin resembling Chico and Zeppo. . . . Generally, the tall good-looking Martin sings ballads in a rich voice that has been described as "Crosby out of Jolson," and he functions with subtle drollery as the handsome, self-possessed oppressor of the Chaplinesque waif, Lewis.
>
> Lewis is a gangling six-foot 130-pounder with a crew haircut, a squeaky adolescent voice, and a long, rubbery face that he can contort into an amazing variety of outrageous expressions. He winks, snarls, pouts, grimaces, and makes cross-eyes—usually behind his partner's back. He is the misfit, the lout, the boy with ten thumbs, the wrongdoer. He is kicked about by Martin and by Fate, and he builds up such a store of pathos for himself that when he explodes into wild and tumultuous revenge, all his impishness seems justified and doubly funny to the audience. This basically has been the formula of all the great Low Comedians since Shakespeare's time—and no one uses it more effectively than Lewis does today.

The encomiums for Martin and Lewis weren't limited to the printed word.

Steve Allen, on one of his early radio shows, said enthusiastically, "If you are fortunate enough to see Dean and Jerry on a nightclub floor, no one will ever make you laugh more."

Jerry's mother said, "My boy's even funnier without that Italian."

A few of Broadway's better-known comics weren't quite so ebullient in their praise of their newest rivals. Milton Berle, for example, complained, "They're using all my best bits. And since I've often been accused of helping myself to everyone else's best bits, then Jerry and Dean's stuff isn't even *secondhand*."

The late Jackie Leonard, the alleged "master of the one-liner," had to take more than one line to verbalize his contempt—contempt probably bordering on envy—for the upstarts. "This is a nothing act," said Leonard. "What Martin and Lewis do isn't basically funny, but nobody else has the gall to do it in a sophisticated café where they're paying you twenty grand a week. When you figure other comics have struggled all their lives to perfect an act, it burns you up that here's a couple of characters that come out and do nothing but tell some old chestnuts, and the customers are crazy for them."

But Jerry, who was already taking it upon himself to be the spokesman for the team, had an answer for that kind of criticism. "If you break down our routines, I guess there's very little in them. There's nothing we do that another act couldn't do, and maybe better. But it's the way we feel for each other that nobody can duplicate. The kind of comedy we do, it's our own fun. We do it for laughs, and we have a lot of laughs, and the audience is part of us. So there can never be another two-act like this because there's never going to be two guys who feel this way about each other. There couldn't be two men who are as close to each other as we are."

But whatever people were saying or writing about Martin and Lewis didn't really matter. Juley Podell's Copacabana never had it so good. Neither had Martin and Lewis. The morning after their opening at the Copa, the phone at the maître d's desk started to ring with people calling for reservations, and it didn't stop ringing until Martin and Lewis finished a record-breaking engagement there eighteen weeks later.

So great was the demand to see the new act that out-of-towners phoned long distance from as far away as Chicago and Los Angeles to make certain they had reservations when they arrived in New York. But, despite the Copa's 800-person seating capacity, many potential customers had to be turned away during Martin and Lewis's initial two-week stand there. As a result, Podell had to extend their engagement to six weeks and raise

Martin and Lewis's salary to $5,000 a week. Five thousand a week! That would buy an awful lot of cocker spaniels.

But that wasn't the whole story. When, after six weeks, people were still queuing up outside the Copa, Podell extended their run to eighteen weeks. Still the Copa couldn't take care of all the New Yorkers who wanted to see Martin and Lewis. So for one three-week period Abbey Greshler had them doubling at the Roxy movie theater.

Between the supper show and the midnight show at the Copa, Dean and Jerry would hop into a cab, ride down to Forty-ninth Street and Sixth Avenue, and dash out onto the stage of the world's largest movie house—just in time to put on their nightclub act between showings of the film being offered.

This additional stint brought their weekly take to an incredible $15,000—a 1,500 percent raise over what they had received at the Club 500. Even the superstars of the nightclub world—like Danny Thomas and Milton Berle—weren't earning $15,000 a week in 1948.

With incomes of that magnitude, a decided change in Jerry's and Dean's personal life-styles inevitably occurred.

Out of pure sentiment, Jerry and Patti kept their apartment in Newark until they officially moved their home base to Southern California, but once Dean and Jerry became important nightclub stars, the Lewises rarely lived in it. Nightclub and theater engagements kept them moving constantly around the country, and, as a result, both the Lewises and the Martins were usually holed up in expensive hotel suites near whatever club or theater they were playing.

When they were playing New York, for example, the Lewises would often stay at the Sherry-Netherland, right around the corner from the Copa, or else at the Waldorf Astoria rather than try to commute between Newark and Manhattan.

The Martins, however, had too large a family to go on living in a hotel room when Dean was in Manhattan. Craig and Claudia were of school age, and Gail soon would be. The Martins needed a more permanent kind of residence. So Betty and Dean rented a ten-room apartment on New York's West Side—One Hundred Sixth Street and Riverside Drive, on the third floor, to be exact.

The more desirable apartments were on the higher floors, but because of a traumatic experience Dean once had when he was trapped in an elevator for a couple of hours, he would not live on any floor he could not comfortably reach by means of his own two feet. To this day, Dean Martin won't ride in an elevator if he can help it, and he has been known to climb as many as eighteen flights of stairs in order to avoid the claustrophobic feeling of riding in an elevator.

But Betty didn't care about being chic as long as the surroundings were comfortable. Their West Side apartment was her and Dean's first real home—a refreshing change from the Bryant Hotel or living with her parents. "It was marvelous to have the space to raise a family the way they should be raised," says Betty. "To have the room to breathe."

With plenty of money rolling in to pay for doctors, clothing, food, and even a few luxuries that the Martins had never been able to afford, Betty could foresee only good times ahead with her new nouveau riche celebrity husband.

Unlike other stars who rose from the ghetto, became big money-makers, and then turned into misers because the specter of poverty was always hovering over them, Jerry and Dean, once the money started rolling in, treated hard cash as if it had no more value than the phony bills in a Monopoly set.

Never carrying less than $1,000 in $100 bills in his pocket, Superstar Lewis started cutting a wide swath through all of Manhattan's finest stores. He lavished expensive toys from F. A. O. Schwarz on his two-year-old son Gary. He bought Patti a diamond ring from Tiffany's and not one, but three, mink coats (to make up for that dyed squirrel she was wearing during their Oliver Twist days). He gave his mother and father a $25,000 check on their anniversary.

He started buying clothes for himself with the abandon of a madcap heiress. At one point not too long after Martin and Lewis's first success, Jerry had over 500 pairs of socks in his dresser drawer and 200 mono-grammed shirts, and he was even having his blue jeans made to order by one of Hollywood's most expensive tailors, Sy Devore.

Jerry's compulsion to corner the haberdashery market had little to do with vanity; it was an outgrowth of his destitute childhood. "When I was a kid, I had a threadbare wardrobe," explains Jerry. "When I'd go to a drawer for a shirt or a pair of socks to wear, I'd usually find one pair of socks with holes in the toes and a shirt with a frayed collar and no buttons, because my mother was too busy in show business to have time to do any sewing."

As a hedge against ever finding himself in that predicament again, Jerry Lewis, even today, keeps his bureau and closets overstocked with a few hundred of every item. In a further nose-thumbing gesture at his early poverty, Lewis has developed another quirk; he never wears the same pair of socks more than once; he throws them away immediately after taking them off. As for his made-to-order monogrammed shirts, he'll wear them just a few times, then lay them all out on the floor of his office, and tell his friends and employees to take their pick. It is a tribute to his unfailing ego that he believes anyone else would want to wear a shirt bearing the initials J L.

Jerry's parents were also taking their "boy Joey's" success in stride. The second night of Martin and Lewis's long run at the Copa, Danny Lewis confronted Lou Perry, who was sitting at a table by himself at the Copa, and said to him rather querulously. "What's the idea of teaming Jerry with Dean Martin?"

Taken aback that the elder Lewis could quarrel with all that success, Lou Perry politely inquired, "Who should I have teamed him with?"

"Me!" answered Danny, without cracking a smile. "I can sing as good as Dean Martin."

Despite the mismating of the wrong singer to Jerry, some residual benefits did accrue to Danny over the next couple of years in the form of better club dates that he never would have been offered if his son hadn't suddenly become so famous.

In June 1948, for example, the formerly unemployable Danny was booked into the Latin Casino in Philadelphia, and this is what *Variety's* June 16, 1948, issue had to say about his debut there:

DANNY LEWIS
Songs
15 Mins.
Latin Casino, Phila.

Success can be retroactive. Skyrocketing of young Jerry Lewis (Martin and) is carrying special premiums for his not-so-old-man, Danny Lewis. After years on the borscht circuit and moderate stage success, Lewis, Sr., is getting his chance for a bid at top niteries.

Break in at the Latin Casino here had sentimental overtones. Singer got a sheaf of wires from virtually everybody at Lindy's. He's due to go into the Glass Hat, N.Y., after his run here.

Lewis has a voice so much like Al Jolson's that it might easily be palmed off as same, if you weren't looking. However, he does it straight, wisely eschewing those worn-thin imitations of Jolie's mannerisms.

He also picked up some bookings at Loew's State and Iceland. So he had little to complain about, except that his son turned out to be more famous than he.

Rea Lewis accepted her son's fame more in the tradition of the typical Jewish mother. Every night before the first show, patrons could hear her not-so-dulcet tones announcing her own arrival to the maître d' as she pushed her plump body through the crowd waiting to be seated. "I'm Jerry Lewis's mother," she would say officiously. "Have you got my table ready?" She and Danny were soon a permanent fixture at the Copa, smiling and applauding from a ringside table every time her boy "Joey made another funny."

Rea's status had taken a leap forward at Lindy's Restaurant. Previously, she and Danny couldn't even get into the kosher eatery, but now they were given a preferred table the moment the head waiter spotted them coming through the revolving door. Once seated, Rea ruled as regally as Queen Elizabeth, barking orders to the waiters ("Bring my friend a corned beef sandwich and put it on my son's tab."), trading wisecracks with Milton Berle, and offering sage bits of advice on how to succeed in show business to young hopefuls who had not yet made it.

Dino, meanwhile, was enjoying success with as much gusto as an actor in a Schlitz Beer commercial. Now that he didn't have to fight Sonny King for nickels and dimes, Dino started buying thirty-five-dollar shirts and having his suits made to order by Jim Balletta, an Italian tailor on Seventh Avenue who catered to the show business trade.

He was probably not paying for any of this because, despite his large income, he was still heavily in debt. He still hadn't conquered his love of wine, women, and gambling. To make matters worse, people from his past were beginning to turn up with not only IOUs signed by Dino but also management contracts where he had agreed to turn over a part of his income in return for immediate cash.

In order to pay some of his old debts, Dino had to make some of his newer purchases on credit. At the same time, he was slowly going into hock to the government, because, in the early days of his and Jerry's success, he had no one managing his business for him. He certainly didn't have time to manage it himself or to think of putting anything aside for taxes. He was too busy having fun, dodging past creditors, and hiding from a number of girls-about-town to whom he'd sung love songs at one time or another and subsequently jilted.

In between all this activity, he managed to squeeze in time to play golf and to work with Jerry, which, in those days, he enjoyed almost as much as his other activities.

"In the beginning of our relationship, Jerry was wonderful," recalls Dino. "And I was doing all the funny things I had always wanted to do. I love to hear laughter, but I couldn't get laughter just singing. Hearing a whole audience laugh is like getting drunk."

But hearing Jerry get most of the credit for that laughter must have been like a bad hangover to Dino. If there was one single note that all the reviewers, magazine feature writers, amateur critics, and other so-called comedy experts sounded, it was that Jerry Lewis was the great clown—at least, he had the potential for greatness—and that Dean Martin was just another good-looking guy with a fair voice who probably wouldn't be missed at all if he left the act, but whose style was a pleasant change of pace from Lewis's frenetic brand of comedy.

Today, in the light of what's happened since that period of his life, it's obvious that that kind of press rubbed the usually good-natured, happy-go-lucky Dino the wrong way. But, in the inchoate stages of the team's turbulent existence, Dino was too much of a gentleman to complain about it. There were real danger signs of future trouble even then, however.

There was a night, for example, when Jerry, in a burst of ambition, cut loose on the stage of the Copa and did a routine by himself that lasted fully an hour, while Dino just stood by with egg on his face and watched. Finally, fed up, Dino ducked into his dressing room, grabbed a suitcase, and started to leave the club through the main entrance.

As he passed the stage where Jerry was still doing a single, Dino called out wryly, "When you're through, lock up!" And he ducked out the door onto Sixtieth Street, as though he didn't mean to come back. The audience roared, taking Dino's quip for just another one of the myriad gags in their fast-paced act.

No one suspected that inside that handsome, easygoing Italian was a churning stomach—churning because even then, subconsciously, Dino resented being Jerry's stooge.

There were other harbingers of future trouble between Jerry and Dean that had nothing to do with an actor's ego. One of these was Dean's sex life.

In the four years that had elapsed since Jerry had baby-sat for the Martins, he and Patti had struck up a warm, personal friendship with Betty Martin as well as with Dino. Now that the partnership was working out so well, the four of them were closer than ever.

"We were together constantly," remembers Betty. "The four of us never had an argument. When the boys were off working somewhere, Patti and I would gather all our kids and drive over to Palisades Park in the Jersey Palisades and spend the afternoon sitting in the sun and talking and watching the kids have fun."

The Martins and the Lewises were Italian food buffs and would frequently have dinner together at the same spaghetti joint; on trips to out-of-town nightclub engagements, they often traveled together and stayed at the same expensive hotels; and, in the evenings, they'd always try to be together at the same table between shows at whatever nightclub Martin and Lewis happened to be playing.

But, as time went on, Betty discovered that being the mother of three children kept her pretty much tied down to her Riverside Drive apartment—that is, if she wanted to raise them properly. Being a conscientious mother, she believed that kids ought to have the company of their parents —certainly, at least one of them—when they were growing up.

The Martins had led a pretty helter-skelter existence in the past. Now that they had a nice apartment in a good neighborhood, Betty didn't feel like yanking the kids in and out of school every time Dino had to fill a nightclub or theater engagement around the country. Besides, she was pregnant with Deana.

So more and more Betty stayed behind when Martin and Lewis took to the road. When they played locally, like at the Copa, she frequently shunned showing up there too in the evenings. She'd had her fill of nightclubs long ago. It was certainly no novelty or pleasure to sit around a crowded nightclub table between shows, watching her husband guzzle booze and Jerry make funny faces at the cigarette girls.

Betty was no teetotaler, of course. Friends who were around her in Jerry's and Dean's nightclub days remember that she could keep right up with her husband when it came to belting down the hard stuff; and that's pretty good company, although Dino is by no means the legendary boozer he's reputed to be.

Dino is what the bibulous rating-takers have classified as a "heavy drinker"—that is, from five to six highballs a night and maybe a couple of beers during the day. You can't have worked around nightclubs as long as Dino has and be a prohibitionist. But like the late Humphrey Bogart, who could drink all day and most of the night and never really show it, Dino has always been able to handle his liquor with admirable savoir faire.

If he's acting drunk, chances are that's exactly what it is—an act—particularly today, when ulcers have caused him to virtually cut out hard liquor. When he lifts a highball glass to his lips in his nightclub act, he's usually only drinking apple juice. "If I drank half as much booze as people think I do, do you think I'd be able to make three pictures a year and do all those TV shows?" asks Dino with good-humored logic.

But Betty didn't have to hang around the Copa until all hours of the night in order to have a nip or two. She could stay home and do that.

Dino, of course, didn't let Betty's absence from the scene stand in the way of his greatest pleasure. He was a celebrity now, enjoying the first fruits of a tremendous success. Much of this fruit was strutting around in scanty Copa Girl costumes, within easy picking distance of Dino's fine Italian hands.

When Betty was "home with the kids," her seat at the Martin and Lewis table was kept warm by a succession of young, pretty women. According to those who were around the Copa in those days, Dino never appeared to be in active pursuit of any of the forbidden fruit. But most women found him extremely attractive, and he did little to discourage their friendship. As his second wife Jeanne remembers, "Dean never had to chase anyone. Girls chased him."

One beauty who Dean frequently squired around was Gregg Sherwood, a blond, statuesque Copa girl, who later married Horace Dodge II, of the automobile family. Another who found the handsome Italian irresistible was Miriam Davelle, a beautiful young and talented "specialty dancer." Whatever her specialty was, Dino liked it—for a while. She never stopped loving him, however, and after Dean and Jerry left New York to make films in Hollywood, she too moved to the West Coast, where she committed suicide, leaving no note of explanation.

Whatever Dino had, and apparently still has, it's no secret to those who knew him that he left a trail of broken hearts from Steubenville to Times Square and from Times Square to Hollywood and Vine.

Patti and Jerry Lewis took a dim view of Dino's loose style of living. It was none of their business, of course, but since they were friendly with Betty, Dino's openness about his relations with other women put them in an awkward position.

In addition, Patti was a good Catholic, who believed a person should take his marriage vows seriously. But, beyond the morality of the situation, she was simply afraid that Dino's flagrant disregard of most of the Ten Commandments might give her own husband ideas.

As far as she knew, she had no reason to worry on this score. But it was a hazard any wife had to consider, especially in her husband's business. Single girls were plentiful in café society; Jerry had to be away from home a lot, living crazy hours; and, although Jerry didn't have Dino's looks, lot of girls thought he was "cute" and wanted to mother him. Certainly, there were ample opportunities if he wanted to take advantage of them.

Jerry had his own reasons for not approving Dean's behavior. Dean was his best friend, his pal. He'd never had a "best friend" until he met Dean, and he was extremely jealous of any girl who got in the way of their Damon and Pythias relationship.

"I loved Dean almost as much as my wife and kids," Jerry once said. "I worked twenty-four hours a day to get him to keep liking me. I'd do crazy things like snipping off people's ties or gluing their shoes to the ceiling. But he never was as warm and outgoing as I hoped he'd be."

Never was Dino less interested in being warm and outgoing with Jerry than when he had a beautiful girl he was romancing. In the team's early days, all of Dino's romances were ephemeral. That suited Jerry just fine. He and Patti could handle that.

But, in 1948, Dean got mixed up with someone who wasn't quite so ephemeral. Her name was Jeanne Beiggers, and she lasted with Dino for twenty years—which was ten more years than Jerry Lewis lasted with him. Jeanne Beiggers was a beauty contest winner from Coral Gables, Florida, and she was just Dean Martin's type: blond, petite, vivacious, and barely nineteen years old.

As in the Japanese film *Rashomon*, the principals in this great love triangle all have conflicting versions of how and when Dean first met Jeanne. Dean claims he first laid eyes on Jeanne the night he and Jerry opened at Slapsie Maxie's in Hollywood in the summer of 1948. Jeanne's story has it that she and Dean met in January 1949, when he and Jerry were playing the Beachcomber Club in Miami. Betty Martin says that although Dean never would tell her the exact circumstances, she knows it had to have happened sometime *before* August 1948, when Deana, their last child together, was born.

After piecing together everyone's account, as well as published records, it is safe to report that it happened approximately as follows. Sometime after Christmas in 1947, Dean and Jerry left Patti and Betty at home in New York City while they went to Miami to play the Beachcomber Club for two weeks. It was the time of the usual Orange Bowl festivities, with its attendant parade of celebrities down the main street and the "big" football game on New Year's Day.

Jeanne Beiggers, an art major at the University of Miami, was the reigning Orange Bowl Queen, chosen, because of her natural beauty, to ride in the first float of the colorful New Year's Day parade. The floats behind the queen were full of celebrities, but Dean Martin wasn't one of them. This was the January before he and Jerry scored their big triumph at the Copa. Along with the rest of the New Year's Day mob, Dino had to follow the parade on foot.

"I can still see him tagging along beside the floats," recalls Jeanne Martin today, in the quiet of her opulent $400,000 pad on Mountain Drive in Beverly Hills. "He was like a big hick, the way he gaped up in wonderment at all the celebrities and the pretty girls." Although he wasn't a well enough known celebrity to ride in the parade, Jeanne recognized him as being the "tall dark good-looking" half of the comedy team of Martin and Lewis.

At nineteen, Jeanne Beiggers wasn't a habitué of nightclubs. But the previous summer, on a trip to New York City with her folks following her high school graduation, she had been taken to Bill Miller's Riviera, across the Hudson, where Martin and Lewis were appearing. Why Jeanne's folks happened to take her there is a mystery, except that Abbey Greshler's wife Vi was a friend of the Beiggers', having come from Coral Gables herself. Anyway Jeanne remembers "laughing herself silly."

Jeanne had never been to any of the Miami Beach night spots, until in January, as part of her duties as Orange Bowl Queen, she had to put in an appearance one night at the Beachcomber Club, along with the winning football team, the mayor, and some other local bigwigs.

Between shows, the manager asked Dean and Jerry to introduce the Orange Bowl Queen to the audience, which Dean did, inviting the pretty Florida girl up on the stage to take a bow.

"And now, ladies and gentlemen, I'd like to introduce to you the Orange Bowl Queen," began Dino, looking her over with his famous male-chauvinist leer. "And I can tell you this, Jeanne Beiggers looks like she's got the kind of oranges that'll make very good squeezing."

The audience laughed, and the Orange Bowl Queen returned to her table, not noticeably upset by the suggestiveness of Dino's introduction.

After the show, Dino dropped by Jeanne's table to ask her for a date the following day, and she accepted. She was awed by the attentions of the witty, suave romantic half of Martin and Lewis.

But when Dean called at her home to pick Jeanne up the following day about noon, her parents were furious. "He's too old for you," Mrs. Beiggers said. When Mr. Beiggers discovered that Dean was not only twelve years older than his daughter but married and the father of three children as well, he wanted to throw the Italian Crosby into an alligator swamp.

But Dean was as persistent as the Orange Bowl Queen was ready to be squeezed, and these two star-crossed lovers could not be denied their first date.

Whatever transpired between them in Miami, they did not see each other again until the following spring, several weeks after Martin and Lewis had opened at the Copa and had become New York's hottest nightclub act.

By then, Jeanne Beiggers had followed Dean to New York and was working in the garment center, "cataloging," in order to support herself while she pursued her man. "Cataloging" does not mean she was a bookkeeper in a musty office. Her job was to model Junior Miss sizes for the Sears Roebuck and Montgomery Ward mail-order catalogs.

One night Jeanne showed up at the Copa with her parents, who had been invited by the Greshlers to sit at their table. After the show, Martin and Lewis stopped at the table for a free drink on their agent. The chemistry between Dean and Jeanne must have been better than ever that night, because a friendship developed that soon blossomed into romance.

The romance didn't blossom publicly for another year—possibly because Dean already had a wife. But whenever Betty didn't come around, which was frequent now that she was in the final months of her fourth pregnancy, it was Jeanne's trim derriere that filled the empty seat at the Martin and Lewis table.

Jeanne insists that Patti and Jerry gave her the cold shoulder from the very beginning of their relationship, sometimes even refusing to acknowledge her presence by speaking to her. "At one point they even had the drummer in the band not speaking to me," claims Jeanne, "which irked Dean and started to cause trouble between him and Jerry even then."

Jeanne won't say why Jerry and Patti adopted this provincial attitude, but it's fairly apparent they considered her "a husband stealer." Technically she was, although Dino swears his marriage to Betty was definitely over by the time he met Jeanne. If it was, Betty Martin wasn't aware of it, or of Jeanne Beiggers either. She wasn't to get that surprise until later in 1948, when Dean and Jerry returned home to New York, after scoring a tremendous success at Slapsie Maxie's in Hollywood.

Dean and Betty in Philadelphia in early 1940s (prior to his famous "nose job").

Betty and Dean (after nose job) in nightclub. (*Photo from Betty Martin collection*)

Betty and Dean at a dinner celebration with her mother and father. (*Photo from Betty Martin collection*)

Jerry doing the comedy
busboy bit that shot him into
the big league as a comdeian
and lead to his teaming up
with Dean Martin. (*Photo by
Pictorial Parade*)

Jerry and Dean doing their
act at the old Beachcomber
nightclub, Miami Beach.
(*Photo by Harold Kaye*)

Laughing it up during their
halcyon days. (*Photo by Art
and Len Weissman*)

Dean and Jerry relax at a
penny arcade between
appearances on the NBC-TV
"Colgate Comedy Hour,"
November 1953. (*Photo by
Pictorial Parade*)

From left: Betty Martin, Mrs. Gus Schaefer and her daughter June (hometown friends of Betty's), and, of course, Jerry and Dean, at the Latin Casino in Philadelphia. (*Photo from Betty Martin collection*)

Dean and Betty with three of their children, Gail, Craig, and Claudia, in their Riverside Drive apartment.

The 1948 B'Nai Brith Annual Dinner, honoring Daryl Zanuck with their Man of the Year Award. On dais: Daryl Zanuck, center; to his right, George Jessel; with Harry Cohn next to last at right. At left foreground table, from left: Dick Stabile, unknown, Jerry Lewis, and Patti. Facing them: Mack Gray, Dean and Betty Martin. (*Photo from Betty Martin collection*)

Dean and Betty before the birth of Deana. (*Photo by Pictorial Parade*)

Betty Martin as she appeared after her hair turned white. (*Photo from Betty Martin collection*)

Jerry Lewis, Jack Eigen, Frank Sinatra, and Dean Martin in the late forties, being interviewed on Barry Gray's WINS talk show, in the Copacabana Lounge, New York. (*Photo from Jeanne Martin collection*)

Dino and Jerry having a little "fun" with their bandleader Dick Stabile. (*Photo from Jeanne Martin collection*)

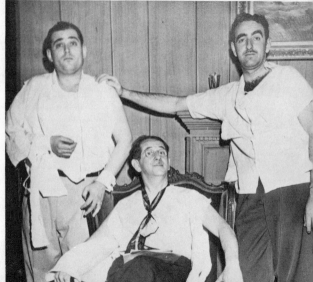

Norman Lear, Ernie Glucksman, and Ed Simmons after a story conference at which Jerry Lewis went wild with the scissors. (*NBC photo*)

Dino with his mother and father, Angela and Guy Crocetti, after they moved to the West Coast. (*Photo by Art and Len Weissman*)

A dinner party at Chez Paree in 1949. Left, top to bottom: Irving Kaye, Dick Stabile, Bob Redd, Sheldon Leonard, Patti, and Jerry. Right, top to bottom: Charlie Isaacs, next person unidentified, Jerry's drummer, production secretary, Jeanne, and Dean.

Patti, Jerry, Jeanne, and Dean putting on a "happy face" for the camera. (*Photo by Pictorial Parade*)

7

We're in the Money

As the Harry Cohn and Joe Schenck letters turning "thumbs down" on Dean Martin amply illustrate, Hollywood has always been the last to recognize potential film talent. Even if it recognizes talent, it is usually too stingy to spend the time and money to develop it. It would rather let some other medium, like Broadway or the book-publishing business, be the star makers. But once a person has made it in another medium and has become a nationally known figure, Hollywood will swoop in and sign that person up for seven times as much as it could have bought them for originally.

Nobody from the movies was exactly swooping in and signing up Martin and Lewis, even after their successes at the Copa, the Chez Paree in Chicago, and the Latin Casino in Philadelphia. The feeling was that, sure, they were funny in a nightclub, but you had to be drunk to like that kind of slapdash comedy—squirting seltzer in customers' faces and tackling the orchestra leader. That would never go over in the same hallowed movie palaces that hawked Cary Grant and hot buttered popcorn—until Martin and Lewis came along, that is. Their success was unprecedented.

By 1948, nightclubs were beginning to sink into a depression from which they have never managed to climb out completely (unless you want to consider topless joints and Las Vegas gambling casinos as being true nightclubs). Late-night radio and its monster child, television, were beginning to sound the death knell for nightclubs. People no longer had to go out to the Riobamba to avoid talking to their husbands or wives; they could get drunk at home and listen to Steve Allen. As a result, nightclubs were beginning to follow the dying route of vaudeville.

Despite this general situation, Martin and Lewis could pack any nightclub they chose to play. As a small example, shortly before they conquered Hollywood, Martin and Lewis were playing the swank Chase Club in the Chase Hotel in St. Louis. There were so many customers on hand for the show that the management had to fill the two extra dining rooms adjoining the Chase Club—the room where they were to perform.

When it was time for the show to go on, the diners in the two extra rooms were herded into the Chase Club and interspersed among the tables and along the walls on folding chairs set up for that purpose (violating all fire laws, of course). Irving Kaye, who was with Dean and Jerry at the time, recalls, "The waiters marched them in like troops. I've been in show business for thirty years, but I've never seen a joint do anything like that."

News of these two men's exploits was slow in reaching the West Coast, but, with that kind of drawing power, it was inevitable that word about Dino and Jerry would eventually be brought back by pony express and stagecoach to settlers west of the Pecos in what was then the entertainment mecca of the movie business—Hollywood.

One of the first to spot their movie potential was Frank Sinatra. He caught their act at the Copa early in 1948, and, upon returning to Hollywood, he told Don McGuire, an actor friend of his, not to miss Martin and Lewis the next time he went to New York.

"Are they that good?" asked McGuire.

"I'll tell you," replied Sinatra, in one of the earliest known instances of the Italian brotherhood not sticking together, "the dago's lousy, but the little Jew is great."

Another one of Martin and Lewis's early boosters was Irving Zussman, who by 1948 was no longer connected with the Havana-Madrid because it had ceased to exist. Zussman was now an independent publicity man, and one of his clients was Hollywood movie producer Hal Wallis.

After seeing Martin and Lewis perform as a team, Zussman phoned Wallis from New York and said, "Hal, drop what you're doing and come back here and see these guys before someone else snaps them up. They're another Hope and Crosby."

Wallis didn't drop what he was doing—he isn't that kind of a man— but, the next time he was in Manhattan, he did stop in at the Copa to see what Zussman was raving about. After the show, Wallis turned to Zussman and exclaimed with considerable annoyance, "Another Hope and Crosby? You've got to be kidding?" whereupon he returned to Southern California, highly disgruntled with his publicity man for being such a bad assayer of talent.

Despite the enormity of their nightclub success, Dino and Jerry might never have signed for films if they hadn't been given a chance to showcase their talents for the West Coast at Slapsie Maxie Rosenbloom's, a large nightclub on Los Angeles's so-called Miracle Mile.

Slapsie Maxie's had formerly been the Wilshire Bowl, where Phil Harris had once risen to prominence as the house orchestra leader. After Harris left the Wilshire Bowl, business fell off, causing its original management to put the place up for sale. Maxie Rosenbloom, the former light-heavyweight boxing champ, bought the place and changed the name to Slapsie Maxie's. But, in the ensuing nightclub depression, it too fell on hard times, even with Ben Blue and Slapsie Maxie performing nightly.

As a result, Slapsie Maxie's was subsequently taken over and refurbished by Sy and Al Devore, a couple of wealthy Los Angeles haberdashers who had a show business clientele. But they needed a draw to pep up business, so when their booker, Sammy Lewis, caught Martin and Lewis's act in the East and recommended them for Slapsie Maxie's, the Devore brothers eagerly signed them to go into their joint in late summer of 1948.

Because Patti didn't feel like making another road trip and Betty wasn't up to it—Deana was due to be born any minute—the two wives elected to stay home and let Dean and Jerry conquer Hollywood by themselves.

Dean and Jerry's arrival in a town where Clark Gable was king didn't generate much excitement—after all, who were Martin and Lewis but a couple of fresh young saloon comics? By opening night, however, the word-of-mouth publicity about their exploits in the sophisticated East Coast clubs like the Copacabana and the Chez Paree was good enough to fill Slapsie Maxie's Wilshire Boulevard nitery. Not only did they fill it, but, as Dino was later to recall, "We stacked people up against the wall that night like cordwood."

In addition to the roomful of celebrities, the reigning heads of all the major studios were on hand: Y. Frank Freeman of Paramount, Hal Wallis of his own production company, Harry Cohn of Columbia, Louis B. Mayer of MGM, Jack Warner of Warner Brothers, and Darryl F. Zanuck of Twentieth Century-Fox.

Also present, by a strange coincidence, was Jeanne Beiggers, who just happened to be on the West Coast, 3,000 miles from home.

It's not necessary to detail again what Martin and Lewis did that night to cause the waves of laughter that roared through Slapsie Maxie's for one hour and fifteen minutes, sending many of the sophisticated Hollywood crowd sprawling in the aisles.

Dino and Jerry hadn't changed the basic ingredients of their act much since they had opened at the Club 500. Dino was still belting out ballads with the insouciance of an Italian wino; and Jerry was just an irrepressible idiot kid whose heckling of his partner came to include everybody in line of sight. What they were doing now was just more polished from two years of constant playing, and they had added a few embellishments, such as Jerry leading the orchestra, and Dino becoming so fed up with his partner's heckling that he finally chases him off the stage, down through the audience, clear around the room, and back up on the stage again.

Opening night at Slapsie Maxie's, Jerry ad-libbed an additional piece of business that neither Dino nor Dick Stabile, the house band leader, was expecting. After being chased back on the stage again, Jerry jumped into Stabile's arms. "Protect me, dear thir," screamed Jerry, as Stabile cradled him in his arms, like an infant.

The bit was such a hit that it was kept in the act, and so was Dick Stabile. They needed a maestro who would go along with their gags and who didn't mind being roughed up for the sake of the comedy muse. So, following their engagement at Slapsie Maxie's, Dean and Jerry persuaded Stabile to give up his leadership of the house band and join their stock company. He remained with Martin and Lewis, playing the part of their musical stooge and traveling everywhere with them until the partnership smashed up on Ego Shoals eight years later.

But such gloomy thoughts of a split-up were furthest from anyone's mind in the heady atmosphere of opening night at Slapsie Maxie's. How could it have occurred to anyone—the way Dino and Jerry seemed to get such a kick out of working with each other? That was true brotherly love, the way Dean let Jerry interrupt his singing and grab most of the laughs. No sibling rivalry there.

By the time Jerry and Dino had taken their final bows and were being congratulated by most of the celebrities in the room, it was obvious to anyone with a sense of humor that they were a logical bet for films.

Abbey Greshler didn't let the feeling cool off. While the boys were relaxing over a much deserved drink, Greshler went from table to table, listening to offers for Martin and Lewis's services from the studio executives most interested in putting their money where their mouths emitting the laughter were.

No deal was finalized that night, of course; it took a week of hard negotiating. But Hal Wallis, who was releasing through Paramount Studios, eventually came up with the best offer—$50,000 a picture for seven pictures in a five-year period. Evidently, Wallis saw something that night that he hadn't seen when he caught their act at the Copa—the eager looks of the other producers, all wanting to have Martin and Lewis at their studios if he didn't snap them up first.

Included in the Wallis deal was permission for Martin and Lewis to make one "outside" film a year through their own production company, which would be called York Productions.

Greshler, who's never been known to overlook an opportunity to pick up an extra buck or two, had a little plan in mind that would benefit Abbey Greshler almost as much as it would his clients.

The first film to be made under the York Productions banner—*At War with the Army*, based on a moderately successful Broadway farce about GI life—would be financed by Sherill Corwin, Ralph Stolkin, and Ray Ryan, who were oil men from Chicago and Houston with whom Greshler had made contact when Martin and Lewis were playing the Chez Paree. A further extension of this deal was that, in return for digging up the money men, Greshler would be given the position of executive producer, which meant that, in addition to receiving his normal agenting fees, Greshler would also be getting a share of the profits, plus a producer's salary.

This practice of taking money from the performers from both ends has since been stopped by the various talent guilds and also the government's antitrust department because of the obvious advantages to a man acting as both buyer and seller, as Greshler was doing. (Several years later, in fact, Greshler himself wound up in two court battles, one involving Martin and Lewis and the other, child singing star Jimmy Boyd, who charged that Greshler had committed a "fraud" by representing himself as a "producer" rather than as an agent in order to obtain 60 percent of his earnings instead of an agent's normal 10 percent.)

Being neophytes in the business at the time and having about as much financial acumen as two kindergarten dropouts, Dean and Jerry went along with Greshler's contractual manipulations because to them the York Productions deal looked like a real gold mine.

As owners of their own company, Dean and Jerry agreed to take just a nominal salary but were to get a substantial cut of the profits—something like 97 percent.

It sounded impressive on paper. But what they didn't realize, and what nobody bothered to tell them, was that there is a substantial difference between "grosses" and "profits." A picture can gross $8 million, but because of the way studios keep their books and tabulate their advertising, overhead, and distribution costs, it can still wind up in the red.

In such a case, anyone on a percentage of the profits won't realize a penny and will end up having worked for nothing—the usual result of most percentage-of-the-profits deals. And if his producer also happens to be his agent and business manager, he's really in trouble.

Dean and Jerry were to find this out the hard way, just as Betty Martin had to have her new baby the hard way—alone.

Dean and Jerry were still playing Slapsie Maxie's when Deana was born in New York City on August 19, 1948. Betty slept for a couple of hours, then awoke and tried to phone the good news to Dean, who was sharing a room with Jerry at the Hollywood Roosevelt.

It was about five in the morning, California time, when the phone in their hotel room rang. Jerry answered it, and Betty said, "Will you please tell Dean he didn't get a Dean, Jr., but a Deana arrived instead."

Jerry screamed, "Who is this—some kind of a nut?" and he hung up. Jerry finally came fully awake.

About ten minutes later, Betty was on the phone calling her mother when a nurse rushed into the room and said, "You have to get off the phone. There are two nuts calling from California and they demand to speak to you."

8

Absence Makes the Heart Grow Fonder – of Somebody Else

With a five-year movie contract tucked securely away in their agent's files and their nightclub act in demand everywhere from coast to coast at a firmly established salary of $10,000 a week, Dean and Jerry headed for an engagement at the Latin Casino in Philadelphia shortly after their highly successful and lucrative eight-week stand at Slapsie Maxie's.

Patti, with Gary, and Betty, with her four children and their nurse, Sue, were to join Dean and Jerry in Philadelphia. This was Dean's first look at his new daughter since she had been born two months earlier, for Deana had been born with a minor respiratory problem and the doctor had advised Betty against taking her on any long trips for several months.

It was a happy reunion for all of them until Dean and Jerry were called to New York to play a benefit one night at the Waldorf Astoria. Betty was in bed with pleurisy at the time and couldn't accompany Dean. Because of that, Jerry tried to persuade Patti not to go on the overnight trip either.

"In looking back at it," Betty recalls with an ironic smile, "I realize they were just trying to get rid of Patti. But I guess she's more tenacious than I am. She went. What I didn't know, of course, was that, while in Hollywood, Dean and Jerry had met two pretty starlets, June Allyson and Gloria De Haven, and the girls were going to be in New York at that time."

When the boys returned to Philadelphia, Patti took Betty aside and told her about June and Dean. "And," she added, "not only that, I hear there's another one."

"Well," relates. Betty, "I'd heard this before about Dean and other women, so I was just going to ignore it, true or not. But a couple of nights later I walked into Dean's dressing room and there was George, a man who was married to our children's nurse, Sue, holding a copy of a telegram he'd sent for Dean. Without having any idea what it was, I took it and read it. It was to June Allyson and said, 'I'm still tingling.'

"I was so mad that I grabbed it and ran out. Dean and Jerry were on stage. I went to the right, where they ordinarily exited, and waved the telegram. Dean saw me and grabbed Jerry over to the left. As he did, I ran to that side. Finally Dean grabbed poor Jerry, who had no idea what was going on, and they went right across the stage and out the front door. Even I had to laugh, mad as I was.

"That was the night I heard about Jeanne. Someone told me that there was a girl in New York who'd just about had a nervous breakdown when she saw Dean out with June. She'd become so upset that Abbey Greshler's wife had to take her to her hotel suite to calm her down. When Dean finally arrived home that night, I said, 'Who's the other girl—the one who had the fit in New York?' He replied, 'Oh, my God, you mean that kid from Florida. She followed me East.'

"Well, anyway, I knew there was really nothing serious between Dean and June, and I took his word that Jeanne was just a fan with a crush on him. So we made up, and I thought that was the end of it. Everything seemed fine between us."

Now that Dean Martin and Jerry Lewis were going to become full-fledged movie stars, working on the same Paramount Studios lot where Bob Hope, Bing Crosby, and Shirley Temple got their start in films, they would, of course, have to pull up stakes on the East Coast and establish permanent residences in Hollywood.

Accordingly, later in the fall, after they finished their engagement in Philadelphia, Dean and Jerry left for the West Coast—again without their wives, who remained home to pack—to start conferring with Hal Wallis about their first picture for him.

While they were out there, the two of them rented furnished houses—not just any old homes but the kind befitting movie stars.

Through the help of a kindly Beverly Hills real estate broker, Jerry rented a modest little place on Tower Road for only $1,500 a month. Built along the lines of a Spanish castle, the Lewises' new home consisted of seventeen rooms, sunken bathtubs, a swimming pool, and several acres of wooded grounds that adjoined the backyard of another graduate of the Catskill mountain resorts—comedian Danny Kaye.

This layout had formerly been the residence of movie actress Maria Montez, until she drowned in one of her sunken bathtubs, and it was considered one of the "must see" spots on the Tanner Bus tours and also on the guide maps to the movie star homes being hawked along Sunset Boulevard.

It was a "must" for Jerry Lewis to have such a sizable dwelling because not only were he and Patti planning a large family (either the normal way or, if that wasn't possible, through adoption), but he'd be wanting his mother and father as house guests from time to time, to say nothing of a desultory band of loyal employees, such as Irving Kaye, whom Jerry had already rewarded for past services by giving him a job in his organization with the impressive title of road manager.

Dino's choice of a homestead was less garish but equally large and luxurious. The home he rented was an English-style dwelling on Stone Canyon Road, in Bel Air, within walking distance of the famed Bel Air Hotel and about a brassie shot from the Bel Air Country Club. According to Betty, Dino phoned her long distance after he had taken the place and told her to start packing. He sounded very happy that she and the children would soon be joining him.

His parents, Guy and Angela Crocetti, were already on the West Coast, living in Long Beach, in a small house Dean had purchased for them soon after he and Jerry had come into the big money, and, according to Dean, they had helped him get the place in readiness for her. "Mom and Pop are putting in all the little things in the house that I don't know about," exclaimed Dino enthusiastically.

"Patti and I came West together with the children," relates Betty, "and the boys met us at the train station. It seemed like the beginning of a beautiful life together in Hollywood. For the first time, Dean and I would have a *real* house—and he'd be home making pictures most of the time instead of traveling.

"I remember Dean taking me through the house. When we got to each room, he'd say, 'Now, Betty, close your eyes,' and I did and opened them only when he told me to. He was like a little kid showing off his Christmas toys. Mom and Pop Crocetti were there, so glad to see their grandchildren. Well, I counted the rooms in the place, and there was an extra bedroom and bath. I said to Dean, 'That's for Mom and Pop.' Well, he got tears in his eyes—he was so pleased about it. And you know, they did move in with us. Of course, on that happy day I never dreamed Dean and I would ever divorce."

That was November 28, 1948. A few days later, Dean and Jerry had a date in San Francisco to add some laughs to the inauguration ceremonies of an ice palace that Sonja Henie was opening.

Betty and Patti wisely accompanied their men on this trip. Somehow that didn't deter Jeanne Beiggers from also being present in the audience.

Betty, of course, didn't recognize Jeanne because she had never seen her before. But Patti remembered those cool Germanic blue eyes instantly and wasted no time pointing out her husband's Number One fan.

With Betty at his side constantly, Dino's extracurricular activities weren't very active that trip. As a result, Betty maintained her cool, and another "incident" was avoided. By the time they returned to Southern California, in fact, the nearly derailed Martin marriage appeared to be back on the tracks again. As far as the outside world knew, the Martins were still a happily married couple a little later in the year, when Dean and Jerry were called upon, along with a number of other high-powered entertainers, to appear at one of those $100-a-plate black-tie affairs that the Los Angeles chapter of the B'nai B'rith was throwing at the Ambassador Hotel. The dinner was to honor Darryl Zanuck and give him the B'nai B'rith Man of the Year Award—probably for producing *Gentleman's Agreement*, a film in which, for the first time, Hollywood had dared raise its voice against such a thing as anti-Semitism as practiced in polite society.

Although they were on the program, Dean and Jerry weren't important enough names yet to sit at the dais with the other celebrities. They were at one of the tables in front of the dais with Betty and Patti, Dick Stabile, and Mack Gray. But Dean and Jerry didn't care where they sat. This was the first time they'd ever been invited to a movie industry affair of this importance, and they were just grateful for the opportunity to do their thing in front of so many Hollywood luminaries.

Unfortunately, the show was overbooked, and the big names—Hope, Benny, Burns, Kaye, and Jessel—stayed on too long. By midnight, Dean and Jerry were still standing in the wings, waiting to get on. So, when it became obvious that some of the scheduled entertainment had to be dropped if there was to be time left to give Zanuck his award, the first names to pop into the producer's mind were Martin and Lewis. Despite their popularity at Slapsie Maxie's, they were not yet in the superstar category, and therefore the audience wouldn't be too disappointed if they didn't appear.

Dean and Jerry did a couple of "slow burns" as they stood despondently in the wings listening to the emcee explain to the crowd that "due to the lateness of the hour, the rest of the entertainment will have to be cut, so we can get on with the main business at hand—honoring our guest of honor, Darryl F. Zanuck."

But Dean and Jerry refused to roll over and play dead for Jack Benny, Bob Hope, and Darryl F. Zanuck. Just as Zanuck was to be presented with his award, a screechy voice suddenly shouted from the wings, "Who the hell is Darryl F. Zanuck?"

To the surprise and eventual delight of the crowd, a youngish-looking man in a crew haircut and sporting a mouthful of dime-store teeth bounded out onto the stage behind his voice. He was followed by a handsome Italian chap, who said, "Yeah, who the hell is Darryl F. Zan NOOK?"

"Now listen, fellows," said the startled emcee, "we have to give Mr. Zanuck his award now, and—"

"We don't care what you have to do," said Jerry. "We came here to do a show, and no one's going home until we do it."

"Is that clear?" added Dino, whereupon he grabbed a seltzer bottle from one of the tables and squirted the bubbly water into the surprised emcee's face.

As the black-tie audience roared its approval, others turned to their dinner-table companions and asked, "Who are those nuts?" They found out by the time Dean and Jerry did their complete act for them and took their bows to a standing ovation, as their adoring wives looked on proud and misty-eyed. That was probably the last time Betty shared a moment like that with her husband.

On December 17, the peripatetic team of comics and lovers was scheduled to take off for Miami and another date at the Beachcomber Club. This was to be another bachelor excursion, sans wives, so Betty and Patti decided to celebrate Christmas early. A party was arranged at the Martin household since they had four children and Dean's mother and father, and Patti only had Gary. It was a real *gemütlich* affair. All the Martins, Lewises, and Crocettis joined in to decorate the house and the tree, eat turkey, and exchange expensive presents.

When Dean left for Florida the next day, all seemed right between the Martins—or so Betty thought. But Betty was either terribly naive or else, like many wives with cheating husbands, she just didn't want to face the truth. And the truth was that Jeanne exited California and returned to Miami at the same time that Dean did.

According to Jeanne Martin, Dean promised her, when he left Florida several weeks later, that his divorce from Betty was in the works and that he would send for her immediately. But Betty insists that she and Dean had never discussed a divorce. Being Catholic, she didn't believe in it. If a fleeting thought of it had ever crossed her mind, she had immediately blotted it out because in her religion people took their vows seriously.

When Dean returned to Hollywood, he went right back to Betty. As proof of his honorable intentions to remain a faithful husband, he rented an even larger and better home for Betty and the kids (and himself) in Holmby Hills, on Beverly Glen Boulevard—one of the highest-priced neighborhoods in the city of Los Angeles. The Holmby Hills place was more of an estate, with countless rooms, a swimming pool, and rolling tree-studded grounds. Their neighbors were Fred Astaire and Bing Crosby.

Dino had come a long way from his Bryant Hotel days to being Bing

Crosby's neighbor. Why a man on the verge of leaving his wife and family needed such a lavish layout not even Betty can explain. Perhaps he didn't know himself what he wanted to do.

At any rate, Jeanne Beiggers knew what she wanted, and evidently nothing was going to stand in her way.

Between January and March, souvenirs from Florida, in the form of miniature crates of oranges, started arriving in the Martins' family mailbox addressed to Dean in a feminine hand. According to Betty, friendly little messages affixed to the orange crates expressed such sentiments as "miss you" and "can hardly wait," and they were usually signed "Love, Jeanne."

Jeanne was so brazen in her approach to the situation that she apparently didn't care whether she got Dean in trouble with his wife or not. Neither did Dean, for that matter.

In March, Jeanne Beiggers herself arrived in Southern California, this time for good. At Dean's request, Martin and Lewis's band leader, Dick Stabile, and his wife, Trudy, took the pretty Florida maid into their house and allowed her to live with them until Dean could make up his mind what he wanted to do about Betty.

When Betty, who admits to being pretty much of a "stoop" not to realize earlier that Jeanne was no "mere fan," finally found out that her husband's little bag of oranges was residing at the Stabiles', she confronted Dean and asked him to leave their home.

Dean willingly obliged and rented a house on King's Road, north of Sunset Strip in Hollywood. Shortly after that, Jeanne moved out of the Stabiles' house.

Being a good Catholic, Betty had no intention of seeking a divorce, but under the circumstances she felt it was necessary to separate for a while. It was her hope that, after a cooling-off period, they would reconcile—not only for the sake of the children but because she still loved Dean, despite his errant ways, and she hoped he felt the same way about her.

Dean had been a naughty boy before and had always returned to the fold. So why should this time be different? But this time it was. Dean never even came back to see the children once he and Betty separated—and, according to Betty, it was a long time before Jeanne would allow "Betty's kids" in her house.

It was a situation that put a terrible strain on Betty's emotions. And if, as some of her friends from that period remember, she started drinking more heavily than was good for a person, to help her forget, who could blame Betty?

She and Dean had been through an awful lot together since she had first seen him crooning in front of the Sammy Watkins Band at the Hollenden Hotel nearly ten years earlier. They had loved passionately and quarreled violently. She'd borne him four children. She'd seen him rise from an obscure band singer, forced to accept charity from Lou Perry, to one of the most successful and famous men in America.

She felt that all their years of mutual struggles must have created a bond between them—a bond that was much too strong for a little girl from Miami to break with a few sweet words and some ardent caresses. At least, that's what Betty kept telling herself, which was what gave her the courage to hang on and not file for a divorce. In fact, in the beginning, Betty was determined to fight any move of Dino's to start divorce proceedings himself, which she'd heard he might be contemplating.

Then two things happened that made her realize the situation was pretty hopeless. "One day," recalls Betty, with a sardonic laugh, "I saw Dean and Jeanne walking down Sunset Strip arm in arm, in *matching* Sy Devore suits. That really started my blood boiling."

The final straw came a few days later. Betty was at her business manager's office picking up her allowance check. The business manager was on the phone when she came in, but pointed to something on the desk and said, "Your check's there, Betty." Looking down to pick it up, she noticed an engraved invitation of some sort next to it. The invitation stated, "Mr. and Mrs. Beiggers invite you to the wedding of their daughter Jeanne to Dean Martin."

Betty shoved the invitation under her manager's nose and demanded, "What is this?"

He shrugged and said, "I figured you must have decided on a divorce. Otherwise, why would I have received this?"

When Betty got home, her phone was ringing. Marilyn Maxwell, Patti and Jerry Lewis, and a number of other friends of the Martins had all received invitations to Dino's wedding and wanted to know what it was all about. Betty wasn't quite sure herself. But she was too angry and hurt to try to hang onto her husband any longer.

The next day she took her troubles to Jacques Leslie, a high-priced Beverly Hills lawyer who specialized in nailing errant husbands to the financial cross, and divorce proceedings were started at once.

But, to this day, Betty Martin, who now lives the life of a recluse in San Francisco, cut off from all of her show business friends, is wondering what would have happened if she hadn't snapped at the bait involving the concocted wedding invitation.

9

Hurray for Hollywood

Because Martin and Lewis became important movie stars almost overnight—motion picture exhibitors in both 1951 and 1952 named them the Number One draw at the box office—few people realize that Jerry was almost fired from their first picture because he couldn't act and that Dino was going to go ahead and appear in it anyway, regardless of their partnership.

Hal Wallis, who doesn't part with money easily, had bought a veritable "pig in a poke" when he signed Dino and Jerry for pictures. He didn't have the faintest idea if they could act in front of a camera. "I just know they were the first nightclub comics to come along in a long time who could break me up," recalls Wallis. "So I decided to take a chance on them."

He wasn't taking too much of a chance. Early Martin and Lewis films were budgeted at around $500,000. The casts were filled with low-budget actors—even Martin and Lewis were only getting $50,000—a bargain when you consider that not one of the first seven pictures for Wallis ever grossed less than $4 million, a blockbuster figure for 1949.

Yet, even with the small salaries he was on the hook for (small compared with Gene Kelly's $300,000 a picture at MGM, for example), Hal Wallis suffered many moments of regret during the weeks when he and his minions were trying to come up with a vehicle that would capture the true spirit of Martin and Lewis on film.

Lewis's comedy was completely undisciplined. He wasn't used to sticking to the written line—mainly because he and Dino had never before used material expressly prepared for them by writers. Any material they didn't ad-lib they had stolen and possibly put a "switch" on.

88

Dino acted as if he had "a breadstick up his ass," in the estimation of one Paramount casting director. He could sing almost as well as his new neighbor, Bing Crosby, but his acting was stiffer than Zeppo Marx's.

Scriptwriters under contract to Wallis were at a loss as to what kind of a vehicle they could put together that would fit the peculiar talents of Martin and Lewis. Wallis, who had been specializing in gangster films and romantic comedies, wasn't sure what to suggest either, despite his many years of producing experience.

One thing he was sure of, however. He didn't want Martin and Lewis to emulate the low-class burlesque style of that other team that was around then—Abbott and Costello. Their grosses were already falling off, which meant the public was tiring of that kind of fare.

Then Cy Howard came up with a novel idea. Why not put Martin and Lewis in *My Friend Irma*, a property Hal Wallis had just acquired from CBS? They could play the boyfriends of Irma and her roommate.

My Friend Irma, starring the very busty Marie Wilson, had been a successful comedy radio series on the CBS network for the past five years —so successful, in fact, that Hal Wallis had bought the picture rights from CBS and hired Cy Howard, who created it, to write the screenplay and act as associate producer.

But now that Cy Howard had completed his screenplay and George Marshall had agreed to direct it, Hal Wallis was having as difficult a time casting the male leads as he was having finding the proper vehicle for Martin and Lewis's screen debut.

Since Wallis owned both Martin and Lewis and *My Friend Irma*, the logical solution seemed to be to put them together. But the question that remained to be answered was, would *My Friend Irma* still be *My Friend Irma* with two slapstick nightclub comics in it?

In its original version, *My Friend Irma* was a light romantic story with no visual comedy scenes. It contained two female roles: Irma, a dumb blond (Marie Wilson), and Jean, her hep roommate (Diana Lynn). The male roles were their boyfriends. Dino could probably play Steve Laird, a straight good-looking guy who ran an orange juice stand. But the other male role, that of Al, a real con man, didn't exactly conform to the character Jerry Lewis could probably portray best—a patsy or a real schnook. Al had been written to be played by a Jack Albertson or a Jack Carson type.

But since Wallis was desperate to get *My Friend Irma* off the ground and just as anxious to see whether or not he had bought two duds in the persons of Martin and Lewis, he ordered George Marshall to make a screen test of Jerry Lewis playing Al, the con man.

The test confirmed Hal Wallis's darkest qualms; in no way could this refugee from Newark, New Jersey, cut the part of a con man.

"He's no good," was Marshall's verdict, and Marshall, being a director-ial veteran of half a dozen of Bob Hope's best comedies, was a man whose opinion had to be respected. "Either we change the part to fit Jerry Lewis or we get another actor to play it."

But CBS and Cy Howard refused to allow one of the series' main characters to be altered to fit the dubious talents of Jerry Lewis, and with good reason. *My Friend Irma* was still a very viable radio property—near the top of the ratings. If a film appeared with different characterizations than its millions of loyal radio fans were familiar with, it was liable to hurt the series.

So Hal Wallis told George Marshall to "try again," and Jerry was put in the hands of an acting coach, who certainly had his work cut out for him. "It was like trying to turn Jane Fonda into Archie Bunker," states Howard today. "Stanislavsky and Lee Strasburg *combined* couldn't have done it."

Nevertheless, a number of tests of Jerry were made—nine in all, remembers Howard—but Jerry's interpretation of the role didn't improve. The verdict was still "thumbs down," and even Jerry was getting discouraged and suffering sleepless nights over his acting inadequacies.

Finally, Cy Howard came up with a solution that both Marshall and Hal Wallis bought. They would hire somebody else—a real actor—to play Al, the con man, and Howard would write in a separate part for Jerry—that of "Seymour," Steve Laird's schnooky assistant in the orange juice stand business. That way Howard could give Jerry all his usual nightclub schtick without committing the heresy of altering Al's character and disappointing *My Friend Irma*'s regular fans.

But Jerry wouldn't buy the idea. It was a blow to his ego. "My contract says I've got to play Al, and that's who I'm going to play," he protested in a conference one night with George Marshall, Cy Howard, and Hal Wallis in the latter's office on the Paramount lot.

"What good is it if your contract says you've gotta play Al if you can't play Al?" screamed Howard.

"I don't care. I won't play Seymour," insisted Jerry.

The screaming went on late into the night, with Jerry infuriating the others by sticking to his frustratingly stubborn attitude.

Finally, around midnight, Wallis said wearily, "All right, Jerry, if you won't play Seymour, I'll have to drop you from the picture. I'll just use Dean."

"My contract says we're a team," cried Jerry. "You have to use us as a team."

"There's no law that says I can't sign Dean for a separate picture," replied Wallis, with King Solomon-like logic. "I'll put Dean in *Irma*, and you'll just have to wait until we find a separate property for the two of you."

The notion that his own partner and bosom buddy might have his name on movie theater marquees before he did quickly brought about Jerry's acquiescence. Howard was told to go ahead and write in the part of Seymour. There must have been something Freudian in Cy Howard's dubbing Jerry's new character "Seymour," for Seymour happens to be Howard's real first name, which, he avows, "I hate."

In the light of what everybody predicted would happen to the two of them individually when they split up, it's a strange bit of irony that in Martin and Lewis's initial venture into films it was Jerry who was almost dropped because he didn't have it, whereas Dean's acting, although it left a lot to be desired, presented no real problems to the Paramount brass.

Jerry, with his penchant for blowing his own horn, was wise to have kept this fact a secret all these years.

One thing Jerry Lewis didn't keep a secret, once he had been bludgeoned into accepting the part of Seymour, was his presence on the Paramount lot in particular and the Hollywood scene in general.

Over the entrance to the dressing room that Hal Wallis had assigned to him, he nailed a plaque with the following inscription on it:

MONSTER'S LAIR

On his handmade shirts, he had "Child Star" monogrammed in place of his initials.

In the new Cadillac he had just purchased, Jerry had a special device installed for passing other motorists. Whenever he wanted another car to move over, he'd press down a pedal near the throttle, and a loud bell would start clanging like a streetcar. For dark and foggy nights, he'd press another pedal. This one sent out the eerie wail of a foghorn, giving other drivers the uneasy sensation that a steamer from the Pacific Ocean was adrift on Sunset Boulevard.

If Jerry were a passenger in somebody else's car—a car that wasn't gagged up with attention-calling devices—he'd place his foot on top of the driver's foot that was working the throttle pedal, and he wouldn't remove it until they were speeding along at some eighty miles an hour through dense traffic. At this point, Jerry would stick his head out the window and scream, "Help, I'm being *kidnapped!*"

Jerry may have been just a twenty-three-year-old wunderkind, but he knew the value of publicity and how to get people talking about *him*. Before long, all his and Dino's wacky antics were making Louella Parson's, Hedda Hopper's, Sidney Skolsky's, and Earl Wilson's columns.

Dino wasn't an activator of publicity stunts. He would rather be out at Lakeside playing golf with Hope and Crosby. But since he and Jerry were partners, he usually went along with his sidekick's impromptu gags—although sometimes a bit wearily. Even then, people got the impression that sometimes Dino just wanted to be left alone, to go about the business of making movies, so he could earn the money to keep him in gals, golf balls, and other hedonistic luxuries.

But Jerry's energy and ambition were just too much for Dean to repress.

If the two of them were being interviewed by a newspaperman, for example, the hapless reporter would soon find them flicking cigar ashes in his hair or applying the flame of a cigarette lighter to any document he might make the mistake of taking out of his pocket. If the man dared protest (or sometimes if he didn't), they'd rip his shirt off.

Perhaps Jerry would resort to another of his favorite gags. He'd ask to see your watch, claiming he wanted to test it. If you weren't familiar with Jerry's tricks, you'd probably give it to him. Jerry would then drop the watch on the floor and "test it" by stamping up and down on it with his foot.

The next day, you would receive half a dozen thirty-dollar shirts in return, or perhaps a Patek Phillippe wristwatch in place of the one destroyed. But what if the destroyed wristwatch happened to have some sentimental value or you had to go to another interview bare-chested? Well, that was just one of the hazards of being in the same room with Martin and Lewis in their halcyon days around Paramount.

Jerry might not have been able to play the part of a con man, but he had no trouble dreaming up many fiendish variations on the "anything-for-a-laugh" theme.

One of Dean and Jerry's favorite victims was their orchestra leader, Dick Stabile. In the first year he was with them, Stabile had to replace eight $200 tuxedos that they destroyed during their nightclub act—an act, incidentally, that they didn't abandon just because they had picture careers to worry about.

Except when they were actually shooting *My Friend Irma* or rehearsing for it, they played their act all over the United States. One of their most successful appearances that year was at Ciro's on Sunset Strip in Hollywood. Herman Hover's Ciro's was Los Angeles's only really first-class nightclub, catering mostly to top-echelon stars and executives. Most saloon comics usually bombed there. Jerry and Dino were the exceptions.

During their first engagement at Ciro's, Dick Stabile rushed into his dressing room one night for a quick change and found his shoes glued to the ceiling and his tuxedo hanging out the window—when he found it, that is. It took him a while to discover his boss's practical joke. By the time he did, Jerry was leading the orchestra in the wrong beat, causing that old roué Louis B. Mayer, who was a devotee of rumba dancing, to trip over the feet of the starlet who was his dancing partner and fall flat on his face on the floor.

Jerry wasn't above including himself in his own practical jokes. For a series of gag photographs for *Esquire* magazine that were to be taken in New York, Jerry had to grow a beard. The photographs were to be shot outdoors, but when the weather turned to icy sleet, Jerry refused to face the elements, despite the photographer's insistence that the layout would be worthless if shot indoors.

To make sure that he wouldn't have to go out into the sleet, Jerry stretched out and stapled his beard to the floor while the photographer ducked into a back room to get his equipment. The photographs had to be postponed until the weather warmed up.

Although Dino was rarely the instigator of this kind of madness, occasionally Jerry's practical joking became so contagious that Dino would be inspired to dream up something of his own.

Once, on the Paramount lot, Dino introduced a gray-haired old gentleman to Jack Rudley, George Marshall's assistant director. "Jack, this is my father," said Dino. "As long as you're not shooting today, would you mind taking him on a tour of the lot and showing him what a studio's like?"

Rudley politely escorted the old gentleman around the studio and even took him to lunch in the Paramount commissary, where he introduced him to all the celebrities as Dean Martin's father. It wasn't until 5:00 in the afternoon, when Rudley was putting the old man into a chauffeur-driven studio limousine to send him home, that he discovered his charge was a janitor from the apartment building across the street from the studio.

During a personal-appearance tour that took them to New York, Dean and Jerry once found themselves alone in a reception room on the eighth floor of an office building on Broadway. A few minutes later, the crowds on the street below were shocked to see two young men—an Italian and a Jew with a bangtail bob—stick their heads out of an open window on the eighth floor and scream at the top of their lungs, "Help—they're killing us!" After a few more frenzied calls for help, the two young men fell back into the office out of sight.

A huge crowd gathered below. The police were summoned and arrived moments later with sirens screaming. The officers quickly and efficiently tracked down the office and, finding the door locked, broke it in. They found Jerry and Dean innocently sitting on a couch, reading magazines.

Back at Paramount Studios, one day at the height of the lunch hour, Jerry and Dino came capering into the commissary in search of a few laughs that they probably hadn't been getting on the set (after all, they were used to the immediate reactions of nightclubs and theater audiences, and it could be disheartening not to hear even the cameraman laugh).

Climbing onto a chair, Jerry rapped for the attention of the 200 or more studio workers in the commissary—an assemblage that included quite a few important stars and front-office executives. "I guess you're wondering why I called you here," he screamed at them in his highest-pitched falsetto. "Well, it's to let you know that we're closing down the studio and that you're all fired."

At the same time, Dean seized a chop from the nearest plate and began an argument with Jerry over the choicest part. Jerry then stuck two french-fried potatoes in his ears—and one up his nostril—and wiggled them at Franca Faldini, a beautiful exotic new Italian import who'd just arrived on the lot to play her first Hollywood role and who was having lunch at a table with Y. Frank Freeman, the dignified southern gentleman who was head of the studio in 1949.

At the time, Miss Faldini was in costume, wearing $500 worth of twenty-four-karat-gold stockings spun for her first role as a Paramount star. While Dean suddenly took Miss Faldini in his arms and embraced her with his full Italian lasciviousness, Jerry whipped out a jar of jewelry polish (which he just happened to have with him) and briskly massaged her legs, ruining the hosiery.

"Stop that, you madmen!" roared Y. Frank Freeman, in his best Southern Comfort accent.

Suddenly, Jerry wheeled around, advancing slowly and menacingly on the studio head. "Freeman, I don't like your attitude," screamed Jerry. "Wash up, collect your pay, and get out!"

Another time, Dino and Jerry were walking down a studio street in the direction of the *My Friend Irma* set when they bumped into Freeman coming out of his bungalow with a dignified-looking old gentleman in a bowler hat. This man happened to be J. Sandler, a member of the board of directors of the Chase National Bank in New York, who was on the West Coast to check into Paramount's shaky financial condition. Chase National supplied the production money for Paramount's pictures in those days.

When Dino and Jerry spied their boss, Jerry walked up to him and said, "Hi, Frank, have you got our cars washed yet?" As Freeman sputtered and stammered in embarrassment, Dino said, "Another thing, Mr. Freeman, how come the studio's so dirty? There's nothin' but cigarette butts everywhere I look."

"Hey, Frank, have you got our cars washed yet?" became a standard greeting whenever Jerry and Dean spied Freeman on the lot.

Freeman soon learned to ignore their disrespectful attitude. Correction: He never really learned to ignore it, just how to cope with it better. Whenever he saw them approaching, he would walk in another direction or duck into the nearest men's room. If he couldn't escape their taunts, he'd simply smile blandly and continue his steady gait to wherever he was going.

Whether or not he was ever amused by their antics, no one ever knew. But Hal Wallis reports that Freeman once offered Martin and Lewis $500 if they would be quiet for five minutes during his lunch hour.

"Five hundred dollars," scoffed Jerry. "We lose that much on one hole at golf. Make it worth our while and we'll talk business."

Freeman made no further offers, and Jerry and Dean continued their harassment of the old southern gentleman for as long as they were at Paramount.

Their immediate boss, Hal Wallis, wasn't spared the ravages of their madness either. They just put a new twist on it for him. They treated him with exaggerated solicitude.

Summoned to his office one day, Jerry whipped out a shoe-shine rag and a bottle of shoe polish, dropped to one knee, and said, "May I shine your shoes, dear thir?"

Before Wallis could say no, Jerry started applying black shoe polish to tan shoes, while Dino wrapped a towel around Wallis's front and began giving him a haircut with a pair of his desk scissors.

On other occasions, they would offer to polish Wallis's car or to mend his socks.

Minor annoyances like that Hal Wallis grew to expect and even to accept resignedly. But one of Jerry's pranks nearly gave him a heart attack.

Wallis was sitting in his office one day, complimenting himself on how smoothly the filming of *My Friend Irma* was going. There was just one more week before shooting would be wrapped up, and so far there had been no major crises, and the picture was still within its established budget.

Suddenly, the door to the reception room was flung open, and in staggered Jerry, his head bandaged and dripping with blood. As he gasped, "Mr. Wallis," in what sounded to Wallis like his final words, he crumpled to the floor.

"Oh, my God," exclaimed Wallis, and he dashed out the door to summon the studio doctor.

Five minutes later, Wallis dashed back, with the studio doctor in tow. They found Jerry Lewis, with not a trace of blood or a bandage on him, sitting behind Wallis's desk, posing as a studio executive.

Hal Wallis was—and still is—a no-nonsense producer. He doesn't like temperamental performers, and he's not particularly fond of practical jokes. To him, making movies is a business. He just wants to get them made on schedule and without going over budget. For him to put up with Martin and Lewis's katzenjammer antics, he must have liked what he saw in the "dailies" and been pleased with their behavior on the set.

"In the beginning, the two of them conducted themselves like real pros," recalls director George Marshall. "They were all business. They just wanted to get the picture done so they could get on to other things."

"Dean never was any trouble," adds Norman Taurog, who directed many of their films after the *Irma* series. "He was always on time when he showed up in the morning, and he always knew his words. His only trouble was he didn't like rehearsing. He'd run through his lines without any feeling. But once the cameras started to roll, he'd do a good job for you."

Everybody recalls that Jerry was a "doll" too, until he got bitten by the bug to be his own writer, director, cameraman, and producer—which ultimately led to his downfall.

But in his early days at Paramount, he'd listen to anybody he thought knew what was right for him.

One who knew what was right for him was Cy Howard. He saw right away that Jerry had to play "the little guy"—the schnook in the tennis sneakers who was always being pushed into trouble by his smart-aleck sidekick, as played by Dean Martin. "Seymour" was the perfect name for "the little guy," and, fortunately for Jerry Lewis, Howard came up with some very funny bits for him.

One was a scene that grew out of his boss's refusal to put in an automatic orange juice squeezer, thereby forcing Jerry to squeeze 1,000 oranges by hand. Because of the way he had to grip each orange while squeezing it, Jerry's hand froze into a claw by the scene's end. It could not be straightened out, and he had to play the rest of the picture with his hand in this paralyzed condition. Since nobody can play paralytic humor any better than Jerry, the bit was a big hit with the audiences—the young kids especially. Young people started flocking to Martin and Lewis's movies after *My Friend Irma* was released with the same passion as later generations went to see the Beatles.

In another bit from *Irma* that became a classic, Jerry played a parking lot attendant who couldn't back cars in and out of tight spaces without tearing off the fenders of brand-new Rolls Royces and Lincoln Continentals. It may not have been *My Friend Irma* kind of humor, but it was hilarious stuff that had sophisticated people in the projection room, including Hal Wallis, falling in the aisles.

Jerry must have felt things were going well too, for now that he didn't have to play a character that didn't fit him, he quickly regained his lost confidence, and he began acting and ad-libbing before the cameras with the same reckless abandon that made Martin and Lewis such a hit in nightclubs and that was to make them even bigger hits on the screen.

One day on the set, director George Marshall complained to Jerry that he was pitching his voice too high. "I have to," Jerry sassed him back, "I'm making love to a tall woman."

10

Everything I Have Is Yours

Although Dean's first marriage was definitely over (at least as far as he was concerned) by the time he moved to Hollywood, it wasn't until September 1949 that he was free to marry Jeanne. It had taken that long for Betty's attorney, Jacques Leslie, to work out a financial settlement that she could live with, even if Dean couldn't.

The chief snag in the negotiations had been that although Betty was rightfully entitled to 50 percent of hers and Dean's community property, there really wasn't anything to divide up except his income. They owned nothing and had nothing in the bank.

Still, Leslie felt that Betty was entitled to something more than straight alimony, which was taxable, because of the huge amounts Dean had already earned in the past and what he was on the verge of making in the future. So he devised the following formula, which Dean eventually accepted:

1. One thousand dollars a month straight alimony
2. One thousand dollars a month child support
3. One thousand dollars a month, nontaxable, based upon a projection of Dean's future income, to make up for there being no community property to divide.

The papers were signed in the early summer of 1949 and were approved by the Superior Court of Los Angeles.

Then Dean and Jeanne became impatient about having to wait a full year for the divorce to become final (which was still the case in 1949). He approached Betty and asked her if she would mind going to Las

Vegas and getting a quickie Nevada divorce on top of the California one so that he would be able to expedite his marriage to Jeanne.

Betty talked it over with her attorney, who saw a further chance for his client to capitalize on Dean's anxiety to make it legal with Jeanne. He advised Betty to play it cool and wait—until Dean agreed to come through with more money.

Betty next told Dean that she would go to Vegas only if he fattened the financial settlement. He recognized it for what it was—legal blackmail—but, evidently, he felt Jeanne was worth it, for he then volunteered to pay Betty another $100 a week for the rest of her life. That brought her monthly take-home pay to $3,400, or $40,800 a year, not bad for a little girl from Morton, Pennsylvania.

Once the agreement was amended, Betty took off for a six-week residency in Las Vegas, leaving her four children in her Holmby Hills home, in the care of Guy and Angela Crocetti, who went on living with her for a couple of years.

The Crocettis were not in favor of the divorce; it upset them to see the family driven apart. Consequently, they sided with Betty during most of the early legal infighting over the financial settlement and child custody. Mrs. Crocetti, in fact, used to tell her ex-daughter-in-law, "You know, Betty, some day it will happen again. Another girl will take Dean from Jeanne." It happened, of course, but Mrs. Crocetti never lived to see it.

After serving out her time in Las Vegas, during which she missed her daughter Deana's first birthday party, Betty divorced Dean on August 24, 1949.

This enabled Dean to marry Jeanne on September 1 in the Beverly Hills home of Herman Hover, the entrepreneur who owned and ran Ciro's, the splashy Sunset Strip nightclub where Martin and Lewis played to capacity audiences a couple of times yearly.

It was a simple civil ceremony, with just a few close friends and business acquaintances (including Abbey Greshler, who was the signatory witness on the couple's marriage certificate) in attendance. Beverly Hills city court judge Charles J. Griffen married the couple in Hover's elegant living room, and Jerry was best man. Patti Lewis was there too, among the well-wishers, although she didn't exactly approve of the match. Relations were still a bit on the cool side between the Lewises and the second Mrs. Martin.

To show that he could be a good sport about the nuptials, however, Jerry kissed Dino's new bride and followed that up by jumping into Hover's swimming pool in the suit Dean was planning to wear when he left on his honeymoon. After all, even a wedding needed a few laughs. Besides, he couldn't tolerate Dino's getting all the attention, even at his own wedding.

Now that the newlyweds could live together officially, Dean and Jeanne moved into a house on the corner of Lomitas and Alpine Drives in Beverly Hills. Their honeymoon was to be a tour around the country, to advertise the opening of Martin and Lewis's first film, *My Friend Irma.*

Martin and Lewis's first stop was New York's Paramount Theater, where only ten years earlier Jerry Lewis had stood in the back of the house in an usher's uniform and dreamed of the day Milton Berle would break his leg so that he could fill in for him on stage. Now he was the headliner himself (well, he and Dino, anyway), playing six shows a day to packed houses.

With six shows a day, Dino could hardly squeeze in the time for squeezing Jeanne. But what did Jerry care? It wasn't his honeymoon. He loved being busy—so much so that in between stints on the stage he donned the uniform of a Paramount usher, plus white tennis sneakers, and stood out front on the sidewalk under the marquee trying to elicit a few laughs from the passers-by he was trying to entice inside. Jerry's appetite for laughs and attention was apparently insatiable.

"Immediate seating at the Capitol and Strand," Jerry would announce in a shrill falsetto. "Keep moving, folks. Buy your tickets. Go away. Step right up here. Well, come on, do something."

The crowd that gathered on the sidewalk—some of whom thought they recognized Jerry—would be somewhat confused by his orders and, consequently, showed no sign of entering the theater at all. They found it much more fun—and also cheaper—to watch Jerry's antics under the marquee.

At one point, Jerry noticed a blond slender young girl standing a few feet away, gaping at him and looking terribly confused. He grabbed her arm and escorted her with mock gallantry to the box office.

"All right, lady," he told her. "How many tickets do you want? Speak up."

The young girl flushed. "Oh, heavens," she exclaimed in a frightened voice.

"Heavens! Heavens!" Jerry repeated. "This is no heaven. This is a movie house. How much dough you got? Can you afford a ticket? If not, I'll take your IOU."

The embarrassed girl ran off and disappeared into the gathering crowd.

At other times Jerry would station himself inside the ticket-taker's box and shout out the circular window at potential customers. "Come on, folks, let's buy some tickets. Let's get a little hustle on," he would exhort the people. "Wonderful show inside. Thirty beautiful girls. Starring Jerry Lewis."

The crowds that gathered for these and other samples of Jerry's extormania would grow to such proportions that they constituted a safety hazard. The policeman on the beat would have to beg Jerry to go inside so he could clear the sidewalk for legitimate traffic.

As author Leo Rosten once wrote about them, Martin and Lewis had "a twenty-four-karat sense of publicity." But publicity without a marketable product won't sell many tickets, and Jerry and Dean were packing them in.

The reviews, with the exception of a few lint-picking critics from *Newsweek* and *Time*, didn't hurt.

The nation's leading movie reviewer, Bosley Crowther, wrote in *The New York Times* on September 29, 1949,

> We could go along with the laughs, which were fetched by a new mad comedian, Jerry Lewis by name. This freakishly built and acting young man, who has been seen in nightclubs hereabouts with a collar-ad partner, Dean Martin, has a genuine comic quality. The swift eccentricity of his movements, the harrowing features of his face and the squeak of his vocal protestations . . . have flair. His idiocy constitutes the burlesque of an idiot, which is something else again. He's the funniest thing in it. Indeed, he's the only thing in it that we can expressly propose for seeing the picture.

The Hollywood Reporter started out with,

> Hal Wallis knows gold dust when he sees it, for in grabbing up *My Friend Irma* he has not only turned out a lilting comedy, but has paved the way for a series that will linger many seasons in the future. Spotting the comedy team of Martin and Lewis for their film debut as buddies of Irma is only one showmanly angle in Wallis's clever presentation . . . the tomfoolery of Martin and Lewis is just as effective on the screen as on the nightclub platform. Lewis is a rare comic whose sense of the ridiculous is simply sublime. Martin sings a lot and clicks with every number.

Variety wrote, in part,

> An important phase of the production is the screen introduction of Dean Martin and Jerry Lewis. Latter is a socko comedian, and with Martin as straight man singer, they form a team that has decided film possibilities if backed with the right material and used properly.

The Los Angeles Examiner, a powerful voice in 1949, said,

> *My Friend Irma* has been transplanted to a motion picture without losing a jot or tittle of her effervescent, maddening, beguiling, ingenuous charm.
>
> The introduction of the zany comedy-singing team of Dean Martin

and Jerry Lewis amounts to an invasion. Frankenstein-faced Lewis
all but steals win, place, and show money in this comedy sweepstakes.
There just hasn't been anything like him ever on land, sea, or celluloid.

His handsome partner, Dean Martin, will undoubtedly be more at
home on the screen with added experience. And he shouldn't oughtta
listen to any more Bing Crosby records—the similarity is uncanny as
Dean sings the tuneful tunes of Jay Livingston and Ray Evans.

Although plenty of kudos went to the team itself, there was never any
doubt, from reading the critics or listening to their fans, about who was
its "star" if one had to analyze its component parts, which most show-wise
people were wont to do. Dino was treated by the press with good-natured
condescension right from the very beginning of their screen careers. He
was just a straight man, a tagalong, a minor talent, perhaps a "half a star"
but not one who could shine by himself in the show business firmament.

All this had to bug Dino, had to gnaw away at his ulcer-prone insides,
for basically Dino is a vain man with a pretty high opinion of himself,
despite his happy-go-lucky facade.

After reading all those accolades to Jerry, Dino was bound to ask himself: Where would Jerry have been if he hadn't been nice enough to let
him join forces with him or if Cy Howard hadn't come up with a brain-
storm that kept Jerry from being dropped from the picture altogether?
He'd probably be off in some second-rate nightclub doing his lousy
record act for $100 a week.

Instead, Jerry was the "socko" half of the team. That additional little
twist of the dagger in Dino's back by the Prince of Irony must have really
hurt—especially when Jerry did nothing to correct that impression with
the public or the press.

But fortunately—or unfortunately, depending on how staunch a Martin
and Lewis fan one is—the combined success of the two was beginning to
snowball so rapidly that there was little time for the melancholy dago to
brood about Jerry's upstaging him, if not deliberately, then with the same
results.

My Friend Irma was an immediate box office smash everywhere it
played. Martin and Lewis's personal-appearance tour to plug the picture
drew larger crowds than the president did. There weren't enough nights
in the year to play all the nightclubs that were willing to pay them
$10,000 a week. On top of that, they now had their own weekly radio series
on the NBC network.

This additional windfall had grown out of a couple of "guest shots"
on Bob Hope's radio show the previous winter; a single appearance on
"The Big Show," a radio program starring Tallulah Bankhead; and three
appearances on one of NBC's first television variety shows, "Welcome
Aboard," sponsored by Admiral Television.

"Welcome Aboard" was a variety show with a nautical flavor, no doubt inspired by the sponsor's name—"Admiral." Its stage setting was a ship and the performers were dressed as passengers and crew members.

The man who put the Admiral show together was Norman Blackburn, newly appointed head of television programming for NBC at the time Abbey Greshler first showed up in his office one day in 1948 to try to sell his clients, Martin and Lewis. Dean and Jerry, of course, had made big names for themselves in nightclubs by that time but were still relatively unknown to people in the broadcasting business.

Blackburn had barely heard of Martin and Lewis, but he signed them for $2,500 a show for three shows on Greshler's assurance that his clients were "a very funny act." The networks had to take what they could get in the way of talent in those days because most of the superstars of radio were afraid of television and were postponing the day they'd have to get into it.

After three shows with Martin and Lewis, Blackburn wished he'd never fallen prey to Greshler's salesmanship. Doing their regular nightclub act, Dean and Jerry were an absolute riot before the television cameras. Unfortunately they didn't know when to quit. With just a minute and a half left of the first show, they were supposed to end their act to leave time for the sponsor's message. But they paid absolutely no attention to the director's frantic signaling to them from the sponsor's booth and just rambled on—right up to the station break—at which point the technical crew simply cut them and the show off the air, puzzling the viewers.

Blackburn naively figured that the network and the sponsor would be pleased that he had come up with such a laugh riot. But when the sponsor phoned, it was apparent that he couldn't have cared less about how funny Martin and Lewis had been. He was furious that he hadn't been able to get his sales pitch about the high quality of Admiral television sets across to the public.

At the beginning of the second show, Blackburn cautioned Jerry and Dean about going past the last minute and a half. "The trouble with us," answered Jerry, "is we know how we're gonna get on, but sometimes we wonder how we're gonna get off."

The same thing happened at the second show. Jerry and Dean blew the commercial, and Blackburn was in even more trouble with old man Admiral, to say nothing of his boss, the network head, Pat Weaver. If it happened again, Blackburn would be out of a job. He'd have to think of something practical to subvert Dean's and Jerry's undisciplined behavior. Just warning them was a waste of breath.

Finally, he got an inspiration, which he put into action at the end of the third show. Two minutes before the sponsor's message, Dean and Jerry were still doing their schtick and showing absolute contempt for the time clock and all the people waving at them from the sponsor's booth. Suddenly, from out of the wings strode a man in a gob's suit, ringing a bell.

"All ashore who's going ashore," announced the gob. Two other sailors picked up Dean and Jerry and carried them down a gangplank and out of camera range, allowing the camera to train its lens on the announcer doing the Admiral Television commercial.

The sponsor was happy. Blackburn's job was saved. And Dean and Jerry were a big hit on their first TV appearances, which didn't actually mean much because very few people had television sets in 1948 and 1949, and consequently the ratings were low.

Nevertheless, Dean and Jerry were beginning to get an overexaggerated opinion of their importance by the time they were hired to do a guest shot on Tallulah Bankhead's "The Big Show."

Goodman Ace, head writer of Tallulah's radio show at the time and one of the most distinguished men of letters in the comedy-writing field, remembers all too vividly his first business dealings with Dean and Jerry.

After insisting that a script be sent over to them at their suites in the Essex House, Jerry phoned Ace and complained that they were bowing out of the show because the material didn't fit him and Dino.

"We'd rather just ad-lib," said Jerry.

"That's probably because you don't know how to read," countered Goody Ace rather acidly.

That hooked them, and they reluctantly agreed to show up for rehearsals, provided they were granted full approval of all musical arrangements.

The rehearsals went smoothly until a few minutes before air time the day of the show. At that point, Ace had to call the cast together to make some cuts in the script. The others in the guest cast, which included such notables as Bob Hope and Ethel Barrymore, cooperatively showed up on stage with scripts and pencils.

Dean and Jerry remained in their dressing rooms. The director had to scream for them a number of times before they finally deigned to appear. When they did, Jerry was completely bare-chested and had an electric razor in his hand with which he pretended to be shaving. The razor cord was plugged into his belly button, held there by tape.

"Where the hell have you been?" asked Tallulah, who was burning because of the delay.

"I'm shaving, Mama," answered Jerry in his "idiot kid" voice and sporting his mongoloid expression.

Tallulah hauled off with her fist and socked Jerry right in his electric razor, nearly breaking his jaw.

Just before the show was to go on the air, Bob Hope informed Goody

Ace that he didn't want "them," meaning Martin and Lewis, on stage when he was doing his spot. They already had a reputation for disrupting everyone else's act, and even the great Mr. Hope didn't want to cope with them on "live" radio.

Ace explained to Hope that there was no way Martin and Lewis could be offstage because the performers wouldn't be making separate entrances and exits. The actors would sit on stage in wooden chairs lined up along the wall, and when it was time for a particular performer to be in a scene, he or she would merely stand and walk to the mike. "But they promised me they'll behave," Ace assured the nervous Hope.

They behaved like two well-mannered Sunday school students—right up to the time Bob Hope rose to do his monologue. But no sooner did Hope open his mouth to spout his first joke into the mike than the studio audience and radio listeners heard Jerry's voice ring out.

"I don't know how much they're payin' him, Dean. Why are you asking me?"

"I thought you knew everything, baby," replied Dino, going right along with his partner's high jinks.

Burning, Hope fixed an icy stare on the two delinquents and snappishly said, "Oh, Arthur Godfrey's Amateur Hour!"

Although no sponsors were willing to take a chance on Martin and Lewis, all three major networks recognized their potential—if not for radio, for TV, which was still in its infancy but was rapidly expanding into the big time—and started making overtures to Greshler for his clients' services.

In February 1949, NBC signed Jerry and Dean to star in a regular weekly radio series. The network gave "The Martin and Lewis Show" a $10,000 weekly budget with which to work (a generous amount for radio) and a preferred time slot, 6:30–7:00 on Sunday nights.

"The Martin and Lewis Show" was first heard over NBC in April 1949. It had the usual variety show format, with Dean and Jerry playing themselves and Dean crooning a couple of songs.

The reactions to Martin and Lewis as radio entertainers were somewhat disappointing. It was the first actual setback in their careers since they had come together as a team.

"The freshness of the Martin and Lewis humor, so evident on the nightclub floor, was, on the air, a sometime thing," wrote *Newsweek* in its April 18, 1949, issue.

The two principal problems seemed to be that Martin and Lewis's humor had to be seen in order to be appreciated and that having to stick to a script seemed to crimp their free-and-easy style of saying and doing practically anything that came into their heads. They convulsed the studio audience by their wild clowning around at the mike, but radio listeners couldn't see any of that.

At one point, when he feared they were laying an ostrich-sized egg, Jerry whined to Dean but loudly enough for everyone else to hear, "In radio everyone gets in for free. At those prices they can afford to hate us." That line got a huge guffaw, which was one of the first encouraging sounds Jerry heard during the entire half hour.

But Jerry and Dean improved with practice, and, by the time their radio series went off the air in the spring, *Variety* wrote, "Potentially the boys have got it."

But whether or not they had clicked on radio was relatively unimportant to them. They had enough other work to keep them busy fifty-two weeks a year.

In the summer of 1949, they made *At War with the Army* at Motion Picture Center for their own York Productions company. It was produced by Abbey Greshler and directed by Hal Walker, and the girl playing the feminine lead was Polly Bergen.

In *At War with the Army*, Dean Martin played a top sergeant, and Jerry portrayed a private first class who was trying to win a three-day pass home because his wife was about to have a child. He wins the pass, but at the last minute it is canceled when his entire division is called overseas.

Although it was a paper-thin story, *At War with the Army* was the ideal vehicle for the schnook character Jerry was becoming a master at portraying. It was such a hit at its first sneak preview that Paramount, which had turned up its collective nose at the project when Greshler first offered it to them, quickly made a deal with York Productions to release it.

With *My Friend Irma* a nationwide hit in its first runs in the fall of 1949, *At War with the Army* had to be kept out of release for another year and a half. But the feeling around Hollywood was that Martin and Lewis had made their second straight film hit, and that they were now the hottest new comics to come along in years.

As a result, NBC started wooing Jerry and Dean for another radio series. Even though their first fling on the ether had been less than sensational, NBC was convinced that they could be giant stars on TV. Dean and Jerry weren't quite willing to go into TV full time yet for fear of overexposing themselves to the public. Besides, most video emanated from the East in those days, and Dean and Jerry were now West Coast residents. Dean, especially, saw no reason to go into TV and take on all that extra work. Radio was easier. Therefore, NBC decided to give them another crack at radio, if only to tie them up until such time as they would agree to make the jump into the more demanding medium.

To entice them back, NBC put a package together that Dino and Jerry couldn't resist (and neither could Greshler because he had wangled a special deal for himself whereby he would receive a producer's salary from NBC). NBC still had no sponsor for the show, but they raised the budget to $12,000 (meaning a bigger slice for Dean and Jerry personally) and hired three of the best comedy writers in the business, Charlie Isaacs, Hal Goodman, and Jack Douglas (who wrote the best-selling book *My Brother Is an Only Child*).

They also gave them a capable supporting cast, consisting of Sheldon Leonard, Ben Alexander, and their very own band leader, Dick Stabile. Moreover, they offered them a more desirable time slot, 8:00–8:30 on Friday nights. Dean and Jerry accepted the challenge, and "The Martin and Lewis Show" was back on the air in the fall of 1949.

But there was another aspect to their signing that never made the trade papers. NBC had sweetened the deal by lending Jerry and Dean $75,000 in cash in return for which they agreed to give the network the exclusive rights to their radio appearances over the next three years.

The availability of a $75,000 interest-free loan was probably the principal reason that Jerry and Dean decided to take another fling at radio. For, difficult as it is to believe, two of the highest-priced entertainers in the business, with a yearly take in the neighborhood of $1 million, were hardpressed for spending money.

The trouble seemed to be that the two of them were living much too high on the hog considering what the government was allowing them to keep after taxes. Their gross take, which put them in about the 90 percent bracket, was merely an illusion. Breaking down their income, with the government getting 90 percent and their agent getting 20 percent of the remainder (10 percent of which was for business management), they were winding up with something like $80,000 each. Dino was spending half that much on alimony alone.

Jerry was supporting a number of poor relatives and about thirty stooges and hangers-on. He was buying expensive cars and paying a huge rent on the Montez house. He was gambling heavily; according to Greshler, "the Las Vegas crowd got healthy when Martin and Lewis came to town." He was also squandering on gifts more than twice the amount that the average family had to live on. In 1950, for example, he was reputed to have spent somewhere in the neighborhood of $35,000 on small gifts and "touches" alone.

One of Jerry's favorite ways of showing his appreciation to a loyal friend or to employees was to give out gold watches with something sentimental engraved on them, like the one he gave to Irving Kaye: "To Irving —I owe my success to you. Jerry Lewis." As his career skyrocketed,

handing out gold watches was to become practically a fetish with Jerry
Lewis. Virtually every person who had ever worked for him or been fired
by him wound up with a gold timepiece as a memento.

Some people received more than one watch. For example, Ernie Glucksman, who produced Martin and Lewis's first television show and who for
many years following that was Jerry's personal assistant and constant companion, has an entire bureau drawer full of gold watches from Jerry
Lewis, all sentimentally engraved with such phrases as "It's you and me
together" or "How could I get along without you?"

At one point in his career, Jerry became so hung up on awarding gold
watches that he kept one closet in his house filled from floor to ceiling with
watches already gift-wrapped so that when people came to his home, he
could hand them out as the feeling hit him. "I thought I could buy love by
giving them a watch," Jerry once confessed in a rare moment of truth.

All of which Jerry might have been able to afford had not the United
States government suddenly reminded Dean and Jerry that they hadn't
paid any federal income taxes for approximately five years. "We thought
Greshler was paying our taxes," Jerry later confided to writer Ed Hartmann in speaking of the financial woes that plagued him and Dean.
"Greshler had led us to believe he was. So we went on spending money like
we were making a fortune."

Suddenly the federal government clamped down on Dean and Jerry,
commandeered the bulk of their income, and put them on a $125-a-week
allowance each. "There I was," relates Lewis, "driving around in a
Cadillac, living in a movie star's home, and sometimes I didn't have
enough money to pay the grocery bills."

According to what Hartmann claims Lewis told him, Jerry was so mad
that he bought a gun and went out looking for Greshler. "He wanted to
kill him." He never did, of course. He probably couldn't afford to buy
bullets.

But, compared with Dino, Jerry was as solvent as the Bank of America.
In addition to the fortune in back taxes Dino suddenly discovered he owed,
his other debts were compounding at such an alarming rate that, in January 1949, he had been forced to file bankruptcy proceedings. This, of
course, meant that he could get no loans from a legitimate source nor any
credit anywhere in the United States except from private individuals who
were trusting enough to take a chance on him.

His future was good, but his past was full of grief and trouble. Besides
the many debts, large and small, that he had never paid off (including
some $40,000 in hard-cash loans he and Jerry had wangled out of
Greshler), people from far back in Dino's past were suddenly crawling
out of the woodwork to sue him, figuring from all they'd read about him
that he could well afford it.

Sammy Watkins, the Cleveland band leader who had given him his start as a vocalist, sued Dean for $32,590. He claimed Dean had signed a paper with him, giving him 10 percent of his yearly earnings for seven years—which Dean obviously did, in order to get the job. Contracts giving band leaders agent's fees was a standard practice in the music business in those days.

Then there was comedian Lou Costello, who had befriended Dean during his sleazy New York days. He took Dean to court and demanded a mere $100,000, claiming he had paid Dean a salary and advanced him the money to have his nose "bobbed." There must have been something to Costello's story, because Dean reportedly settled with Costello for $20,000.

A number of other suits were also pending. Several of these actions were initiated by record companies, each claiming exclusive rights to peddle his singing on their label. Dino, it seems, would sign a contract with one record company, accept an advance, and record a few songs for them. Then he would wander over to a rival company in Tin Pan Alley, repeat the numbers for another label, and pick up still another advance. It wasn't that Dino was trying to get away with anything; he just couldn't be bothered with keeping track of what he had signed.

In addition to suits and settlements and the demands of Uncle Sam, Dino was still obligated to shell out $3,400 a month to support Betty and the four kids, come rain or shine. Despite the big money he and Jerry were making, it wasn't easy to part with $3,400 in hard cash every month. In fact, it proved to be such a back-breaking load early in his marriage to Jeanne that he took Betty to court to try to get his alimony and child-support payments reduced. The Superior Court judge not only upheld the original agreement but saddled Dino with an additional $8,000 in legal fees. Dino just couldn't win in those days.

All told, he and Jerry figured they were being sued for something like $12 million at one point early in their careers. Stories about their legal troubles made all the front pages and were even the subject of quite a few jokes and practical jokes.

While dining in a Boston restaurant, Dino once opened the menu to look for lasagna and sausages, his favorite dish, but, instead of seeing the normal bill of fare offerings, his eyes read,

> Defendants Martin and Lewis are hereby ordered to appear in the Superior Court of Boston on Thursday, December 1st.

Dino soon recognized it as a gag, but it had struck close enough to home to spoil his appetite. He settled for poached eggs and milk.

Then there was the joke that was going around about Dean's wedding to Jeanne.

The judge asked, "Do you take this woman to be your lawfully—"

"Look, Judge," interrupted Dino, "can't we settle this out of court?"

Although Martin and Lewis didn't lose every case and frequently settled for a fraction of the amounts being asked, their legal expenses alone were keeping them just one short step ahead of the sheriff. Occasionally the sheriff caught up with them.

It will be a long time, for example, before Jeanne Martin forgets the embarrassing day, just a few weeks after her wedding to Dean, that a Los Angeles city sheriff called on them at their Beverly Hills residence, presented them with a writ of attachment, and drove off in their brand new Cadillac. One of their many creditors had put a $5,000 lien on the car, an amount that was about $4,999 more than the Martins had in their checking account at the time.

The two of them immediately started making frantic phone calls to friends and acquaintances who might be in a position to lend them $5,000. When the frantic appeals brought no sign of financial aid, they contacted the nightclub owners for whom Dean and Jerry had worked and done record-breaking business: Herman Hover, Juley Podell, and Skinny D'Amato.

"But none of them would help us out, because we had no collateral," recalls Jeanne. "And after all Dean and Jerry had done for them by racking up such large grosses when no other comics could do any business!"

Jeanne still speaks with considerable bitterness about the forgetfulness of supposed "friends," even though today she is sitting on about $6 million worth of collateral given to her by Dino in their recent divorce settlement.

One man didn't forget: Harold Kopler, the owner of the Chase Hotel in St. Louis. The moment the Martins told him about their predicament, he lent them $6,000 and wanted no collateral—just Dino's promise that he and Jerry would work off the debt by playing a week in his swanky Chase Club the first week they were free. Of course, Jerry and Dean filled the engagement, and the Martins got their car back.

"That was one marvelous thing about Dean and Jerry," remembers Jeanne, with a faraway look in her blue eyes. "If one owed someone a free booking, the other would always go along and work for nothing to help him pay off the debt."

As Ernie Glucksman told Jerry and Dino soon after he went to work for them on "The Colgate Comedy Hour," "You guys are the Damon and Pythias of show business."

Jerry shot him a puzzled look and asked, "Who the hell's Damon and Pythias?"

Bob Hope takes a turn at the mike with Martin and Lewis. (*Photo from Jeanne Martin collection*)

Jerry and Dino rehearsing for one of their first radio shows. (*NBC photo by Herb Ball*)

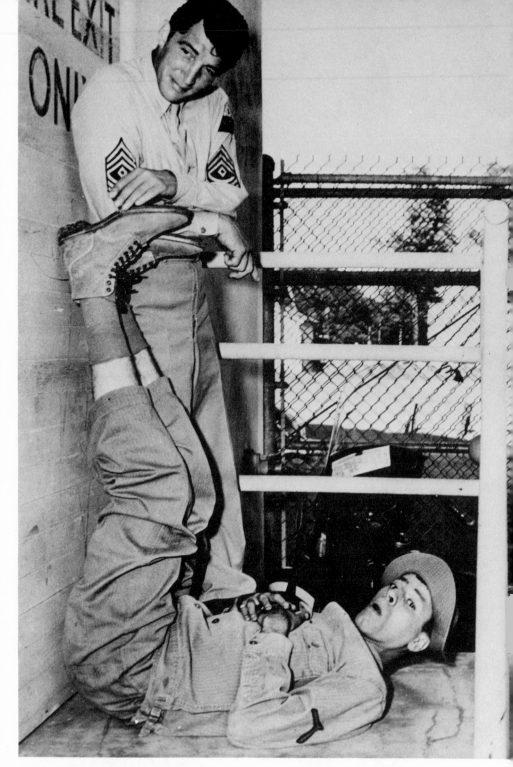

A scene from *At War with the Army*. (*Photo from Jeanne Martin collection*)

The Martins and the Lewises on a personal appearance tour of the Midwest to plug *At War with the Army*. (*Photo from Jeanne Martin collection*)

An evenings at Ciro's. Rear, from left: Tony Curtis, Janet Leigh, and Dean. Front, from left: Jerry and Patti Lewis, Jeanne Martin, and Marie McDonald. (*Photo from Jeanne Martin collection*)

Partners share fifty-fifty: Jerry Kisses Jeanne, while Dean waits his turn. (*Photo by Art and Len Weissman*)

Anyone for softball? Shelley Winters, Marilyn Maxwell, Dean Martin, Jerry Lewis, and the world's greatest catcher, Elizabeth Taylor. (*Photo by Darlene Hammond*)

Ed Simmons, Norman Lear, and Jerry Lewis on the comedian's front lawn in the Pacific Palisades, celebrating Norman Lear's birthday.

Dean and Jerry wrestling for a gag shot. (*Wide World Photos*)

Noel Coward's not the only one who can be suave. (*Photo by London Daily Express*)

Bing Crosby, Bob Hope, Jerry Lewis, and Dean Martin in 1953. (*United Press International Photo*)

Dean and Jerry measuring actress Tracy Morgan to see if she shapes up for part on "The Colgate Comedy Hour" TV show, 1955. (*Photo by Pictorial Parade*)

Dean Martin, Natalie Wood and Bob Hope on Bob Hope TV show, 1959. (*Photo by Darlene Hammond*)

Dean and Jeanne's second son, Ricci James Martin, born September 20, 1953, poses for his first picture. (*Wide World Photos*)

Dean with Jeanne and their daughter Gina, 1957. (*United Press International Photo*)

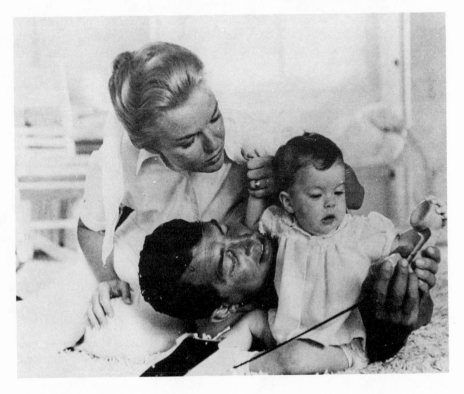

The children gather around as the Martin family celebrates the first birthday, December 20, 1957, of its newest member, Gina, held in the arms of her mother Jeanne Martin, as father Dean beams proudly. The other children are, left to right: Claudia, 13; Ricci, 4; Dino, 6; Gail, 12; and Deana, 9. Another son, Craig, 15, was not present. Dino, Ricci, and Gina are children of his marriage to Jeanne. (*Wide World Photos*)

Left to right: Grandfather Guy Crocetti, Dean, Gina (at age three), Jeanne Martin, and grandmother Angela Crocetti, in the Martins' dining room, 1959. (*Photo by Mel Traxel*)

11

♪People

All work and no play might make Jack a dull boy, but not two fellows named Dean and Jerry.

Since forming their partnership in 1946, the two of them had worked fifty-two weeks a year, without a single vacation. Between their radio series, nightclub engagements, personal appearances at theaters to plug their first picture, and filming a sequel to *My Friend Irma* in Hollywood, Dean and Jerry were kept so busy in 1950 crisscrossing the nation to meet their various commitments that they barely had time to see their wives and families. Somehow Jeanne Martin wound up pregnant shortly after her marriage to Dean, but, except for that, the statement still stands.

The only thing that wasn't going well for Dean and Jerry professionally was their radio show. It wasn't exactly bombing, but Dean and Jerry just couldn't compete with the well-established giants of radio: Jack Benny, Fred Allen, Bob Hope, and Red Skelton.

"The Martin and Lewis Show" was still suffering from the same malady that had plagued it in the spring. Dean and Jerry had to be seen to be appreciated. No matter how well written they were, straight "stand-up" joke routines, with strict adherence to the time clock, inhibited their comedy and prevented their true personalities from getting across to the public.

On one program, they were doing a satirical version of the Martin and Lewis story. The following exchange took place between them in a schoolroom where they supposedly met:

DEAN: Say, what's your name?
JERRY: Joey Levitch. What's yours?

DEAN: Paul Crocetti.

JERRY: Gee, I can just see our names up in lights someday—
MARTIN AND LEWIS.

Later in the same sketch, on the subject of a nightclub they were planning to open, the dialogue went as follows:

JERRY: Our nightclub will be a smash. And before I forget it—we'd
better get a big neon sign outside. We want the folks to be
able to find us, you know.

DEAN: You mean—our names up in lights?

JERRY: Sure—I've got the whole thing all worked out. As you drive
up to the club at night, the first thing you see is this big neon
sign: "Now appearing—Jerry Lewis, the world's youngest
comedian."

DEAN: (disappointed) That's all the sign says?

JERRY: Neon costs money.

DEAN: I know, but what about me? Doesn't the sign say anything
about me? What about my singing?

JERRY: Oh, yes—your singing. Well, right below where this big
neon sign says, "Now appearing, Jerry Lewis, the world's
youngest comedian," . . .

DEAN: (anxiously) Yeah?

JERRY: It says, "Also, the world's oldest Dean Martin."

After one of Dean's song renditions, the following banter was heard:

JERRY: That was pretty good, Dean.

DEAN: Like it, eh?

JERRY: Yeah, someday you're gonna be a really great singer. Why,
you'll be like Carmen Lombardo, Vaughan Monroe, and Mel
Torme rolled into one.

DEAN: What would that sound like?

JERRY: Peggy Lee.

Although the humor creaks plenty after twenty-five years, one thing is
apparent from glancing over those old scripts: Jerry was the dominant
character, the one the writers depended on to deliver their punch lines.
Dino was thrown a bone occasionally, but for the most part he had to be
satisfied with straight lines and the chance to sing a couple of numbers,
which was probably why, even as long ago as 1949, Dino started to lose
interest in rehearsing very seriously.

In his radio days, Jerry was pretty subdued for Jerry—probably because his show wasn't catching on. Nevertheless, every once in a while, his

behavior showed indications of the monster he would turn into when he could no longer handle his own success.

One week, a seven-year-old child actor named Donny Richards played the part of a precocious child on "The Martin and Lewis Show." Donny was one of those surefire kid actors who comes along every once in a great while, like Rusty Hamer on the old "Danny Thomas Show." Donny had a brilliant sense of timing and a natural instinct for upstaging adult actors.

During the preview performance, Donny was getting bigger laughs than Jerry was. This induced Jerry to take the kid aside after the preview and warn him to "quit trying to be so funny!" Donny promised not to do so much mugging, but, once the show went on the air, he couldn't resist the temptation to get bigger laughs than the stars. "Suddenly," recalls one of the script writers, "I saw Jerry sidle over to Donny, mutter something under his breath to him, and then push him away from the mike."

Between the show's low ratings and the lack of a sponsor to pick up the costly tab, NBC wisely allowed the show to die a slow death come February "pick-up" time.

By then, Dean and Jerry were willing to concede that radio was not their best medium, and they began to pay serious attention to proposals from the network that they get their feet wet in TV.

Consequently, Norman Blackburn, newly crowned national director of TV programming for NBC, hired Charlie Isaacs and Hal Goodman to create a TV format for Martin and Lewis and dispatched them to Chicago to discuss it with the two comedians. Dean and Jerry were doing a personal appearance at the Chicago Theater at the time to plug their latest picture, *My Friend Irma Goes West*, which was getting rave reviews, but again the kind that bugged the hell out of Dino—for example, "Most of the laugh meat is tossed to Jerry Lewis, and the young comedian knows just what to do with it. As the film's mainstay, he grooves the guffaws in sock fashion," etc., etc.

On an NBC expense account, Charlie Isaacs and Hal Goodman checked into the swanky Ambassador-East Hotel and notified Abbey Greshler, who was "mother-henning" Jerry and Dean's activities in the Windy City, that they were in town to discuss a TV idea.

"When can we get together with Dean and Jerry?" Isaacs asked Greshler.

"To hell with the TV show," snapped Greshler. "I want you to write the boys some new nightclub material."

"But that's not why NBC sent us here," protested Goodman. "They're paying us to come up with a TV format."

That could wait, Greshler explained to them. Dean and Jerry needed some fresh nightclub material first.

He wasn't kidding about that, judging from the review editor Abel Green had given them in *Variety* the second time they played the Copa in the spring of 1949:

> Maybe their best friends won't tell them, or their management seems unable to see it or control it, but fact is that people are beginning to talk about Dean Martin and Jerry Lewis's dialectics. The ever-growing accent on Martin's Italian extraction and Lewis's Yiddishisms are annoying and unshowmanly.
>
> The personable singer, furthermore, is evidencing his dialectic predilections by throwing in some other Bronx patois, and all this tends to make for a needless hurdle for two of the freshest, upcoming comedians extant. In between are some other *paisan* lyrics, evidently of spicy origin judging by the gustos from the Americans of Italian extraction. And that goes ditto for Lewis. Fact is they are extraordinarily talented, particularly in the visual medium. But when the new things that have been added become increasingly flavored with kosher or antipasto hors d'oeuvres, it's time to mention it.
>
> Team has gotten so that their chatter and patter put emphasis on "some of my people are here tonight too," and wheezes like "even the tables go to shul" (synagogue), etc.
>
> The boys would be smart to leave out the Lindy's trimmings, before they die of indigestion.

Since forming his alliance with Dean, Jerry had stated many times, both publicly and privately, that he and the Steubenville Romeo didn't need material. Unlike Jack Benny, Fred Allen, and Bob Hope—all of whom expended thousands of dollars a week for first-class comedy writing—Dean and Jerry seemed to feel that they were so talented that, out of all the great comedians in the business, they alone could get away with making up their own jokes on the spur of the moment or putting fresh twists on somebody else's.

Jerry's line to Billy Rose ("Dean and I don't need material!") the night of Martin and Lewis's smash opening at the Copa was coming back to haunt him now. Maybe they had been able to get by with their own gags and skits for a while, but, at the pace they were now using up material, they were discovering that they could no longer rely on their own inventiveness to keep the laughs going. As a result, they found themselves sinking into the bad-taste quagmire of dialectic and racist humor, and now, suddenly, they were screaming for someone to save them.

Charlie Isaacs and Hal Goodman informed Greshler that they were aware of some of those bad reviews Dean and Jerry had been getting and that they were sympathetic with their problem. Nevertheless, that was not why NBC had sent them to Chicago, so would Greshler please get them together with his clients and stop wasting valuable time.

"First write some nightclub material; then I'll put you together with the boys," countered Greshler.

Having little choice in the matter, Isaacs and Goodman agreed to knock out a few pages of nightclub material for Dean and Jerry. They wanted to know who was going to pay them, however, and how much?

"Don't worry, we'll work something out," promised Greshler, exiting quickly to impart the good news to his clients.

Well-established experienced comedy writers don't usually work on "spec," but "We trusted them," recalls Isaacs today. "After all, Dean and Jerry were big stars, making at least $10,000 a week at the Chez Paree, not to mention their other income. We figured they had to be good for it."

So on Greshler's word that they would be paid, Isaacs and Goodman locked themselves up in their hotel room, opened their portable typewriters, and began pounding out jokes.

A couple of days later, they presented about ten pages of new material to Greshler, who perused it quickly, nodded his approval, and turned it over to Dean and Jerry.

"How'd they like it?" asked Isaacs when Greshler returned to the Ambassador-East after privately meeting with Dean and Jerry in their dressing room at the Chicago Theater.

"Fine," replied Greshler.

"Now can we see them about the TV show?" asked Goodman.

"First they want more club material," countered Greshler.

Figuring they'd never get to see Martin and Lewis about the TV show any other way, Isaacs and Goodman invested a few more days of their time on the nightclub act.

"That's fine, but we still want more," said Greshler after they'd turned in a second batch of material.

So again they sat down at their typewriters, and again Greshler informed them after they'd completed their work that it wasn't enough.

This pattern continued for a couple of weeks, with Greshler always dangling the same carrot in front of the two rabbits but never quite letting them catch up with it because there was always more nightclub material to write *first*.

Finally, Isaacs and Goodman reached the end of their patience. They phoned Norman Blackburn on the West Coast, explained their problem to him, and asked him to send them a wire calling them back home.

Blackburn complied, and Isaacs and Goodman retreated to the Coast, but only after exacting a promise from Greshler that they would be well compensated for the good job they had done as soon as Martin and Lewis returned to Hollywood, where they were going to open at Ciro's.

A couple of days before Martin and Lewis's opening at Ciro's, Charlie Isaacs phoned Greshler and brought up that always unpleasant subject, money.

"We're not going to pay you," answered Greshler. "Dean and Jerry aren't going to use any of your stuff."

"You mean, they don't like it?"

"No. They like it. They just don't want to be bothered memorizing anything new."

Isaacs and Goodman then informed Greshler that whether Martin and Lewis used their material or not had nothing to do with it. He'd asked them to write an act, they'd cooperated, and now they expected to be paid. But Greshler brushed off their request by again repeating that Martin and Lewis didn't have to pay because they weren't using the material and hung up.

Having a natural suspicion of comedians and agents after many years of association with them, Isaacs and Goodman and their wives attended the Martin and Lewis opening at Ciro's. They had to see for themselves if Greshler had been telling the truth.

What they saw on the stage confirmed their suspicions. Greshler had only told them *half* the truth. The true half was that Dino and Jerry couldn't be bothered memorizing anything new; the lie involved Greshler's claim that they weren't using Isaacs's and Goodman's material.

Instead of memorizing the new stuff, Dino and Jerry simply put Isaacs's and Goodman's typewritten manuscripts on the piano and referred to them during the act. For example, when Dean was doing his soft-shoe dance routine, Jerry leaned casually on his elbow on the piano, glanced down the written manuscript, and picked out an appropriate one-liner. "Hey, Dean, you shouldn't be doing that without your truss," exclaimed Jerry, reading off the paper.

Similarly, while Jerry was bouncing around the stage, Dino would rush over to the piano and pull out a joke for himself. "You'll notice, folks, that at no time does Jerry's head leave his body," was one of Dino's new lines that he pretended to be ad-libbing.

When a particular piece of business didn't receive the proper response, Jerry brought down the house with a line of his own—a put-down of the writers. "How do you like that? I paid $5,000 for that joke."

Of course, the truth of it was that he'd paid nothing, and, the following morning, Isaacs and Goodman were on the phone with Greshler, demanding payment for the act they'd written that, when augmented with their regular material, had been such a smash the previous night.

"We'll pay you in a few weeks—as soon as they get back from playing the Copa," Greshler stalled them. "The boys are a little short of dough right now."

"We hope so," said Isaacs, "otherwise we're going to see a lawyer."

Martin and Lewis's third Copacabana stand gave Isaacs and Goodman more ammunition for taking legal action. Fortunately for them, Earl Wilson had dropped into the Copa one night and, the next day, printed a column filled with the best jokes from Martin and Lewis's new act. The jokes he had quoted had all been written by Isaacs and Goodman, which they could easily prove.

They confronted Dino and Jerry with the facts when they returned to the West Coast. Jerry still insisted they weren't using their material. Dino, in keeping with his noninvolvement policy, didn't want to discuss it at all and suggested they take it up with Greshler. Greshler, backed to the wall, promised the two writers that there'd be a check in the mail very soon.

When no money was received after a month of additional stalling, Isaacs and Goodman took their troubles to Max Sturges, a lawyer. Sturges first sent Martin and Lewis a letter demanding immediate payment of $7,500 to Isaacs and Goodman or else he was going to take them to court. This was not an exorbitant sum for a nightclub act for two stars making the money Martin and Lewis were pulling in.

Nevertheless, the check wasn't forthcoming, and Sturges decided that his only recourse now was to "freeze" Dino's and Jerry's assets. Luckily for Dino and Jerry, they had no assets, which Sturges quickly discovered. They were still renting their homes; their cars were owned by the General Acceptance Company, a finance company; and they owed money to just about everybody in town.

After doing a little more sleuthing, Sturges discovered that Jerry Lewis had a private bank account containing approximately $800. Sturges promptly tied up the account so that Jerry couldn't get his hands on any of his money.

A few days later, Charlie Isaacs received a frantic telephone call from Jerry Lewis, asking him to come over to his home to "talk things over."

Jerry was still living in Maria Montez's Spanish castle. Isaacs remembers that Jerry greeted him at the door very warmly. He was very apologetic for what had happened as he invited Isaacs into the huge den and closed the door. Then, in a troubled voice, he started pleading with Isaacs to release his bank account. "Patti and I haven't had a vacation in three years," he cried out, seemingly on the verge of tears. "We'd been saving that money to go on a trip to Hawaii."

Jerry promised Isaacs that he and Goodman would get their money if only he'd have mercy on him and release his back account. It was his old sob-story act, but this was Isaacs's first experience with it, and he fell for Jerry's histrionics. "Okay, I'll tell Sturges," Isaacs relented, and Jerry and Patti were soon drinking mai tais on the beach at Waikiki on Isaacs's and Goodman's money.

The postscript to the story is that Isaacs and Goodman never got the $7,500 to which they felt they were entitled. When Jerry returned from his Hawaiian vacation, Isaacs and Goodman made a deal with Jerry's new attorney, Joe Ross, to settle for $2,500. Of the $2,500, Sturges received $1,000 for his services. The remaining $1,500 was paid to the two writers in $200 monthly installments, "which stopped, I believe," recalls Isaacs, "with their still owing us $500."

12

Who's Afraid of the Big Bad Wolf?

Nobody has ever been any bigger on TV than Milton Berle was in the spring of 1950. Although Berle had been a failure on radio, his "Texaco Star Theater" on Tuesday nights was Number One in the television ratings. To millions of Americans, Berle was suddenly and affectionately known as Uncle Miltie. The night of the week following Monday was no longer Tuesday but, rather, "Milton Berle Night"—that is, until Martin and Lewis appeared as Uncle Miltie's guest stars one week in the spring. That Tuesday night turned out to be Martin and Lewis night.

Berle had the same reputation as Martin and Lewis had for wild ad-libbing and speaking through closing commercials. To get his star off, the producer of the Texaco show employed a tactic he'd seen Norman Blackburn pull on Martin and Lewis—only, instead of using a gob ringing a bell announcing "all ashore who's going ashore," he "buttoned" Berle's last spot by sounding off a loud fire chief's siren, which people, even today, still remember as Uncle Miltie's special badge of identification.

Like most comedians, Berle didn't appreciate other people's ad libs. So, before he would consent to having Dean and Jerry as guests, he made a pact with them: Under absolutely no circumstances would there be any ad-libbing from anybody, including himself.

Dean and Jerry agreed to behave themselves, and did—until Uncle Miltie broke the pact the first minute they were on the air. From that moment on, there was absolute bedlam, and Uncle Miltie still hasn't quite recovered.

Dean and Jerry ordered him out of the studio to buy cigars, cigarettes, and candy bars for themselves. They imitated his own routines. Jerry screamed at him in his idiot voice. Jerry cut off his clothes with a huge scissors while Dino stripped him down to his undershorts. When Berle tried to deal with Lewis, Dino stepped in and took over. When Berle stepped between them and the camera, Dean and Jerry jumped there ahead of him—practically climbing into the camera itself.

When Berle mugged, Jerry would mug better. When Berle tried to introduce another act, Dino or Jerry would interrupt with things like, "Just a minute, I'm talking with the band" or "Shut up, Uncle Miltie, whose show do you think this is?"

In a fast soft-shoe routine, they outdanced the older comedian, who ran completely out of breath trying to keep up with their zany steps.

Finally, Berle threw in the towel. For the first time in his TV career, he stood by helpless on stage, with a sheepish grin on his face, and watched two other comedians take complete charge of his own show. The last thing the King of Television's fans saw on their sets that night was Jerry Lewis's face popping right into the middle of the commercial and saying, "Milton Berle Night: *Big* deal!"

Norman Blackburn, who was working out of NBC's New York offices at the time, was impressed with Dean's and Jerry's performance with Berle and decided he would like to have them on a new show he was putting together for the fall, to be called "The Colgate Comedy Hour," sponsored by the Colgate Drug Company.

Blackburn had been wanting to use Dean and Jerry since the time they had worked for him on "Welcome Aboard," which was sponsored by Admiral Television. But, after moving to Hollywood, Dino and Jerry had shied away from becoming involved in a regular weekly TV show, claiming too many other commitments.

For the last couple of months, however, Blackburn had been fooling around with a new concept for a television show that would permit Martin and Lewis the freedom they needed. Instead of using the same comedian week after week, "The Colgate Comedy Hour" would feature four different comedians, who would alternate with each other on four different Sunday nights of the month.

Blackburn had already signed Eddie Cantor, Donald O'Connor, and Abbott and Costello for three of the weeks, but one week was still open. What would be nicer than to be able to fill it with the hottest new act in show business—Martin and Lewis? They would ensure big ratings for the new show, which would please his bosses and therefore make his own position with the network more secure.

Consequently, he got in touch with Abbey Greshler, who said that, yes, his boys would be interested in doing a TV show once a month if the price was right. Their price would be $25,000 a show—quite a jump from the $2,500 a month Blackburn had paid them on the show sponsored by Admiral. But the Colgate Drug Company said yes to the $25,000 price tag, so Blackburn flew to Hollywood and signed Martin and Lewis for four shows spread over the fall and winter months.

Following that, Blackburn returned to New York and proudly announced to the other network heads and also to Colgate that Martin and Lewis were in the NBC fold. Shortly after the news hit the trade papers that Martin and Lewis had signed to do four Colgate shows for $25,000 a show, Blackburn received a phone call from Lew Wasserman, vice-president of MCA. Wasserman was phoning from Los Angeles.

"We understand you've signed Martin and Lewis for 'The Colgate Comedy Hour' for $25,000 a show," began Wasserman in a tone that Blackburn knew boded nothing but trouble.

"That's correct," admitted Blackburn uneasily.

"Well, we'd like to renegotiate the deal," said Wasserman. "We want $75,000 a show or there's no deal."

"That's impossible," stated Blackburn. "They're already signed for $25,000. Besides, what has MCA got to do with it? Greshler made the deal. He's their agent."

"He *was* their agent," Wasserman informed him. "The boys are no longer with Greshler. MCA's handling them now."

It was, of course, the same MCA that had once owned a "nebbish" singer named Dean Martin and sold him to another nebbish, Lou Perry, for a few hundred dollars in back commissions because it couldn't be bothered with him.

It wasn't, however, quite the same Dean Martin. With his partner, Jerry Lewis, Dino had developed into half of one of the hottest comedy acts in show business—an act that could do "Standing Room Only" business at a sophisticated place like Ciro's and whose first film, *My Friend Irma*, was turning out to be an enormous box office bonanza all over the country.

MCA had also grown. It was now (with the possible exception of the William Morris Theatrical Agency) the largest and the most powerful talent agency in the business, with tentacles reaching out like an octopus into every corner of the theatrical world.

MCA had had its collective eyes on Martin and Lewis ever since the time they had scored their first big success at the Copa in 1948. But, before making any overt moves to sign them, MCA had been biding its time to learn whether or not they were merely flashes in the pan.

Time had proven that Jerry and Dean had the real staying power of champions. By early 1950, they had ripened into just the kind of clients the bigwigs of MCA were ready to swoop down on and pluck—the kind you didn't have to go out into the "field" and "sell." Martin and Lewis sold themselves. You just had to wait in your office for buyers to start bidding for their services.

There was one slight hitch. Dean and Jerry were still legally tied to Abbey Greshler, and, for all MCA knew, they were satisfied to remain with him.

Early in 1950, however, Lew Wasserman and Taft Schreiber, the reigning heads of MCA, were tipped off by Freddy Fields, Greshler's assistant, that Martin and Lewis were no longer completely happy under Greshler's management. Today, Fields heads Creative Management Association (CMA), one of the largest agencies in the business, but at the time he was little more than Greshler's office boy. He was, however, privy to most of Greshler's business secrets, not the least of which was that Martin and Lewis were terribly disillusioned with Greshler's management after their little contretemps with the Internal Revenue Service.

Fields said he would try to steer Jerry and Dean in Wasserman's direction. All he asked in return was a job at MCA—preferably handling Martin and Lewis personally.

With that to go on, Wasserman and Schreiber began romancing Dean and Jerry in their usual subtle manner. They sent them expensive gifts, invited them to all the "in" Hollywood parties, and filled them with glowing promises of how much more they could do for Martin and Lewis than could Abbey Greshler.

Greshler was small potatoes, a one-man operation, they said. Moreover, that one man wasn't too well. He couldn't possibly wheel and deal with the same efficiency as fifty of MCA's black-suited, button-down-collar boys, who had all of MCA's dignity, resources, and that long list of super-star clients behind them to give them the muscle needed for making million-dollar deals.

For a time, Dean resisted MCA's overtures, feeling a certain amount of loyalty toward the man who had helped to get him and Jerry where they were. "But just where were they?" Jeanne Martin finally made Dean ask himself after the sheriff drove off in their new Cadillac.

Dean and Jerry were big names in show business, their incomes were high, and they were in demand everywhere. But what did they have to show for it? No money in the bank, unpaid debts, a bankruptcy, a lot of responsibilities—she would soon have her first child with Dino—and an agent who, many people felt, wasn't doing right by his only important clients. Better management seemed to be the answer, indeed.

Because of his laissez-faire attitude of never taking direct action and just letting things slide, Dino didn't exactly leap when Jeanne suggested that he and Jerry dump Greshler and give MCA a chance because their affairs couldn't be in a "worse mess."

But Jerry, whose hatred for Greshler has not cooled to this day, was eager to dump him. Jerry was more ambitious, more subject to MCA's flattery, and, consequently, more vulnerable to Lew Wasserman's opinion that the $25,000 Colgate contract Greshler had negotiated was "chicken feed" for stars of his and Dino's magnitude.

Wasserman was confident that he could increase that figure by a considerable margin if Dean and Jerry would just give him the chance to prove it. He also promised that MCA would lend them money to help get them out of their income tax difficulties. So with Jeanne nudging them, Dean and Jerry gave Lew Wasserman the green light to see what he could do. If the results were half as impressive as his sales talk, they told him, he could have them for clients.

As a result of all these machinations, Norman Blackburn, in the company of George Halbert, a young lawyer who had recently joined the NBC legal staff, found himself on a plane heading for California to renegotiate a deal that Colgate already assumed was locked up for $25,000 a show.

In California, Blackburn and Halbert taxied directly from Los Angeles International Airport to a meeting with Taft Schreiber and Lew Wasserman in the latter's office in MCA's Beverly Hills headquarters. In keeping with the dignity of MCA, this was not an ordinary office building but, rather, a stately, imposing-looking white-brick colonial edifice, which any important southern governor would be lucky to have for his executive mansion.

Like its New York City counterpart, every office was furnished with authentic Chippendale and Queen Anne antique pieces personally selected by Mrs. Jules Stein as a hedge against inflation and the day the agency business might go sour.

A secretary ushered Blackburn and Halbert into Lew Wasserman's office, which was fit for a governor himself. It was thickly carpeted, expensively draped, and furnished with leather chairs, an English breakfront filled with antique bric-a-brac and leather-bound classics, and a large burnished walnut antique desk with a tooled leather working surface that had not a single scrap of paper on it. This was in accordance with the rules laid down by the grand master of agentry himself, Jules Stein, who operated on the theory that it was bad business and extremely unwise to leave papers on desk tops for prying eyes (some experienced at reading memos and contracts upside down) to see.

Stein, however, was a mysterious figure, who devoted most of his time to raising money for the Jules Stein Eye Hospital. He never showed up for conferences on this level. Straight bargaining he delegated to his two most able vice-presidents: Lew Wasserman, a tall angular man with a boyish face and the heart of a Watergate conspirator; and Taft Schreiber, who was somewhat older than Wasserman, with graying straight hair, spectacles that gave him an owlish countenance, and a paunchy middle-aged figure that was expertly camouflaged in an expensively tailored black suit.

After the opening introductions, Wasserman wasted little time on amenities.

"We want to renegotiate the Martin and Lewis deal," he began brusquely.

"You can't renegotiate it," said Blackburn. "I've got a deal for three shows at $25,000 a show."

"We're sorry," said Wasserman. "We want $75,000 instead of $25,000. It's as simple as that."

"They signed a contract with us," insisted Halbert, "and we intend to hold them to it."

"Yeah, but they're bigger names now," pointed out Wasserman.

"They don't think their old agent asked enough," added Schreiber.

"If they can't get seventy-five grand, they'd just as soon not work at all," concluded Wasserman.

"We stand absolutely firm," said Halbert, ready to blow the deal.

At this point Blackburn said, "Excuse us a minute" to Wasserman and Schreiber. Then he took Halbert into a neighboring anteroom for a private council of war.

"They're just bluffing—they'll never be able to break our contract," insisted Halbert with the intransigent pragmatism of a man not many years out of law school. "They'll work for $25,000 a show and like it."

"Sure, we can make them stick to the contract," said Blackburn. "But you know what'll happen? Right before we go on the air, Jerry'll come down with a stomachache, and Dean'll have laryngitis, and we'll be stuck with sixty minutes of air time with nothing to put on the tube but the NBC test pattern."

"But they'd be lying," said Halbert.

"It doesn't matter. You can't prove they're not sick unless you send them to Mayo Brothers. Believe me, I know what I'm talking about. I've been in show business a lot longer than you. So you'd better let me renegotiate or we'll lose the two hottest commodities in the business."

"But we're liable to lose Colgate."

"Well, we'll have to take that chance," said Blackburn, striding back into the next room to beard Wasserman and Schreiber once again.

When he came out again, the smooth-talking Blackburn wasn't exactly bloodied, but he was a little battered. The results were that NBC got to keep Martin and Lewis for $25,000 for one show but had to pay them $75,000 for every appearance on Colgate thereafter. "Which Colgate wasn't too happy to pay, but Martin and Lewis turned out to be well worth it," Blackburn now admits.

The second result of all that negotiating was that Abbey Greshler was no longer Martin and Lewis's agent. Like Lou Perry before him, Greshler lost out to someone a little bigger, a whole lot more aggressive, and with more standing in the show business world.

It would, however, take several more years of law suits, bitter accusations and counteraccusations between Greshler and Martin and Lewis, and many thousands of dollars in legal fees before the agent would accept that verdict officially.

In August 1950, Greshler petitioned the Superior Court of Los Angeles for "permission to take deposition testimony" from Dean Martin and Jerry Lewis and various MCA officials, including Jules Stein.

According to the *Los Angeles Times*, Greshler needed the testimony for the prosecution of a damage suit he was about to file against MCA over loss of their account. His petition asserted that he had represented Martin and Lewis in all theatrical matters for many years. It charged that MCA got the two to sign with the corporation through "gifts, loans, and other inducements."

While the various lawyers, agents, and participants were dealing with this matter, another action was started against Martin and Lewis, York Productions (their producing firm), Hal Wallis, and Paramount Pictures by Screen Associates, the independent company Greshler had put together with Sherill Corwin, Ralph Stolkin, and Ray Ryan for the purpose of producing *At War with the Army*. This suit asked for $10 million in damages—$2 million from Dino and Jerry personally.

The story and headline about the case appeared in *The Los Angeles Times* on August 4, 1951:

FILM COMEDY PAIR
SUED FOR $10,000,000

Dean Martin, Jerry Lewis Defendants in Action
by Screen Group Charging Breach of Contract

Dean Martin and Jerry Lewis, the zany and newly popular film comedians, were sued for $10,000,000 breach of contract damages in Superior Court yesterday by Screen Associates, Inc.

The complaint asserted that on April 5, 1950, the two comics, acting through York Pictures Co., which they are described as controlling, agreed to make seven films for Screen Associates.

One of these pictures, the document adds, was made and released under the title *At War with the Army*. But since then, Screen Associates contends, Martin and Lewis have refused to make any other films and have entered into a conspiracy with others to breach the agreement.

When called on to perform the services for the remaining six pictures, Martin and Lewis have reported themselves "unavailable," the complaint adds.

Included as defendants in the suit were York Pictures Co. and Hal Wallis, film producer who held a contract with the comedians, signed September 1, 1948.

The suit demands $8,000,000 damages from York Pictures and Hal Wallis, but asks $2,000,000 from Martin and Lewis.

The legal battling and maneuvering between Abbey Greshler and Screen Associates, on the one hand, and Martin and Lewis, Hal Wallis, Paramount Studios, and MCA, on the other hand, was to go on for the next several years in courtrooms, courthouse corridors, and various law offices all over the city of Los Angeles and Beverly Hills before it was finally settled.

One of the suits culminated with Freddy Fields's taking the stand in open court and testifying, in Martin and Lewis's behalf, against Abbey Greshler's questionable agenting practices. In exchange for his testimony, Fields received the plum he was after: a job at MCA and an antique desk of his own.

Screen Associates and Greshler eventually negotiated out-of-court settlements from both MCA, Paramount, and Martin and Lewis, but what Greshler wound up with didn't nearly approach the $10 million figure he felt he deserved.

The exact amounts of the settlements will probably never be known, for the documents themselves are buried somewhere deep in the MCA and Paramount Studios legal archives; the details were never reported in the newspapers; and those people directly involved seem to have extremely faulty memories when it comes to recalling who got what from whom. Therefore, at the very least, it would take a Sam Ervin to ferret out the figures from the many participants who do know but whose memories have conveniently "failed" them in respect to these convoluted maneuvers.

It is the consensus of most people connected with Martin and Lewis at the time, however, that Screen Associates and Abbey Greshler wound up doing all right for themselves.

According to Herman Citron, who took over Martin and Lewis's personal management after they moved to MCA, the Screen Associates suit was settled by him in the following way: Dean and Jerry gave up *all* of their 90 percent interest in *At War with the Army* (which turned out to be an enormously profitable movie) in exchange for not having to make the other six pictures for Screen Associates that they had contracted for under Greshler's management.

"Legally, the Screen Associates contract was no good and probably wouldn't hold up in court," states Herman Citron today, "but I figured the only clean way I could get them out of it was for them to give up all their interests in *At War with the Army* and walk away."

And so they did, and everyone connected with *At War with the Army* wound up making a handsome profit on it, except Dean and Jerry, who were the ones responsible for its tremendous success at the box office. Abbey Greshler, of course, had a percentage-of-the-profits deal for producing it and today rides around in a chauffeur-driven Rolls Royce.

In addition to Greshler's profits on *At War with the Army*, writer Maurice Zolotow reported at the time that the agent also received something in the neighborhood of $2 million from MCA for relinquishing Martin and Lewis's contract. It is unlikely that he received this in a lump payment. Al Melnick, a veteran agent around Hollywood, believes Greshler received from Paramount, as part of the Screen Associates suit, considerable cash and a house in West Los Angeles worth about $250,000 (complete with 35mm projection room) that had once belonged to the studio.

What is positively known about the results of all this is that Abbey Greshler did not receive an engraved gold wristwatch (or even a Mickey Mouse watch) from Jerry Lewis after all those years of service.

Instead of the customary gold watch treatment, Jerry, lest anyone be unaware of his hatred for the man, had toilet paper printed with Abbey Greshler's picture on every tissue, handed the rolls out to his friends as gifts, and decreed to his wife and children that thereafter no other kind of toilet paper could be used in the Lewis household.

13

I've Got the World on a String

With Abbey Greshler "deep-sixed" and MCA taking over the helm, the good ship Martin and Lewis was now ready to sail through the dangerous shoals of television in quest of Mr. Neilsen's Golden Fleece. To accomplish this feat they needed a stout crew, good writing, and a stomach for traveling.

In its first season, "The Colgate Comedy Hour" originated in New York City because the largest population centers were east of the Mississippi and there were no coaxial cables or orbiting satellites to transmit entertainment from the Atlantic to the Pacific in 1950, which was still the horse-and-buggy era of television. (The Pacific states usually got the same broadcasts a week later—by kinescope.)

The actual broadcast site was the Park Theater, a former legit house just off Columbus Circle that had been converted to a TV studio, and rehearsing was done in a large wide-open hall called the Paramount Caterers located on the second floor of a building in the West Forties.

This arrangement meant that Dean and Jerry had to spend the 1950–1951 television season practically commuting between New York and Hollywood, where they had not only families but movie-making commitments to keep with Hal Wallis. In addition, they were still accepting nightclub engagements in Chicago, St. Louis, Miami, and any other place that would pay them $10,000 or more a week.

As for the crew, NBC hired Ernie Glucksman to produce the Martin and Lewis segments of "The Colgate Comedy Hour," Kingman Moore to direct, and a young man just out of college, Bud Yorkin, to be the stage manager.

Considering that it was a new medium, Glucksman was a TV veteran. He'd worked on the Sid Caesar–Imogene Coca "Show of Shows," had produced the Phil Silvers "Arrow Show," and had worked in "experimental" television for Dumont as early as 1943. He'd also had considerable legitimate-theater experience, staging shows at the Green Mansions Playhouse, a summer theater in Warrensburg, New York, where such names as Cheryl Crawford, Marty Ritt, and Elia Kazan had served out their apprenticeships painting drops and playing bit parts.

But Glucksman had had absolutely no experience in dealing with such offbeat characters as Dean Martin and Jerry Lewis. Furthermore, he didn't seem to be the type to cope with their antics and practical jokes.

Soft-spoken, bespectacled, and middle-aged, Ernie Glucksman in 1950 appeared to be the epitome of the dignified Madison Avenue advertising executive: he dressed in Brooks Brothers suits, complete with tie, button-down shirts and suspenders, and he was never without an expensive homburg hat on his head and an attaché case full of papers in his hand.

In other words, he was the perfect foil for a Martin and Lewis gag.

Once Dean and Jerry got to know Glucksman well, they singled him out as the main target for their practical jokes.

Whenever they'd meet him in his office or on the street, they'd pull his homburg down over his ears and eyes, and cut off his tie with a large pair of scissors, which Jerry carried in his pocket at all times. In keeping with their "destroy and replace" policy, they would send him a new homburg the following day and a dozen of the most expensive ties they could pick out. Nevertheless, the wear and tear on Glucksman's wardrobe and patient disposition was enormous.

After several of these tie-snipping confrontations, Glucksman reached a point where, when he saw either of them approaching, he would sigh, automatically pull his hat down over his ears, take a scissors from his pocket and cut off his own tie.

But Glucksman couldn't anticipate all their gags.

On one occasion—this time they were rehearsing their TV show in front of the full cast—Jerry produced a pair of scissors and snipped the left side of Glucksman's suspenders. As the surprised Glucksman turned toward Lewis, Dino whipped out his own pair of scissors and snipped the right side of the producer's suspenders. As Glucksman leaned down to pick up his fallen trousers, Jerry snipped off his tie just below the knot.

Funny stuff, to be sure. But it is the theory of several people who worked on "The Colgate Comedy Hour" that Jerry's outrageous treatment of Ernie Glucksman was motivated by something deeper than just a desire to get laughs from his co-workers. They felt that Jerry looked upon the older Ernie as a "father substitute." Resenting his own father because of his miserable childhood, Jerry did all the things to Glucksman, including cutting off his necktie and humiliating him in public, that he had always wanted to do to Danny but never quite had the nerve.

In the beginning of their long relationship, however, Jerry treated Ernie Glucksman with more respect—but not much.

Glucksman's first meeting with Jerry and Dean took place in August 1950, in a conference room at MCA's Beverly Hills headquarters. Because Dean and Jerry were too tired to come East, NBC sent Glucksman to the West Coast to "talk about a television format for the boys' first show."

Lew Wasserman and Herman Citron had requested that they be allowed to sit in at the meeting, to look after their clients' interests, which was why everyone met at MCA. Wasserman, Citron, and Glucksman were punctual, but Dean and Jerry blew in about an hour late. Dino was carrying a golf club, and Jerry a candid camera. Photography was his new hobby, and he took candid shots of everyone during the meeting. There wasn't much of a meeting, however. Neither Dean nor Jerry seemed capable of settling down to serious discussion. Both were more interested in cracking jokes about how uncomfortable Mrs. Stein's antique chairs were and getting off silly non sequiturs to Wasserman and Citron, such as "Where is Jules, anyway? We'd like him to wash our cars" and "You guys promised us service when we left Greshler—not conferences." When he wasn't talking, Jerry was stuffing pencils up his nostrils to amuse the secretaries.

By the time the meeting started to break up, nothing tangible had been accomplished except that Citron had recommended that they hire Harry Crane to write the show. Crane was a local gagman with a good reputation, so Dean and Jerry said okay to that, glanced at their watches, and rose to leave.

"Wait a minute," said Glucksman, catching them in the hall. "Where are you going?"

"I'm taking Patti to Hawaii," explained Jerry. "I have to buy some swimming trunks before the stores close."

"And I'm going on a hunting trip," added Dino, taking a swing at an imaginary golf ball with the driver he was carrying.

"But we haven't decided on a format."

"And Dean and I haven't had a vacation in three years," said Jerry. "I promised Patti I'd take her to Hawaii."

"Yeah, baby," said Dino, "we need some rest before we get into this TV thing."

Following the pair to the parking lot, Glucksman grabbed Dino by the coat sleeve and said, "When you get back, Dean, let's have lunch sometime. I'd like to get to know you a little more closely, so I can tell the writers how to write for you."

"Nobody gets to know me closely," replied Dino, without cracking a smile. "Not even my wife."

Panicking because the September 17 air date was only a little over a month away, Glucksman asked Jerry if he could just talk to him for a few minutes that evening. Jerry said, "Sure, Ernie," and invited him up to the Maria Montez house to have dinner with him and Patti.

Promptly at the appointed hour, Ernie Glucksman showed up at Jerry's front door in his homburg hat and carrying an attaché case. To his surprise, the door was opened by Danny Lewis, who Glucksman knew from around Broadway but wasn't aware he was Jerry's father.

"What the hell are you doing here?" asked Glucksman.

"What do you mean—what am I doing here?" exclaimed Danny indignantly. "Jerry's my kid!"

If Glucksman was surprised at that, he was shocked to learn what a pushy stage father Danny turned out to be. All during the early part of the evening, Danny kept taking Glucksman aside and saying things like, "I'm a great comedian, too. Why don't you have the writers write a spot for me on the show?" and "You know, Ernie, if it wasn't for me, Jerry wouldn't have the talent he has today."

After dinner, Jerry told his old man to "get lost" and then invited Glucksman into the den for their conference. Again there wasn't much of a conference. Jerry spent most of the few minutes they had left showing Glucksman his mountainous collection of scrapbooks, press clippings, photographs, leather-bound scripts, and records and tapes of the various shows he and Dino had done in the past. All this was neatly stacked on book shelves or filed in cabinets, and, according to Glucksman, the meticulous Jerry knew in an instant where to find any piece of memorabilia he was seeking.

"He amazed me with the organized fashion he had everything categorized and catalogued," recounts Glucksman today. "Every appearance he and Dean had ever made . . . comments on how they had performed . . . how much money they got . . . who was on the bill with them. Any radio or TV things they had done he either had a kinescope of or an audio tape recording. . . . He was better organized than IBM."

But although Glucksman was impressed with Jerry's filing genius, he was no closer to locking in a show format by the time he left the house than he was when NBC first assigned him to "The Colgate Comedy Hour."

Having accomplished little on the West Coast except the hiring of one writer whose credits did not impress him to any great degree, Ernie

Glucksman returned to New York to start preparing the show with Harry Crane.

If he was depressed about his stars' lack of interest in their own TV careers, Glucksman didn't have to worry on that score long—at least, not about Jerry. He soon discovered that Jerry Lewis wasn't the type to leave important decisions about his career in the hands of anyone else.

Rejuvenated from two weeks of loafing on the beach at Waikiki, Jerry tuned in his television set his first night home to the "Ford Star Review," a summer replacement show starring Jack Haley. On it he saw a comedy sketch that literally had him doubled over with laughter.

He immediately grabbed the phone and called David Susskind in New York. At the time, Susskind was an agent for MCA, working out of their New York office, and it was his job to "service" "The Colgate Comedy Hour."

"I just saw a sketch on the Haley show that would have been perfect for Dean and me," said Jerry. "Find out who wrote it. I want him to work for me."

The next morning, Susskind got back to Jerry with the information that the sketch he liked had been written by two unknown young comedy writers named Ed Simmons and Norman Lear.

Today Ed Simmons is one of the top comedy writers in the business, and Norman Lear is half of the Bud Yorkin–Norman Lear writing-producing-directing combination that is responsible for turning out such hits as "All in the Family," "Sanford and Son," and "Maude." But, in 1950, Simmons and Lear were working in television for the first time. Prior to their coming onto the Haley show, Simmons and Lear had earned their living in the daytime as door-to-door baby photographers for the same company. In the evenings, they speculated in comedy writing, submitting their material to the various comedy shows, until they finally got lucky and were hired by Jack Haley to write the "Ford Star Review."

"But they signed with Haley for eight shows," Susskind informed Jerry.

"I don't care—I have to have them," insisted Jerry, who'd evidently had second thoughts about his and Dino's not needing material.

Luckily for Jerry, it turned out that Simmons and Lear hadn't signed an exclusive contract with Haley, and they were able to double on "The Colgate Comedy Hour" for Martin and Lewis until the "Ford Star Review" was buried in the graveyard of canceled shows at the end of the summer.

Simmons and Lear remained with Dean and Jerry for three seasons, along with Bud Yorkin, who, at Ernie Glucksman's request, stepped in and took over the show's direction after Kingman Moore quit.

A lot of good things came out of Yorkin's coming on the show as its director. It led to his and Norman Lear's becoming friendly and finally teaming up to become the Number One writing-producing-directing team in the business.

It also led to Jerry Lewis's becoming the ardent spokesman and tireless fund raiser for the Muscular Dystrophy Association that he is today. It was Yorkin who first told Jerry about the disease, for Yorkin had a sister whose son had succumbed to it. This motivated her to begin raising money for research and treatment of the disease, about which very little was known in those days. She enlisted her brother's aid in getting the local Muscular Dystrophy association's publicity help, and he, in turn, asked Jerry one day while they were rehearsing if he would do a plug for muscular dystrophy on the air that Sunday.

"Jerry had never heard of muscular dystrophy, wanted to know how you pronounced it, and how it was spelled," recalls Yorkin.

Yorkin told him a little bit about the disease and filled him in on how desperate the foundation was for research money. Jerry said he'd plug it if there was time at the end of Sunday's show. As the director, Bud Yorkin saw to it that there was time, and Jerry did a minute-and-a-half commercial asking for donations to help fight muscular dystrophy.

The muscular dystrophy people were so grateful that they inundated Jerry with all kinds of literature on the subject. They also sent him a plaque to hang on his wall.

"I knew the plaque would get him," says Yorkin. "Jerry's crazy about plaques and awards saying 'Thanks, Jerry Lewis' on them."

From that day on, Jerry started reading everything he could find that concerned muscular dystrophy and plugged the cause regularly on his show.

Jerry never does anything halfway. Soon he was running around the country putting on telethons and benefits for muscular dystrophy and raising at least $10 million for the various local and regional associations annually.

Jerry's enthusiasm and unflagging spirit in behalf of these associations has inspired other comedians to quip that "Muscular dystrophy is Jerry Lewis's very own personal disease."

But, for some reason known only to Jerry (and possibly Patti), he has always resisted efforts to worm out of him the exact reason he became interested in the muscular dystrophy cause in the first place. If someone asks the question on a talk show, for example, he usually avoids answering by saying, "It's something very personal I'd rather not talk about."

Perhaps he's just trying to avoid giving Bud Yorkin the publicity. For when the director left the show three years later, "It was under very unpleasant circumstances," admits Yorkin.

In the early days of the Colgate show, however, there was good rapport between Jerry Lewis and the whole creative staff.

"We had a real romance going," remembers Norman Lear today. "Eddie Simmons and I and Dean and Jerry were like four fraternity brothers. We were all around the same ages—the late twenties and early thirties—and we had fun together. Eddie and I were friendly with both of them, but socially we saw more of Jerry—at least in the beginning. No one ever saw much of Dino. As a matter of fact, when we had to be in California without our wives, Eddie and I stayed in Jerry's house. I remember that Jerry used to come into our bedroom—the guest bedroom—in the morning in his pajamas.

"We were in twin beds, and Jerry would jump from one bed to the other. We'd have pillow fights and free-for-alls. When we had to go on the road with them and we checked into a hotel, Jerry would take the fire hoses off the walls in the hotel corridors and we'd have water fights. Of course, we'd pay for the damage later. But we were really like a bunch of fraternity boys."

Dino rarely took part in any of their hijinks, preferring his own company or that of his friends. "Dino came from a school where it was considered unmanly to display emotion," states Ed Simmons. "He doesn't even believe in shaking hands."

At rehearsals, Dean was a very sober, hard-working young man in those days. "He was always punctual, he did what he was told, and he didn't fool around," recalls Lear. "It was Jerry who sometimes wouldn't settle down."

"But his practical jokes aside Jerry was a good boy then," recalls Glucksman. "He hadn't tried to take over yet. He'd listen to those who knew better—the writers, the director."

"He was getting involved a little though, even then," admits Yorkin. "He was very inventive—he couldn't help it."

His "take-over" of aspects of the show in which he had no business meddling was an evolutionary process that occurred during several TV seasons. It mainly grew out of the writers' considering Jerry the "funny" member of the team. As a result, they threw most of the comedy routine his way, because it was easier to write for him and comedy had a better chance of paying off if he was doing it.

Since he was carrying the main comedy burden, it was only natural that the staff would check out ideas for sketches or gags with him rather than with Dino. Besides, Dino always discouraged actual involvement. If Glucksman or the writers asked him for an opinion, he'd usually say, "If it's okay with Jerry, it's okay with me."

In effect, he was releasing his costarring rights of approval to Jerry by default. He'd rather play golf or pal around with his Italian cronies than stay in the studio and act like a big shot.

Gradually the writers stopped asking Dino for his opinion altogether.

But Jerry didn't stop volunteering his. "And he eventually worked himself into acting like the producer and director as well as the costar," recalls Lear. "But he was a costar who really worked harder than Dean to make sure that his costarring role was a bigger costarring role than Dean's was. Dean just did his 'thing' and left. Jerry worked and improved what they were doing together—especially his end of it."

But during the preparations for the first program of "The Colgate Comedy Hour," Jerry did his best to treat Dino as his equal. As proof of Jerry's good intentions, Ernie Glucksman cites one of the first things Jerry told him after Simmons and Lear had been hired.

"Now remember, Ernie," said Jerry, completely in earnest, "when you talk to the writers, I want you to be sure to remind them that Dean and I are *two* comics—not a comic and a straight man."

That it was necessary to give Glucksman that advice at all is indicative of how sensitive—and resentful—Dino must already have been about being considered only Jerry Lewis's straight man. Moreover, it shows a surprising amount of awareness of Dino's problem on Jerry's part. Too bad he wasn't able to maintain that awareness over the years and behave himself accordingly. If he had, he might not today be known mostly as Dean Martin's ex-partner.

But Jerry had an indomitable ego that even time spent at fifty dollars an hour on a psychiatrist's couch couldn't deflate. As much as he loved Dino, he loved himself even more.

For example, few people outside the business realized until Dean went out on his own what a fine sense of humor he really has. But Jerry realized it, and it bugged him.

"I remember," says Lear, "realizing as long ago as when we were rehearsing our first show at the Paramount Caterers that Jerry, who was supposed to be the 'funny one' couldn't stand it if Dean got any laughs. Dean could be insanely funny with a line. Any morning that Dean would come in and start being funny with the lines or do funny things, Jerry would wind up in a corner on the floor someplace with a bellyache. And a doctor would have to come. This was always true. Whenever Dean was very funny, strange physical things happened to Jerry. Sometimes he would go to the extreme of calling Marvin Levy, who was his doctor at the time, to fly in from California to treat him."

Jerry's envy of Dino's ability to be funny on his own manifested itself in peculiar ways for a fellow who professed to be so fond of his partner. Bud Yorkin remembers another trick Jerry would pull on his beloved Dino that wasn't especially admirable.

"Very often Dean would ad-lib an exceptionally funny line at Monday's rehearsal, and everybody around would fall on the floor, laughing. We'd never hear it again until we went on the air on Sunday. Then Jerry would do *Dean's* ad lib, before Dean could, and Jerry would be the one to get screams from the audience and even applause.

"Dean would just stand there dumbfounded and look at Jerry as if he couldn't believe his ears. That happened on a number of occasions. It was unbelievable how he could pull that on his own partner."

Because Dino was the easy-going half of the team—"the quiet one," as Ed Simmons labeled him—he had a tendency to allow other people on the staff to walk all over him too.

The finale of the first show, for example, was a large musical production number that was supposed to be a satire on "Frankie and Johnny." But instead of treating Dean as one of the costars in the number, the man who staged it used him as just a "production" singer—like the no-talent tenor who sings "Girls of All Nations" at the beginning of one of those Miss Universe beauty contests. Not realizing how he would come off, Dino went along with the idea, and as a result ended up looking like a $100-a-week stooge of Jerry Lewis's in the number.

Dino had one funny bit at the opening of the show, which took place at a supposedly very ritzy party, with all the men in tuxedos and the women in long dresses. At a point early in the proceedings, a dignified old gent asked Dean for his autograph and handed him a fountain pen that wouldn't write. Dino shook the pen to force some ink down into its point, and the ink splattered all over the man's white tuxedo front. As a result, the party turned into a shambles, with all the dignified guests (who were actually stunt men and women) tossing each other around in a comedy-style Mack Sennett ballet.

But despite a few high spots for Dino, it was Jerry Lewis who got the lion's share of the reviews the day after "The Colgate Comedy Hour" went on the air for the first time.

Writing in *The New York Times*, Jack Gould, the nation's Number One television critic, said,

> Dean Martin and Jerry Lewis took up a regular television assignment at 8 o'clock last night, and it may be a long time before the National Broadcasting Company is quite the same again. A pair of mad zanies of the first rank, they frolicked through sixty minutes of slapstick and horseplay that for the most part were swell nonsense.
>
> It is the Lewis half of the partnership who is the works, and he certainly put on a demonstration last night. On stage for practically the full hour—in fact, the show had little besides Martin and Lewis— he was a one-man Hellzapoppin who clowned his way through everything and everybody.
>
> It was virtually a marathon through bedlam. If he can repeat his performance on ensuing programs—he will be seen once a month

in rotation with Eddie Cantor and Fred Allen—Lewis will be the real whiz kid of TV.

For all its madness, there is method in the Lewis artistry. If he mugs outrageously and takes stage falls with an elementary aplomb, his antics are seasoned by a real sense of the comic and a rare appreciation of the non sequitur. His is basically roughhouse panto-mime in the old tradition of the Mack Sennett movie short. After the long siege of wisecracking masters of ceremonies on television it should be fun to have him around.

With Mr. Martin, who is a competent straight man and has a bari-tone voice that should not offend either the Crosby or Como fans, Mr. Lewis did a wonderful sketch about an empty movie house where mention of video produced an immediate crisis, and a knockabout scene in the dressing room. The closing takeoff on "Frankie and Johnny" was less successful.

In fairness to Mr. Lewis, however, he should have more support on future programs. Apart from a single song by Marilyn Maxwell and one number by Martin, he was in all the scenes. That's too much of a load for any one comic, even with the energy and resourcefulness of Mr. Lewis.

If Dean Martin were feeling slightly paranoid about his contribution to the act *before* Jack Gould's review appeared, what could he have been thinking after reading such unqualified encomiums about his partner as "the Lewis artistry," "It is the Lewis half of the partnership who is the works," and the final put-down of all, "Mr. Lewis should have more sup-port on future programs"?

With a partner who got raves—and who still felt it necessary to steal your best ad libs—who needed an enemy? No wonder Dino was already beginning to wish he'd let Jerry bomb himself into oblivion on his own in Atlantic City in 1946.

14

Pennies from Heaven

As happened to him once before, the success of Martin and Lewis during the two-year period following their first appearance on "The Colgate Comedy Hour" scaled such unprecedented heights that Dino was forced to swallow his great Italian pride and do as the old Chinese saying recommends when one is getting raped, "Lie back and enjoy it."

After just three appearances on television, the Martin and Lewis segments of "The Colgate Comedy Hour" reached a 48.8 rating, which put them far in the lead in the rating race. What amazed people in the business even more was that Martin and Lewis accomplished this feat opposite the very highly rated "The Ed Sullivan Show" on CBS. Until Martin and Lewis appeared opposite him, old Mr. No Neck thought he had Sunday night to himself. Instead, his rating plummeted.

At the same time, Dean and Jerry's first three films—*My Friend Irma*, *My Friend Irma Goes West*, and *At War with the Army*, which was released in 1951—were causing the public to flock to the box office in such droves that the movie exhibitors of the country voted them Number One in *Motion Picture Herald*'s tenth annual Stars of Tomorrow poll. Aside from winning an Oscar, that was about the most important honor they could be accorded in the film world, for it meant that several thousand movie-house proprietors rated them the trade's biggest box-office money-makers.

Movie exhibitors in those days still wielded an enormous amount of power and influence within the industry. To illustrate how much, Dean and Jerry did a sketch on their first Colgate show called "Movies Are Better Than Ever," satirizing the plight of movie exhibitors now that TV was taking away so much of their audience.

In this particular sketch, Dino played the part of a manager of a movie theater that was so empty it had bats flying around in the balcony. Spotting a potential customer walking by on the sidewalk, Dino tapped the shoulder of his sexy-looking girl ticket seller in the booth and said, "Here comes one now." The girl immediately jumped into action to lure the fellow into the theater. She went after him, twirling her purse and swinging her fanny provocatively at him like a two-dollar hooker.

All the TV critics agreed that the sketch was brilliant, not only in concept but in actual execution. But the movie exhibitors of the nation seemed to feel that Martin and Lewis had dealt them a mortal blow by emphasizing the plight of their dwindling box office. Screams of outrage—all wondering how Dean and Jerry could bite the hand that was feeding them so well—were heard from Times Square to Grauman's Chinese Theater.

The exhibitors' complaints were voiced on the front pages of most of the country's leading newspapers, editorials were written in the trade periodicals condemning Martin and Lewis's premeditated and callous disregard of the business that was keeping them in Cadillacs and mansions, and some theaters were even threatening to boycott their films. Apologies were demanded.

Reacting to criticism the same way most people do—not very well— Dean and Jerry at first defended themselves by taking the offensive and calling the exhibitors a bunch of washed-up old has-beens who oughtn't to be in show business at all if they couldn't stand a little kidding. "After all, we're comedians and satirists," stated Jerry pompously.

But when the furor refused to die down, Jerry apologized both publicly and in a contrite letter to the exhibitors. He promised that, in the future, Martin and Lewis would choose as targets for their satire institutions better able to stand the heat—like General Motors or Joe Stalin.

Once Martin and Lewis rode out that storm, they had nothing to look forward to but hard work, lots of fun, and plenty of income taxes. Mostly, however, they were having fun during the heady days of 1950, 1951, and 1952—fun with themselves, their associates, and the public.

Whenever they were in New York and had to take a cab, they would choose one with a sun roof. During the ride, the two of them would slide the top open, stand and poke their heads through the opening, and play gin rummy on the roof—much to the astonishment and amusement of their fans walking up and down Fifth or Madison avenues.

At television run-throughs at the Park Theater, they would chase after the cameras and stick pornographic photos in front of the lenses while the crew was trying to line up the shots.

Between shows at the Copa or the Chez Paree, they would chase each other through the crowded customers on the dance floor, wearing nothing but socks and underwear.

Another favorite gambit of theirs was to play practical jokes on the passengers of trains on which they were riding. Once, on the Twentieth Century Limited bound from New York to Chicago, they went through their Pullman car at 3:00 in the morning, knocking on all the compartment doors, flapping the curtains of the single berths, and announcing, "Arriving at the La Salle Street Station, Chicago, in twenty minutes."

The half-asleep passengers hurriedly dressed and were standing in the aisle ready to debark, while Chicago was still five hours away, before they discovered the hoax. By then, of course, Dean and Jerry were sound asleep in their drawing room, or so they pretended.

Meanwhile, Dean and Jerry were not averse to playing tricks on each other. One time when they were playing two weeks of personal appearances at New York's Paramount Theater to plug a picture, Dino fell into a habit that disturbed the more conscientious Jerry. Dino started arriving at the theater just a split second before they were scheduled to go on the stage, allowing himself no time to change out of his street clothes or to put on makeup. Arriving in his dressing room, he'd simply kick off his street shoes, slip into his tap shoes, and skip out onto the stage after Jerry.

Jerry kept warning him about being late, but Dino shrugged it off, saying, "Aw, well, Jer, you can do a single until I get there."

The next time Dino was late, Jerry decided to teach him a lesson. He broke some raw eggs into Dino's tap shoes, then added crumpled-up soda crackers and a bottle of ketchup, and stirred it around with a cigar butt until it was a gooey mess.

Just before show time, Dino dashed into his dressing room, slipped into his doctored-up booties, and soft-shoed his way onto the stage. In front of the audience for the first time, Dino did a huge take as he realized he was standing in a good deal more than just his shoes and socks. He was helpless, of course, to do anything about it during the show. He just stood there, up to his ankles in eggs and ketchup, and crooned "Oh, Marie," as Jerry looked at him in baby-faced innocence.

None of this horseplay—nor their enormous success—would have been possible, however, if there hadn't been exceptional chemistry between Dean and Jerry—the kind of chemistry that makes for a real love affair.

The feelings the two of them had for each other during the early days of their romance no doubt stemmed from nothing more than the usual "latent homosexuality" that psychiatrists claim exists between all close friends of the same sex.

"But whatever you want to call it, it was a case of real infatuation just the same," believes Ed Simmons in looking back on their relationship. "Especially on Jerry's part. Everything he did was either to amuse or please Dean. At a party, if he was doing some schtick for the company,

Jerry would have one eye on Dean to see how he was reacting to it. He didn't care if anyone else laughed—it was just Dean he wanted to break up."

Simmons goes on to point out that even some of the comedy scenes Jerry devised for their early pictures had a mild homosexual flavor to them—something akin to the humor in Neil Simon's *The Odd Couple*.

An example of what Simmons is talking about is a scene from *The Caddy*, in which Jerry cooked an elaborate meal for Dino, only to have Dino tell him he wouldn't be home for dinner. "I'm going out to play golf," he informed Jerry at the last minute. Jerry started to sniffle. "You mean, you're going out to play golf after I've spent the day over a hot stove?" he replied, wiping away a tear on the hem of his apron.

Jerry was always the "wife" or "girl friend" in those situations, whereas Dino was the he-man, the protector, the husband, the complete male. In real life, too, they played those identical roles.

While filling a vaudeville engagement in Minneapolis in the winter of 1951, Jerry became a little too frisky on the stage during an acrobatic dance number, fell down, cracked his spinal cord, and knocked himself unconscious.

When smelling salts and ice packs failed to revive him, an ambulance had to be called to take him to a hospital. After the ambulance arrived, Dean would let no one else touch Jerry. He carried him out to the vehicle himself, then rode to the hospital with him in the back of the ambulance with the attendants.

At the hospital, a doctor managed to revive Jerry but ordered him to remain in the hospital overnight. As Jerry slept, Dino sat in a chair beside his bed. Around midnight, the door swung open, and the manager of the theater barged in, looked down at the sleeping Jerry in disgust, and exclaimed to Dino, "What am I supposed to do for my next show?"

"How about putting on a boxing exhibition," suggested Dino, and with that he swung a haymaker at the manager and knocked him flat on his back.

It was during their picture-plugging tours that Dean and Jerry created a kind of show business history—not only for breaking box office records but for pure zaniness.

It all began at New York's Paramount Theater in the spring of 1951, where a picture named *Dear Brat* (a sequel to *Dear Ruth*) was playing. It was not a Martin and Lewis picture, but they were booked into the theater for two weeks to play six shows a day on Sunday through Friday and seven on Saturday. For that, MCA had managed to get them $50,000 a week plus 50 percent of the theater's profits over $100,000.

Under an arrangement like that, a rapid audience turnover was the key to big money. But during their first appearance on the stage, Dean and Jerry were such a hit that few patrons budged from their seats when the show was over.

Not only did their comedy "wow" the audience, but, as *Life* put it, "Martin and Lewis affected their following—both adults and bobby-soxers —like sexy pied pipers."

The appeal to the bobby-soxers wasn't only Dean's languorous singing. Jerry's innocent boyishness seemed to arouse feminine emotions as well— so much so that when the show was over, some of the bobby-soxers tried to storm the stage to touch Jerry. Dino tried to ward them off by shouting, "Girls—girls, Jerry is a married man. He has two children," to which the girls merely screamed back in emulation of one of Jerry's routines, "We *like* him, we *like* him!" And nobody made a move to leave the theater.

All this adulation was indeed flattering to the refugee from Irvington High, but it didn't take any mental giant to figure out that he and Dean would be losing thousands of dollars if the customers stayed through the second show—which most of them did, much to the consternation of Bob Weitman, who was managing the Paramount Theater at the time.

When the same thing continued to happen all through the first day, the management (as well as Dean and Jerry) started to grow alarmed.

"It was the old question of the immovable body," recalls Jack McInerney, who was director of publicity for the Paramount Theater then. "Some of the kids were staying for four and five shows. It was suggested that we remove the candy stand and popcorn machines, so the kids would be facing starvation, but the smart ones brought sandwiches. Then we decided to do what we did with Frank Sinatra and Danny Kaye—lure the kids out into the street with a free, unrehearsed, spontaneous show."

Following the first performance of the second day, Jerry stepped to the footlights and announced, "The next show will be done from Dean's and my dressing room window!"

A squeal went up, followed by a general exodus of the audience to Forty-fourth Street, just below Dean's and Jerry's second-floor dressing room window.

Climbing out onto the fire escape, the seemingly tireless twosome put on an impromptu show, featuring Dean singing, Jerry playing "Ciribiribin" on the trumpet, and a good deal more of their general horseplay. They also threw down to the mob thousands of 8″ x 10″ glossy photos of themselves, Dean's thirty-five-dollar shirts, and Jerry's Sy Devore bow ties. Mixed in with the souvenirs, they dropped about $1,000 worth of twenty-dollar bills onto the street below.

"The response was almost orgiastic," recalls director Norman Taurog, who happened to be on the scene that day. "Little girls were practically having orgasms every time Dean or Jerry opened their mouths."

Climaxing the act, Jerry aimed a shotgun out the window at the screaming bobby-soxers and dared them to come up and get him.

Halfway through their first impromptu performance, such a traffic jam
resulted on Forty-fourth Street that mounted policemen brandishing billy
clubs had to be summoned to untangle the mess. And it didn't become
untangled until Dean and Jerry ducked back into their dressing room to get
ready for their next show inside the theater.

According to the police lieutenant in charge of the local precinct station
at the time, "Forty-fourth Street wasn't the same until Martin and Lewis
left New York two weeks later."

By that time, they had smashed a Paramount Theater box office
record set by Frank Sinatra, taking in $289,500 in two weeks. Of that,
they were paid jointly $144,700, which also set some sort of a salary
record.

Dean and Jerry repeated their triumph in Detroit and Chicago, where
their alfresco acts between regular performances not only continued to
cause traffic jams but also accomplished their main purpose—emptying
out the theaters so fresh money could flow into the box offices.

In four weeks, Dean and Jerry earned $260,000 for themselves, estab-
lishing them as the highest-paid act in show business.

A fifth week of the tour had to be canceled because Dean and Jerry
had worked themselves into such a state of exhaustion that their friends
and agents—and their wives—were beginning to worry. Even Jerry's energy wasn't unlimited.

But, in just those four weeks, Dean and Jerry's fame reached a new
apogee. *Life* featured their pictures on its cover one week, and the
sophisticated *The New Yorker* devoted four full columns in its "Talk of
the Town" section to covering Martin and Lewis's "happening" at the
Paramount.

Until the Beatles came along a decade later, no entertainers had ever
made quite the impact on this nation's under-thirty set as Martin and
Lewis did, and on the over-thirty set too.

All this success and adulation notwithstanding, Jerry did not quickly
forget his humble beginnings. Once when he and Dean were playing the
Capitol in New York City, Jerry took time out from their six-a-day-and-
seven-on-Saturdays schedule to walk across the street and drop in on the
man who made much of this possible—Lou Perry.

"See, Lou, I haven't forgotten you," screamed Jerry as he pranced into
the sparsely furnished office located in an old building off Times Square.
"Here we are across the street with our names up in lights, and I'm coming to say hello to you, who made it possible."

Bouncing around the room, Jerry stopped dramatically and pointed to
a corner. "Gee, Lou, it looks bare there," he said. "What you need for

that corner is a nice bar. As soon as I get back to Hollywood, I'll send you one."

That was over twenty years ago, and Lou Perry still has the same bare corner in his office that he had then.

In fairness to Jerry, it wasn't like him to renege. Jerry may have a few bad points, but no one has ever accused him of not being generous.

When bandleader Dick Stabile's mother was desperately ill in New York, Jerry saved her life by having her flown to California on a chartered airliner so she could be treated by a top specialist he knew. Naturally, Jerry paid the bill.

One week when Martin and Lewis were doing their radio show from Chicago, Ben Starr, a young writer who had just joined the show, decided to marry his fiancée, Gloria.

Jerry not only attended the wedding and stood under the *chuppah* with the young couple as the service was being performed but paid for the rabbi and also for a large wedding reception afterwards at the Ambassador-East Hotel. In addition, he gave Ben and Gloria a $100 check for a wedding present. (He also called in the press, but then what is the fun of giving if nobody knows about it?)

"He really couldn't have been more generous," recalls a grateful Ben Starr, who is one of Hollywood's top comedy writers today. "The only trouble was, when Gloria and I went to bed that night, Jerry took the room next door and banged on the wall with his fist and yelled suggestive remarks at us all night."

Over the years, it has been estimated that Jerry has given away nearly $5 million—not always wisely.

Once, when an unemployed actor he knew was down on his luck and living with his large family in a one-room apartment, Jerry felt so sad he went out and bought him a big house in the country. The man moved in, but because Jerry wouldn't give him a part in one of his pictures, he never spoke to Jerry again.

On another occasion, Dean and Jerry had a publicity man working for them named Jack Keller, of whom Jerry was particularly fond. Keller, like Jerry, was a yachting buff, and Jerry knew he had had his eye on a particular yacht for some time but couldn't afford to buy it. On Keller's birthday, Jerry suggested that the two of them take a drive to San Diego for the day and have dinner to "celebrate" the event. Keller accepted, and the two of them drove down the coast that afternoon.

But, in San Diego, Jerry didn't stop at the restaurant where he allegedly had made a dinner reservation. Instead, he drove straight to the waterfront and parked his car beside a dock at the Coronado Yacht Club. Moored to the dock was the sleek forty-foot power yacht, costing about $50,000, that Keller had been coveting. "Happy birthday to you," said

Jerry, dangling the boat keys in front of the stunned and overwhelmed Keller.

Even though this kind of generosity has kept him in constant hot water with the Internal Revenue Service for inability to pay back taxes, Jerry continued to be a soft touch all during the years of his and Dean's mutual success.

"Giving is selfish," Jerry used to say. "My wife has a proverb: 'The things you keep, you lose; what you give away, you keep forever.' "

If Jerry had a compulsion to give, he had an even more compelling need to buy—and in large quantities.

Ed Simmons remembers an incident that took place when he and Norman Lear and the rest of "The Colgate Comedy Hour" production staff had to accompany Martin and Lewis to San Francisco because the show was being broadcast from the City by the Bay one week.

During a break in rehearsals one afternoon, Jerry decided to take a stroll down Market Street, and he insisted that his entire entourage, consisting of about twenty people, come along.

Suddenly he popped into one of the many Army and Navy stores that make Market Street such a delight to the eye and started ordering merchandise from one of the clerks in such quantities that the man couldn't believe his good fortune: 40 pairs of jockey shorts, 50 T-shirts, 200 pairs of socks, 30 wool sweaters, 300 handkerchiefs, 40 pairs of blue jeans, and just about anything else that caught Jerry's fancy.

"He had the stuff all gift-wrapped into the same amount of packages that he had people in his entourage," relates Ed Simmons, who was along on that particular trip. Then he started tossing the prize packages to each individual, with no regard to sizes or even what anyone wanted— not that any of us wanted any of that Army and Navy store crap."

Each person in the group caught his package with sycophantic resignation, exclaiming with false enthusiasm, "Gee, thanks, Jer"—everyone, that is, except Ed Simmons, who was the last to be favored with a present and who was completely turned off by Jerry's display of hauteur.

When Jerry got around to tossing a package at him, Simmons flipped it right back with all his might. "I can buy my own jockey shorts," he exclaimed to the surprised Jerry. "My mother says I shouldn't accept gifts from strange *men*."

If Simmons couldn't reconcile his own personal pride with Jerry's "big man" complex, he had an even more difficult time becoming adjusted to the way comics will frequently denigrate the efforts of their writing staffs —especially when they think the writers aren't around.

One time when they were all on the road together, Dino was being interviewed by a newspaper man in his hotel room just as Ed Simmons happened to walk by the open door.

"Sure, Jer and I have writers," Simmons heard Dino telling the reporter, "but we just use their stuff as a blueprint. We ad-lib all the really funny stuff."

"And that's why you've always been one of my boyhood idols!" quipped Simmons, poking his head through the door.

A few other writers who later contributed to Martin and Lewis's ad libs were such lightweights as Mel Brooks, Mel Tolkin, George Axelrod, and Neil Simon.

Dean and Jerry weren't any worse about this than were most performers. It happens to all of them eventually. They begin to believe their writers' words are their own.

In the beginning, however, Jerry remembered his writers a few times. At the end of the first season of "The Colgate Comedy Hour," Martin and Lewis bought a full-page ad in the trade papers thanking Simmons and Lear for contributing to the show's success. Along with that went the customary gold watches: "Thanks, Dean and Jerry."

And in a large brown envelope came an additional expression of Jerry's gratitude. It was an 8″ x 10″ color photo of Dean Martin and Jerry Lewis, modestly autographed as follows:

To Eddie and Norm—

the guys who make it
easy to be so great!

/s/ Dean and Jerry

15

Ain't We Got Fun

In 1951 Martin and Lewis traveled 50,000 miles and grossed over $1 million from stage, motion picture, and recording income, as well as from television appearances for NBC. They were also back on radio again, for now that they were such a hit on television, Chesterfield Cigarettes had decided to sponsor them in a weekly prime-time radio variety show. With Simmons and Lear writing it, Martin and Lewis's radio show captured a good audience rating among those people who still didn't have television sets, and the series stayed on the air for two years—or until prime-time big-budget radio emitted its final death rattle and succumbed to television for good.

Somehow during all this frenetic activity, Jerry Lewis found time to have a home life with Patti, his six-year-old son Gary, and a menagerie of some thirteen springer spaniels, all fathered by Jerry's special pal of the lot, Chipper. As has been previously noted, Jerry does nothing halfway—not even his dog loving.

Jerry also found time to go house hunting—now that it was certain beyond a shadow of Hal Wallis that Martin and Lewis weren't flashes in the Hollywood pan.

Although Jerry enjoyed being able to drop in on his neighbor, Danny Kaye, and discuss their mutual beginnings in the Catskill Mountain summer resorts, Jerry felt that the Maria Montez establishment was much too elaborate for a man of his "simple" tastes. So, in October 1950, he and Patti began looking for a house to buy.

They wore down a dozen real estate agents and looked at more than fifty houses before they found a home the following spring that they not only liked but could almost afford.

It was a twelve-room rambling brick-trimmed California-style ranch house, with five and one-half bathrooms, on the Palisades near the Pacific Ocean, in a community called, of all things, Pacific Palisades. The property was within a few blocks of the Riviera Country Club, where Dean Martin plays golf today, sometimes for as much as $5,000 a hole, and on a clear day it was possible to see the azure blue ocean, and perhaps Catalina Island, from Jerry's backyard, if he stood on Patti's shoulders.

The house itself was on North Amalfi Drive, taxwise the most highly assessed property in the city of Los Angeles, and the $65,000 price tag reflected it. (Today, of course, you can barely buy a steak for $65,000, but, in 1951, it was still a bundle.)

The $65,000 price, however, did not include a swimming pool. Jerry quickly altered that situation by calling up the Paddock Pool Company soon after they took possession and ordering an Olympic-sized watering hole for the backyard.

He also bought the vacant lot next door and later put a Little League baseball diamond on it complete with a professional backstop, so that his kids and the kids in the neighborhood (including himself and his movie star friends) would have a decent place to play ball without having to pedal their bikes two miles along much-trafficked Sunset Boulevard to the Pacific Palisades municipal playground.

Jerry may have had a rotten childhood himself, but he was determined that his own youngsters would never feel the pangs of deprivation and loneliness that he experienced when he was growing up as the Irvington, New Jersey, "idiot."

Because he was still paying off his tax deficit to Uncle Sam, Jerry didn't have the funds to meet the 50 percent down payment on the house or to buy furniture fit for a movie star. But Paramount Studios had enough faith in the futures of Martin and Lewis to advance Jerry the necessary cash to set up housekeeping and to settle down to the suburban life of a typical American husband earning $1 million a year and keeping hardly any of it.

The new home's interior was tastefully furnished, mostly with Early American reproductions and colorful hooked rugs, but combined with a few contemporary pieces as well. Among its many features were separate bedrooms for all the young Lewises, a large modern kitchen with plenty of built-in modern appliances, and a knotty-pine family room, where Jerry liked to romp with his kids and entertain his rapidly expanding circle of friends and desultory moochers.

There was only a small bar in the family room, but that didn't much concern Patti and Jerry, for neither of them cared much about drinking, and Dean Martin wasn't a very regular visitor any more.

The social chasm between the Martins and the Lewises was widening as the team grew more successful. This was more or less deliberate, for they were trying to live by the advice once given them by another comedy team—Olsen and Johnson, of *Hellzapoppin* fame. After seeing the Martins and the Lewises feuding in public, Olsen and Johnson took Jerry and Dean aside and warned them, "If you guys want to stay together, do what we do—stay away from each other after hours and keep your wives apart."

So except on special "occasions" or when it was particularly incumbent on the Martins and the Lewises to be seen together and to "put on a happy face" for appearance' sake, they led completely separate social lives after hours.

Although much money and love were lavished on making the Lewises' first house a home, the key word to the decor was "comfort." According to Patti, Jerry insisted on a house in which every room had a place where he could pull off his shoes and flop—"his favorite indoor sport." If the latter were completely true, it is doubtful if Jerry Lewis today would be the father of five kids of his own and be considered somewhat of a bon vivant when he is away from Patti, but it can't be denied that he liked to relax as much as possible when he left the cares of the day behind him at Paramount Studios.

Working in as many mediums as they did, Dean and Jerry were under terrific pressure every day of their lives (including Sunday, which was when they broadcast "The Colgate Comedy Hour."

Jerry was under a little more tension than Dean was, for, as time went on, he started evincing more and more of an interest in getting involved in the production end of all their enterprises, whereas Dean, in about the same ratio, tried to decelerate his activities. Dean, in fact, as long ago as 1951, said he didn't want to become involved in a regular television show at all. He also would have preferred to drop most of his and Jerry's nightclub work and just concentrate on making movies. After all, he was approaching forty; he wanted to spend more time basking in the California sun and playing golf.

It was Jerry who insisted that they maintain a rugged nightclub and TV schedule in addition to their film activities. He was only twenty-six, but his capacity for work was staggering, even for a man of his age. According to Patti, he was always thinking about his work even when he was sleeping. If an idea came to him after he and Patti had gone to bed, he'd switch on the lights and write it down on the pad he kept next to him on the nightstand.

If he were sufficiently inspired, he'd leap out of bed, sit down at a typewriter, and peck away at the keys all night, sometimes not giving up until 5:00 in the morning—often to the dismay of his high-priced scriptwriters, who would see their best efforts thrown out and replaced with a scene of Jerry's when he arrived at the studio. If there was any argument about it, Jerry would usually scream at them (with more and more frequency as time went on), "Mine's the best because *I* wrote it!"

Jerry was usually in such a keyed-up state after coming home that he found it impossible to unwind from the fast-paced activities of the day or to stop tapping the reservoir of nervous energy he'd built up.

"Even when he sleeps, he moves around so restlessly, swinging his arms and tossing the blankets off, that I usually have to get up and re-cover him," complains Patti.

What kept Jerry in a state of perpetual motion was that he was beset by a neurotic fear that his success was only temporary. "I was afraid," says Jerry, "that I would wake up some morning, and everything would be gone—my house, my swimming pool, my job at the studio."

He felt that the safest way to forestall that day was to keep his nose to the movieola and drive himself to the brink of collapse.

For years, Patti tried to get Jerry to relax at breakfast time and forget his work, but he couldn't do it even then. When he was shooting a picture, he'd be up at 6:00. Although the Lewis household was staffed with a cook, a butler, and a cleaning maid, Patti would get up with Jerry at 6:00 in the morning to make sure he ate something before leaving for Paramount. But even at 6:00 Jerry would ignore his food and start making telephone calls and having long frenzied conversations with his writers.

"The eggs would get cold, so I'd cook another batch," says Patti. "And that batch would get cold while he thought of another dozen calls to make. I usually cooked three breakfasts before he finally settled down."

Jerry had the same case of telephonitis at dinner time. Home from a hard day at the studio, he'd be so busy talking on the phone that he rarely sat down to dinner with the rest of the family. When Patti complained, he suggested installing a telephone next to his chair in the dining room so he could eat and talk at the same time. Patti flatly put her foot down. "Nothing doing," she told Jerry. "If the phone comes in, the food goes out."

Typical of most hyperthyroid people, Jerry has never been much of a gourmet, nor does he care about sticking to a nourishing diet. In the middle of a project, he's usually content to grab a hamburger and a coke on the run and chain-smoke a few cigarettes. Since he was always in the middle of a project, his health and weight reflected his complete indifference to the demands of his stomach. Shortly after he and Patti moved into their new abode, Jerry's weight dropped down to 135 pounds, frighteningly slim for a man over six feet tall.

Always on the frail side, Jerry collapsed twice in 1951 from overexhaustion. The second time, Patti had to put him to bed, with firm instructions from their doctor to keep him there for at least two weeks. On the second morning, Patti found a note on her vanity, reading: "Have gone to visit a sick friend." The sick friend was Dean Martin. He was so ill that the same day he and Jerry turned up at the studio, playing more practical jokes on Y. Frank Freeman.

Although he admits that he can take eating or leave it, Jerry confesses to one weakness—Italian fried chicken, prepared by his favorite chef, Patti.

Aside from trying to curb Jerry's activities, Patti's two favorite hobbies are knitting and cooking. According to Jerry, she's superb at both of them. "My wife is the greatest," he boasts. "She's got every cookbook that was ever written, and she can cook anything—any style you want. Have you ever tried matzoh balls with veal scallopini?"

Patti's culinary artistry is one of the reasons Jerry finally insisted that Patti give up golf. He wanted to be sure she'd spend her afternoons in the kitchen.

At one time Patti played golf every afternoon, but once Jerry phoned her from the studio during some kind of a family emergency and wasn't able to reach her. It upset the worrisome Jerry so that he told her he wanted her to stay home in the afternoons after that so she'd always be within reach of a phone. Being a nice Italian housewife (who wasn't that crazy about golf anyway), Patti complied with the boss's wishes.

It was because of Jerry's ever-protective nature regarding his family that Patti also gave up traveling around the country with Jerry and Dean when they were making personal appearances.

The Lewises' original plan was to have five children. When it looked as if Patti couldn't have any more of her own, she started investigating the possibilities of adopting a baby. Jerry was on tour with Dean in Miami when the adoption agency phoned Patti and informed her that a baby was available. Patti wired Jerry for approval. He wired back simply, "YES! YES! YES!"—which was how Ronnie wound up as the second Lewis child.

A few months after Ronnie moved into the North Amalfi Drive residence, the accident happened that ended Patti's traveling days for good.

Leaving the kids in charge of their housekeeper, Patti went off to New York to be with Jerry, who was playing the Paramount Theater with Dean.

Around 8:00 one night, a telegram from the Lewises' housekeeper arrived at the theater saying that Ronnie had fallen off his bathinette in the nursery and fractured a leg and a thigh. The housekeeper had called in the family doctor, who had assured her that Ronnie would probably be all right, but she urged them to come home anyway because "Ronnie needed" them.

Jerry frantically tried to get his release from the show, but the manager of the theater said, "Impossible," so Patti flew home by herself. After personally hearing the doctor's assurances that Ronnie would be all right, she relayed the news to Jerry by phone.

Jerry consented to remain with the show only after Patti sent him a full set of Ronnie's X rays, installed a phone by Ronnie's bed, and called in California's best bone specialists, Doctors Danny Leventhal and Fred Ilfeld.

Curtailing Patti's travel with her husband put an additional strain on their marriage, for, in order to make up his enormous tax deficit, Jerry had to be away from his home almost as much as he was in it.

"But he was a very devoted husband, nevertheless," avers Ernie Glucksman. "No matter where he was, or how many girls he was fooling around with on the road, he'd always be phoning Patti—sometimes fifty times a day."

Having spent quite a bit of time on the road as a single girl before she met Jerry, Patti was not blind to the pitfalls that can befall a man when he is away from home—especially if he is a celebrity, making big money, and the idol of the bobby-soxers.

She once told Jerry, "I know there are temptations—it can't be helped. Just don't do anything that'll make people feel sorry for me."

Just hearing that from Patti gave Jerry such a pang of guilt that thereafter, whenever he had to be away from home, he tried to bring some members of the family along with him to keep him from being lonely. If he couldn't have Patti, then he'd try to take one of the kids; if not one of the kids, then Chipper, their springer spaniel.

Once, while playing Chicago, Jerry was afflicted with such an attack of homesickness that he phoned Jack Keller, who was on the West Coast, and instructed him to ship Chipper to him on the next Super Chief. And "not in the baggage car"; he insisted that Keller book a "drawing room" for the animal.

Despite the temptations of a traveling man, Jerry enjoyed being at home the best, and when he was there, he had no trouble falling into the role of a normal husband who putters in the garden and personally gives his boys swimming and boxing lessons in the backyard.

One kind of instruction he never gave his progeny was religious instruction. Although he has a gold *mezuzah* on the front door to bring the Lewis family good luck, Jerry made up his mind from the outset that he would never foist his own religion on his children—perhaps out of deference to Patti, who is a devout, practicing Catholic.

"We've told them all there is to know about both religions," Jerry used to say in response to those who wanted to know whether the Lewis children were Jewish or Gentile. "They can decide for themselves what they want to be when they're old enough to know what they want."

Considering his reputation for being a round-the-clock puck, Jerry always made it a point to soft-pedal humor around his kids as much as possible. He never believed that a father's first function with his children was to be funny.

At the age of six for example, little Gary, who had butch-cut dark hair and a countenance not dissimilar to his father's, was turning into a born mimic. His favorite bit (naturally) was to imitate all the funny faces he saw his father make on television. If encouraged, he'd continue the mugging all day. But he soon learned that pouting his underlip to touch his nose or crossing his eyes won him less praise from Jerry than did a well-executed left jab in their boxing class, a good crawl stroke down the pool, or a few A's on his report card.

As a parent, Jerry didn't think only of his own children. If something important was at stake, he frequently became involved in neighborhood problems.

Shortly after the Lewises moved to the Pacific Palisades, a neighborhood boy was killed at the unguarded intersection of Amalfi Drive and Sunset Boulevard, where there wasn't even a stop-and-go signal. When the police department refused to do anything about the situation, Jerry took time off one day from his work at the studio to drop in at a meeting of the Los Angeles City Council and make an eloquent plea for the installation of a stoplight. He got it.

When there was no Little League in the Pacific Palisades, Jerry organized the parents into a group large enough for their demands to be heard. The Pacific Palisades soon was the proud possessor of a "last-place" Little League team.

When there wasn't enough money in the public coffers to put up a branch of the Los Angeles Public Library in the Pacific Palisades, Jerry did a benefit with Dean at the Riviera Country Club and raised the necessary funds.

The grateful community eventually bestowed on the former Irvington High dropout the rank of honorary mayor.

The pupils of nearby Emerson Junior High School voted Jerry "the prize" they wanted for winning a Parent-Teacher Association membership drive. This so overwhelmed Jerry that he showed up in the Emerson school auditorium and did his entire nightclub act, solo, for the pupils.

"The only way we could get the kids home before dark," complained the principal, "was to give Mr. Lewis a lifetime PTA membership, and push him off the stage, and out the back door and into his car."

"Kids have such a short time as kids," Jerry was fond of saying. "It should be the most wonderful time of their lives."

It was his deep concern for his own children that was primarily responsible for the Lewises' garnering the reputation among the Hollywood social set as the champion stick-at-homes. Remembering his own loneliness as a child when his parents were off working, Jerry made it a point to turn down social invitations and be home in the evenings with Gary and Ronnie as much as possible.

Quite aside from those considerations, Jerry has never been much of a social lion; and neither, for that matter, has Dean. Despite an outward display of enormous self-confidence, both Dean and Jerry have always suffered from inferiority complexes, stemming from a lack of education in both schooling and the social graces. This has kept them from accepting any more invitations to parties than could be avoided. At large dinner parties that they felt compelled to attend, both men worked hard to cover their insecurity.

Dean, for example, would often get through an unpleasant social ordeal by pretending to be drowsy from too much liquor so he wouldn't have to talk too much or become involved in "group" discussions on politics or other subjects he felt he didn't know anything about. This is responsible, in part, for building his reputation as a heavy drinker. If he was feeling particularly unsociable, he'd disappear into a room uninhabited by the other guests, slump into a chair in front of a TV set, and stare at the tube glassy-eyed or else fall asleep sitting up until it was time to go home or (if he were the host) for the guests to leave.

Jerry's defense would be to clown his way through an evening. For example, he'd appear at a formal dinner gathering in a tuxedo and tennis shoes. Then he'd rush out to the kitchen and kiss the cook, pretending that he had mistaken her for the hostess. When he didn't know which fork to use, he would cover up by pretending to eat the seafood cocktail with the serving fork—until he saw which fork the others were using.

Jerry had a third reason for preferring to stay home in the evenings. It allowed him more time to indulge in his Number One hobby—making home movies.

According to Dean Martin, Jerry's interest in photography dates back to a time when a friend gave him a camera for a birthday gift. "Jerry took a picture with it—I think it was a picture of a lamp. When it turned out well," recalls Dino sardonically, "I could see him saying to himself, 'Hey, I'm a great cameraman!' That started him down the path to thinking he could do everything connected with making motion pictures."

Throwing himself into photography with the enthusiasm with which he approaches every new enterprise, Jerry not only started taking lots of candid snapshots of his family and friends but also bought a camera store on Vine Street in Hollywood and called it the Jerry Lewis Camera Exchange.

On his days off from the studio, Jerry would often take a turn behind the counter, waiting on customers or giving advice on photography.

Frequently, he'd drop into the shop after a late-night rehearsal at NBC radio studios, which was just down Vine Street from the Exchange, until a little contretemps with the police forced him to give up this practice.

One night around 12:00, he invited his close friend and singer, the late Mario Lanza, to the shop to show him some color equipment he had just installed in the darkroom. Prowling about the shop in the dark looking for the light switch, Jerry tripped the burglar alarm.

A half hour later, Patti received a phone call from the police, asking her to "identify a joker with no credentials who claims he's Jerry Lewis."

Jerry's voice suddenly came over the wire as he grabbed the phone from the policeman and screamed, "Patti, I've made a boo boo!"

Being his own best customer (and most of the time his only one), Jerry brought home the most expensive piece of home movie-making equipment in his store—a 16mm Auricon sound camera—and began practicing with it assiduously around the house.

When the results of his early work revealed that he had some promise as a cameraman, Jerry decided to make a full-length home movie to show at the housewarming party for his and Patti's new home in the Pacific Palisades.

Leaving nothing to chance, Jerry persuaded Don McGuire to write a screenplay for his first "really big" home movie. At the time, McGuire was a young good-looking unemployed actor whom Jerry had met and taken a liking to shortly after he and Dean had moved to the West Coast.

McGuire used to hang around Jerry's house a lot, hoping one of the comic's prestigious friends would see him and give him a break in films. He hadn't done much writing, but he was the possessor of a sardonic wit and he had great determination to succeed—at something. So when Jerry asked him to collaborate on the screenplay of the housewarming movie, McGuire willingly agreed.

The result was a screenplay titled *How to Smuggle a Hernia Across the Border*, based on an original idea by Jerry Lewis. The film was a satire of Army life. Jerry, naturally, played the main role—that of a homosexual recruiting officer. For the other major roles, Jerry enlisted the services of his and Patti's closest friends in Hollywood—Tony Curtis and Janet Leigh. For the minor parts, he employed Patti and Don McGuire.

Don McGuire can't remember, or perhaps he just doesn't care to, all the bits in Jerry Lewis's first solo attempt at picture making, but one scene in which Jerry played an American Indian is still vivid in his memory.

Jerry came out from behind a tree, stark naked except for a thin loincloth; his normally snow-white skin was made dusky from an application of Man-Tan.

A policeman saw him and said, "I'm going to arrest you."

"What for?" asked Geronimo Lewis.

"For being an anti-Seminole!" replied his tormentor.

When Jerry ran his epic for the first time the day before the party, he discovered, to his horror, that there was no sound track. He had forgotten to turn on the sound button when he was running the camera. Without sound, the action was meaningless.

This threw Jerry into a panic, for the home movie was supposed to be the party's main entertainment. Jerry had only two options: Call off the party or dub in the voices overnight.

Option number one was out because the caterers were already busy making hors d'oeuvres and Beef Stroganoff; the backyard tent had been set up by Abbey Rents; and the Lewises would be socially ostracized if they canceled out on such important guests as Hal Wallis and Elizabeth Taylor at the last minute.

That left option number two. But how could Jerry gather the actors together to remake the sound track? The problem had a solution: Jerry and McGuire stayed up all night and dubbed in the voices themselves, taking both male and female roles.

Despite production difficulties, *How to Smuggle a Hernia Across the Border* received an enthusiastic response from its first audience. In fact, it was considered the highlight of the party (which ought to be some indication of the depths to which social life in Hollywood had sunk).

As a result of the picture's success, Don McGuire got a job as a screenwriter at Universal, and Gar-Ron Productions–USA (named after Jerry's two sons, Gary and Ronnie) was born. Its business slogan was "Just for Laffs," and its chief aim (aside from giving Jerry something to do on evenings and weekends) was to lampoon public movies.

As in his first venture, Jerry enlisted the acting talents of all his friends in the business—Tony Curtis, Janet Leigh, Van Johnson, John Barrymore, Jr., Mona Freeman, his wife Patti, himself, sometimes his kids, and once he even persuaded Dean Martin to come over and play a part in *The Reinforcer*, a takeoff on a 1930s gangster film.

In *The Reinforcer*, Janet Leigh played a gun moll named Mary Muck and Dean played a cliché gangster called Joe Lasagna, who spoke in an Italian dialect and kept spewing lines like, "Where's-a my broad?" and "Make-a look-a like-a accident."

Other films conceived, written, directed, photographed, and edited by Jerry Lewis for the consumption of his friends had such lofty titles as *Watch on the Lime, Fairfax Avenue* (a takeoff on *Sunset Boulevard*),

Son of Spellbound, Streetcar Named Repulsive, and *Come Back, Little Shiksa.*

To make certain that each production was given the proper send-off, Jerry would hold a regular Hollywood premier at his house, complete with all the trimmings, including klieg lights, bleachers for the fans, a red carpet to the front door, and a radio announcer in the patio interviewing the celebrated guests as they arrived.

The first time Jerry pulled this stunt, he forgot to tell Patti. She came home from a weekend in San Francisco to find the driveway clogged with cars. At the curb, a giant revolving klieg light shot a brilliant beacon into the sky, and a six-foot sign erected on the front lawn proclaimed, "Gala Premier Tonight—Jerry Lewis Production of *The Reinforcer.*"

As Patti pushed her way through the crowd to the front door, a uniformed doorman stopped her and demanded to know if she had a ticket. At that moment, Sam, the Lewises' butler, wandered by and arranged entrée for Patti, but he warned her, "You'd better dress, Mrs. Lewis. This is a black-tie blowout."

In the entry hall, a red plush carpet of the kind used at Grauman's Chinese Theater for legitimate Hollywood openings led to the patio, where hundreds of guests were milling around and a radio announcer was interviewing Corinne Calvet and a barber friend of Jerry's.

Lest anyone in America be unaware of Jerry's picture-making talents, he had also invited all the film critics and Hollywood columnists, like Hedda Hopper, Louella Parsons, and Sidney Skolsky, who later wrote, "Never at the conclusion of a picture has an audience applauded so heartily."

(That just might have been the best review a Jerry Lewis picture has ever received. For although Martin and Lewis's films were all big moneymakers, they did not elicit raves from the critics. *Time,* for example, in reviewing *At War with the Army* wrote, "*At War with the Army* was not much of a play on Broadway, but scripter Fred F. Finklehoffe's film version shows that it could have been much worse.")

In keeping with the magnitude of his home movie-making enterprises, Jerry soon found it necessary to have a tremendous playhouse built in the backyard. He named it the Gar-Ron Playhouse. Its spacious interior was comfortably furnished for entertaining and also contained a projection room and a film-cutting lab.

The Gar-Ron Playhouse was his special pride and joy, for not only could he now pursue his hobby in comfort, but it gave him additional wall space to display his many plaques, trophies, and pictures autographed by his superstar friends and political figures, as well as a place to store his camera and recording equipment and his voluminous records of his past and present work, including his collection of leather-bound scripts and cans of kinescopes of the Martin and Lewis television shows.

It also was the perfect spot for entertaining their multitudes of friends. As a rule, however, they did not entertain on the grand style adopted for Jerry Lewis's gala premiers.

But, as far as Patti was concerned, the "surprises" never stopped. Often when the Lewises were having guests to dinner, Jerry would come home late—sometimes as much as an hour after his friends arrived. Since Patti frequently didn't know half the guests Jerry had invited, this used to annoy her. It also puzzled her, because, on most other occasions, Jerry was always very punctual.

Then, in a moment of great insight, the reason for his tardiness finally dawned on Patti: Being a comedian twenty-four hours a day, he liked to walk in only when his audience was all there, so he could make an "entrance."

Knowing this, however, wasn't especially comforting when Patti had to sit in a room with someone she hardly knew—for example, the night Jerry had invited Joan Crawford over to the house for dinner for the first time.

Being somewhat awed by movie stars in her early days in Hollywood, Patti was understandably nervous at the prospect of meeting Miss Crawford.

Miss Crawford arrived on time, but Jerry didn't show up for two hours. By then Patti had exhausted her imagination making small talk, she couldn't drink another drop of liquor without passing out, and she began to fidget in her chair.

Suddenly the front door flew open, and Jerry bounced in. Pointing his finger at Joan Crawford, he shrieked, "Get in the kitchen! The help isn't allowed in the living room."

Miss Crawford howled with laughter, but for Patti the ordeal still wasn't over. Anxious to make a good impression on the glamorous movie star, Patti had the dining table set with her finest silver and china and had spent the afternoon showing the help how to serve correctly.

As the three of them sat down, Patti asked Jerry to ring for the maid. Jerry nodded, "Yes, honey," pulled out a huge cowbell, which he'd hidden under his chair, and clanged it like a fire chief on his way to a five-alarm conflagration.

On another occasion, Patti and Jerry were entertaining Jack and Mary Benny, in whose home they had been wined and dined sumptuously the previous week. The Bennys had a large house, decorated very formally by Bill Haines, and their parties were always dignified affairs, with the women attending in long dresses and the men in dark suits.

Naturally, Patti wanted to prove to the Bennys that the Jerry Lewises were no country bumpkins, so she had warned Jerry to be on his best behavior and not to wear tennis sneakers. He promised to be good, but halfway through dinner, Jerry's prerecorded voice boomed out through the hi-fi speaker in the dining room: "I hope you're enjoying your dinner. Don't complain about the food. You're getting it for nothing!"

Benny collapsed with laughter, and from that moment on the ice was broken.

Being a sentimentalist, Jerry would throw large blowouts on family birthdays and wedding anniversaries and invite all his close friends, plus the business associates he hadn't yet tired of, such as Hal Wallis, Simmons and Lear, and a host of stooges.

Like the Magi bringing gifts to the Savior, the guests would stream into the Lewis house bearing the most expensive presents they could find —a $500 shotgun (because, after having Greshler for an agent, guns were one of Jerry's favorite hobbies), a $700 camera, a wristwatch from Tiffany's, or anything else they could find to prove that it wasn't the thought that mattered but the price of the gift. The people whose jobs were the most insecure naturally brought the most expensive gifts.

Feeling no particular need to toady up to the boss, Ed Simmons and Norman Lear, one Jerry Lewis birthday, were at a loss as to what to buy the "Comedian Who Had Everything." They didn't want to come empty-handed, and at the same time they'd be damned if they'd spend hundreds of dollars on something Jerry didn't really need or want anyway.

"The whole idea of having to give him expensive presents used to aggravate the hell out of us," recalls Norman Lear. "Finally, we decided as kind of an ironic thing to give him something he never had—a live man. But the ironic part of it was that he really owned about thirty of them— human beings, that is. So we were going to give him his very own human being as a gift. And the day we thought about the idea, a little man about eighty years old, built like Popeye, strong as could be—and he looked like Popeye—came to fix a window in our office, and we asked him if he wanted to make twenty-five dollars that night. He was thrilled.

"He was French, and spoke broken English. We took him down to Fairfax and Santa Monica and had him gift-wrapped. He was very small and weighed about 110 pounds. So they constructed this box that he could squat in, but that he'd only have to get in at the very last minute. When we put the top on the box, the ribbons would fall into place with a big bow on top. It looked like a completely wrapped package.

"So we went out to the birthday party, and the little man sat in the car until we needed him. Toward the end of the evening, about fifty people gathered around a big coffee table in what was called the Gar-Ron Play-house behind Jerry's house. They started to open up these very expensive gifts. 'Oh, a gun!' somebody would exclaim, as Jerry would pull a $500 rifle out of a package, or 'Oh, a record player!'

"As they got to the end of the presents, Ed and I ran out to the car and brought the box and the little man back to the playhouse. Just before we got to the door, we put the man in the box. Before I closed the lid I said, 'We'll give you five extra dollars if you don't smile when they open you up.' I thought that if he smiled, it would ruin everything. 'So try not to smile,' I told him. He said OK and we put the lid on and carried it into the playroom.

"I remember as Ed and I carried the box in, somebody yelled, 'Hey, look at Simmons and Lear—they got him a television set.' Our package looked like the size of a big console television. We put it on the coffee table, and Jerry took the top off. But the old man, in order to keep himself from laughing, had his eyes closed and his head cocked down, and was totally motionless.

"Marvin Levy, who was the only doctor in the room, was standing on the perimeter of this crowd peeking over the heads of everybody into the box. Being a doctor, he harked back to the pranks of his med-school days and exclaimed out loud: 'It's a cadaver!' Well, you never heard such screams and cries—and Jerry almost passed out from the shock, because the man remained motionless.

"I kept yelling into the box, 'You can get up now. It's OK to smile. Get up! Smile. Laugh!' Well, finally he did, but he had played dead so realistically that, during the time he was lying motionless, a complete pall had come over all the guests at the party. They went along with Patti's and Jerry's fears that it really was a cadaver. The party was ruined. The only two people who got a kick out of the gag, besides Eddie and myself, were the old man and Hal Wallis, who roared."

As a host, the honorary mayor of the Pacific Palisades had one additional fault that Patti couldn't stand. He would invite people over to dinner without telling Patti about it and promptly forget he'd issued the invitations.

One night the Lewises were having Judy and Ernie Glucksman to dinner. Since they were the only guests, as far as Patti was aware, she decided to give them a Long Island duckling she'd been saving for an occasion when they just had another couple over. Just as the four were ready to sit down at the dining table, the doorbell rang.

"I wonder who that is!" exclaimed Patti.

"Oh," replied Jerry with a sheepish smile, "I just remembered, I think I invited a couple of guys from the studio."

With the arrival of not a "couple" but eight more friends, Patti was thrown into a panic. She signaled Jerry to follow her into the kitchen.

"Just what do I do now?" asked the enraged Patti. "I have just *one* duck."

"Don't get excited," said Jerry, without loss of aplomb, "Just put more stuffing in it!"

16

Mr. Wonderful

Not content with being a star of movies, television, radio, and nightclubs —to say nothing of being the producer of the most lavishly produced and exploited home movies in the history of the 16mm camera—Jerry was, by the beginning of Martin and Lewis's third season on "The Colgate Comedy Hour," starting to throw his creative weight around in areas that were clearly outside his domain.

He was telling the production head of Paramount what to produce; directors how to direct; writers what to write; cameramen how to focus; his partner what to sing; and casting directors how to cast.

He was even putting his father Danny on "The Colgate Comedy Hour" at regular intervals during the TV season to do his Jolson imitation—not because he thought his father was particularly talented or because he loved him that much, but because, as the show's star, he enjoyed being in a position of pushing his father around and giving him directions. In a sense, he was getting back at his old man for giving him a rotten childhood—but at the expense of his television audience.

Dino, who is no sentimentalist, didn't think Jerry had any right to put his father on the show, but there was so little communication between them by this time that he never mentioned it to his partner. His disgust was evident, however, in a remark he made to Ed Simmons during a rehearsal of the program at the El Capitan Theater in Hollywood one afternoon.

Dino and Simmons were standing at the rear of the theater, watching Danny run through his big "April Showers" number on stage. Jerry was directing him. After listening to a few bars of Danny's corny imitation of

Jolson, Dino turned to Simmons with a cringe and remarked, "I think I'll put my mother on the show—she can sew."

It was evident from a few of Dino's other remarks that he was becoming increasingly embittered with having to toil in his partner's ever-lengthening shadow.

Once he took Jerry by the hand and introduced him to a friend by saying, "I'd like you to meet the lad who—well, he didn't exactly kill Christ —he just contracted for the lumber."

Dino isn't any more anti-Semitic than many Roman Catholics—he was simply finding it more and more difficult to conceal his hostility for Jerry.

It was also becoming harder for Dino to accept the role usually handed to him by scriptwriters. He was always the "friend of the hero's," with nothing very funny to do or say.

"I remember when I was still writing for them," recollects Cy Howard. "I'd bump into Dino on the Paramount lot, and he'd say very bitterly, 'Have you written any funny lines for me today—like, "Who's that fellow who just walked in the door?" or "Hey, you can't treat my buddy that way." ' "

It couldn't be helped. Dino had no particular character in those days (his "drunk" character wasn't to be conceived until he and Jerry broke up), so writers had a difficult time writing for him—a fact of life that Jerry, as the "take-charge guy" of the team, quickly exploited for his own benefit.

By the beginning of the 1953–1954 television season, Jerry was also usurping most of Ernie Glucksman's and Bud Yorkin's power on "The Colgate Comedy Hour." Everyone was noticing it and feeling it—not just Dino.

In a feature article covering a Martin and Lewis television rehearsal, Hal Humphrey wrote in one of the Los Angeles papers,

> A tired-looking little man by the name of Ernie Glucksman holds the title of producer for that comedy hour, but when Dean Martin and Jerry Lewis are on deck, Glucksman's job could be more accurately compared to that of a nut-house attendant who has been stripped of his authority.

A typical first rehearsal would begin with Jerry grandstanding for the cast and crew, usually at his writers' expense. He'd walk into the studio like Mr. Big Shot, pick up the script, which Simmons and Lear had labored over for weeks, and exclaim in his shrill voice, "I don't like this script."

"It stinks," Dino would say, not really meaning it but imitating his partner for lack of anything better to do.

"But," the director would start to say.

"Shut up," Jerry would scream. "Shut up when we're talking."

Glucksman would finally get them settled down around a conference table for the first reading with the cast.

"It's no good sitting around, reading words," Jerry would say, jumping up. "Let's get into a set."

"Yeah," Dino would drawl. "No use reading words. We're not going to use these words, anyway," and he'd throw his script out the window.

In the middle of a reading, Jerry would look at Simmons and Lear and shout, "I can't stand it. Those horrible faces. Out! Out! Out!"

With the aid of a couple of his stooges, Jerry would then grab Simmons and Lear by the arms and legs and shove them into the Men's Room and slam the door.

So Dean wouldn't get cocky, Jerry would then whip out a fountain pen and start playing tic-tac-toe on the sleeve of his partner's thirty-five-dollar shirt or else he'd cut off Ernie Glucksman's suspenders.

Finally, Dean would get so fed up with Jerry's horsing around that he'd finger the dark circles under his eyes and say, "I'm tired. This rehearsal has worn me out. I'm going home." He'd shuffle off and not come back possibly until Sunday at show time.

Meanwhile, Jerry would be seriously going through the script with a red pencil and saying, "This is out, and this is out, and this is out." As a final gesture of contempt, he'd perhaps touch a match to the script.

Although he was very clever in the way he concealed his disdain for the writers under a veneer of hokum, Jerry's treatment of them left little doubt about his true feelings.

It is the classic stance of most comedians to keep their writers off balance and in a subservient position so they'll never really suspect how valuable they are.

Despite this, Simmons and Lear negotiated a new seven-year contract with Martin and Lewis for the third season of "The Colgate Comedy Hour" that called for them to get what was, until then, the highest price ever paid a writing team—$10,400 a program. (Nat Hiken, the creator of "Sergeant Bilko," was getting $7500 a week on "The Martha Raye Show," and Goodman Ace was making $4,000 a week for writing the Berle program.)

Simmons and Lear were able to command such a figure only because "The Colgate Comedy Hour" had maintained high ratings and a consistently high level of comedy during the two years they had been writing it. They'd proven invaluable to Martin and Lewis in other ways too—for example, by "punching up" their movie scripts after the original authors had gone on to other assignments.

Accordingly, even though Jerry Lewis was loathe to admit to the world that he was dependent on writers, people in the trade knew differently. Simmons and Lear were in big demand—so much so that they had even been able to get a "nonexclusive" clause in their new contract with Martin and Lewis.

After the signing, items about Simmons and Lear being "television's highest-priced writers" started to appear in all the trade papers and TV columns in the daily papers. *Variety* and *Billboard* mentioned their salary and gave them headlines, and the *TV Guide* of November 27, 1953, devoted an entire editorial to them, citing how writers were finally achieving the status that they deserved in the business.

None of this publicity was by dint of sheer accident or good fortune. Simmons and Lear, as the early champions of the "TV Writers' Liberation" movement, had hired a publicity man. They felt—perhaps because of the demeaning way Jerry had been treating them—that they had as much right to be known to the public as did the stars who got laughs with *their* material.

Jerry Lewis had other ideas. He has always been the kind of a man who loves hard and hates hard. If he likes you, you're the "greatest" and will soon be loaded down with gold watches; if you dare cross him in the slightest way, you'll be on his blacklist forever. For some reason, it bugged him that Simmons and Lear, who he had started out "loving," were suddenly getting all that publicity.

One day, when Jerry was sitting in Ernie Glucksman's office, he suddenly picked up the phone, dialed Simmons's and Lear's press agent, and screeched into the mouthpiece, "This is Jerry Lewis. I have a hot news item for you. Simmons and Lear are fired!"

Jerry wasn't kidding, although Glucksman's first thought was that he had to be.

As it must to all men who have ever had anything to do with Jerry Lewis, the "love" part of their relationship was over; it was time for hate.

After banging down the receiver, Jerry turned the scriptwriting chore over to four other writers who were currently enjoying his favor—Artie Phillips, Rocky Kalish, Harry Crane, and Danny Arnold.

Then Jerry's lawyers and agents informed him that Simmons and Lear couldn't be summarily dismissed; they had an ironclad contract, and he was obligated to keep them on at $10,400 per show until their deal ran out.

Legalities have never stopped a determined Jerry Lewis bent on revenge, however. He found another way to rub Simmons's and Lear's noses in the dirt. Big Spender Jerry paid them their full $10,400 per script, but each time they turned one in, he dropped their creation into his wastebasket and used the other writers' material.

Variety ran the following news item on January 12, 1953:

MARTIN & LEWIS
BYPASS SCRIPTERS
IN EXPENSIVE FEUD

For the first time since they've headed their own show on "Comedy Hour," Dean Martin and Jerry Lewis went on the air last Sunday without material written by Norman Lear and Ed Simmons. They contributed a script as per their contract but it wasn't used.

Many versions are abroad on the reason behind the break between M & L and their writers, but the one most frequently quoted is that the comics resented an exclusive Page One story in *Daily Variety* noting the writers' precedential deal in terms of money. Understood M & L figured that made them too important and also pointed up they needed the most expensive writers in the business to hold their rated positions.

Publicly, Jerry Lewis kept announcing that all "was well" between him and Simmons and Lear and that they were "hard at work" on subsequent shows, but it simply wasn't true.

The men who made it so easy to be "great" rode out the 1953–1954 television season writing scripts for Jerry Lewis's wastebasket. They were paid in full although not until they retained the services of an attorney. Hell hath no fury like a comedian who's fallen out of love with his writers.

The January 12 story in *Variety* alluded to a fatal flaw in Jerry Lewis's character: He definitely did not want people of stature around him. They were liable to tell him what they thought, which was one of the reasons he had to get rid of Simmons and Lear.

They didn't appreciate his taking liberties with their material and frequently straying so far from the script during the actual performance that it was barely recognizable. Moreover, if Jerry lapsed into bad taste or low-comedy routines through his own bad ad-libbing, they were the ones who had to take the blame for it. This annoyed them, and they told him so.

"What's the difference? The people in the audience laughed, didn't they?" would be Jerry's attitude.

Bud Yorkin was having similar trouble in his capacity as the show's director. Jerry didn't feel he needed a director; he could tell himself how to "act" funny. "So after some unpleasantness between us," relates the soft-spoken Yorkin, "I quit the show at the end of the season and went with George Gobel."

Jerry just wouldn't listen to anybody. But the critics were listening and watching. After seeing a few bomb shows, they were beginning to fall out of love with Martin and Lewis with as much passion as they had once taken them to their hearts.

A critic for *The Hollywood Reporter* started out his review of "The Colgate Comedy Hour" by saying,

> The Martin and Lewis show that opened up the season last night should be called "The Low Comedy Hour." When they have to fall back on such crude devices as slobbering over an out-sized sandwich, wrestling around in a tub full of crushed grapes, and blowing the furniture around with an overly powerful fan—then they've either slipped badly or figure they can take these shows in their stride.

Covering the same show, *Variety* said, "Mediocre material plus an apparent lack of rehearsal resulted in a N.S.G. opening for 'The Colgate Comedy Hour.' "

Apparently Dean and Jerry—but mostly Jerry—figured they could get by with anything. In the middle of their TV season in 1953, Jerry broke his leg in a fall from a motor scooter that Dean had given him for his birthday. (Was there something Freudian in Dean giving Jerry such a dangerous plaything?) Contrary to all advice but in true show business tradition, Jerry, who was confined to crutches for several weeks, insisted that the Colgate show must go on regardless of his immobile condition.

But what kind of a show could he do if he couldn't walk? The irrepressible Jerry Lewis had it all figured out. He'd sit in a wheelchair and recall some of the "high spots" of Martin and Lewis's TV career to date, and they would run kinescopes of the same.

The "high spots" turned out to be low spots when viewed out of context, and time had eroded the freshness of much of the material. Jerry got an "A" for "courage" from the critics but flunking marks for trying to foist "reruns" on the public during prime time.

In July 1953, Dean and Jerry made a quick trip to Great Britain to pick up some extra change playing London's famed Palladium. But the staid British didn't understand their brand of uninhibited madcap humor. In addition, on opening night they had trouble with a heckler in the balcony who just wouldn't quit.

In their first bout with the British critics, Dean and Jerry came out bruised and bloodied but not tongue-tied. Before leaving London after two unprofitable weeks at the Palladium, both the mild-mannered Dino and the volatile Jerry blasted the British press. And after shocking Londoners with outbursts extremely critical of British hospitality, they repeated the same blasts once they arrived on the other side of the Atlantic aboard the French liner *Liberté*.

"They called Jerry a gargoyle and a gorilla and said he had no one to work with—meaning me," sputtered the wounded Dino as he stepped off the gangplank in New York. "We will never go back to England to work.

British critics stink—all capitals—and they have warped minds. We gave a party for the critics the day before our opening. They came and drank all our booze but didn't review our show. All they reviewed was how much money we made."

According to Jerry, he and Dean didn't make enough to cover their expenses. They made $19,600 for two weeks at the Palladium, but their eighteen-person entourage cost them $60,000.

"Jerry did some bits in Jewish dialect and I used Italian dialect, but the critics reviewed our nationality and not our show. The press didn't like us," concluded Dino in one of his most impressive outbursts of eloquence.

David Niven, who came back with Dean and Jerry aboard the *Liberté*, listened sympathetically to what Dino had to say to the New York press about his countrymen and then observed philosophically, "I say, dear chaps, you can't expect good copy because of a bottle of Scotch!"

Dean and Jerry's uncompromising stance against the British was probably the last time the pair was ever on the same side.

The trouble between them started to grow really serious following the release and success of *That's My Boy*, their fourth film for Hal Wallis and unquestionably the best the two of them ever appeared in together.

The other abrasives previously alluded to—principally the inability of their wives to get along and the critics' constant reminders that Jerry was the "important" one—certainly did nothing to cement the partnership. But their professional marriage might have survived those two obstacles if Jerry hadn't fallen victim to the Charlie Chaplin syndrome of wanting to be everything—actor, writer, director, producer, film editor, and a greater singer than Dean Martin.

Dino, in discussing the problem with Pete Martin of *The Saturday Evening Post*, speculated that it all happened because Jerry read a book on the life of Charlie Chaplin.

That's open to question because Jerry admits that the only book he's ever read in his life is Quentin Reynolds's *Courtroom*, "and the only reason he read that," according to his former close friend Don McGuire, "is that someone told him he was mentioned on page 568."

It's much more likely he started to nurture wild dreams of becoming a second Charlie Chaplin because of something actress Paulette Goddard told him during the filming of *That's My Boy*.

That's My Boy, conceived and written for the screen by Cy Howard, was a departure from the usual Martin and Lewis film fare in that it wasn't just a clothes line from which to hang a series of their old nightclub routines and gags. Its story was slight, but it had a serious underlying psychological theme. Moreover, the story required Jerry and Dean to play parts—not just themselves.

In this picture, Jerry portrayed the bespectacled and weakling son of Jarring Jack Jackson (Eddie Mayehoff), a former All American who never let his family forget it. Like many of his breed, he was determined to relive his youth again through his son's exploits on the college gridiron. But, in addition to being hopelessly overawed by his father's reputation, Jerry was unathletic and only interested in studying animal husbandry. Disappointed but unwilling to take "inability" for an answer, Jarring Jack first sent Jerry to a psychiatrist and then hired the college football star (Dean Martin) to room with him, take him under his wing, and make a second Jarring Jack out of him.

Because the part required him to mug less and to get his comedy out of the character he was supposed to be playing, Jerry didn't feel comfortable in it at first. He kept reverting to his old ways—relying on funny faces and spastic gestures.

Concerned that his very good script might be ruined by Jerry's nonstop mugging, Cy Howard, who was the film's coproducer as well as its author, used to drop into the set every day and remind Jerry between takes, "Stop making with the funny faces, Jer. Try to imagine you're really Jarring Jack's son and that you really do have an inferiority complex."

Trying to imagine himself inferior to a $750-a-week character actor wasn't an easy task for a man making $5 million a year. Jerry might never have been able to capture the pathos the part required if Cy Howard, by a strange twist of irony, hadn't been going around with Paulette Goddard, who had just broken up with Charlie Chaplin.

At the time, Howard and the curvaceous actress were seeing quite a bit of Jerry Lewis socially. Having authored *My Friend Irma* and *My Friend Irma Goes West*, Howard was still near the top of Lewis's "love" list, and he had a jewelry box of gold trinkets ("To Cy—nice guy. Gratefully, Jerry Lewis") to prove it. "He even gave me a pair of gold garters," recalls Howard. "I was so weighted down with watches and Dunhill lighters I could hardly walk."

Being familiar with Jerry's "mugging" problem on the set through her close association with Howard, Paulette Goddard took Lewis off in a corner one evening and said, "You know, you don't have to do all that mugging. You're a great talent. You're better than Charlie Chaplin."

From then on, every chance she got until *That's My Boy* was in the "can," Paulette Goddard would try to build up Jerry's confidence by comparing him with the one and only Charlie Chaplin—until finally he began to believe it.

That was good for *That's My Boy* but ruinous to the already shaky Martin and Lewis relationship.

The reviews of Martin and Lewis's fourth picture for Hal Wallis were mostly excellent, but, in the opinions of the critics, Jerry was developing into an "actor," whereas Dino was singing the same old song.

The Los Angeles Times wrote, "*That's My Boy* at the Paramount theaters is one of the funniest film comedies to screen in a long time."

The Los Angeles Herald-Express reported,

> What the boys and gals have been laughing themselves sick about in Jerry Lewis and Dean Martin now comes out in *That's My Boy*, the new Hal Wallis picture.
>
> It isn't Jerry's idiotic cutups at all. It's all tied up with something about a little guy putting up his best face against tough odds. More important, Lewis has a real character to portray and he knocks it off with conviction and consistency to make you realize all over that behind every good comedian is a good actor.

The Los Angeles Examiner said,

> Dean Martin has a few moments as the personable football hero who has been subsidized by Mayehoff to be his sickly son's chum. He sings a couple of numbers and carries on a romance with Marion Marshall, the campus cutie.
>
> But as always most of the laughs come from the antics of Jerry Lewis, who can fracture an audience by the mere lift of an eyebrow.

Although none of the critics mentioned any resemblance between Jerry and Chaplin, Jerry's behavior during the next series of Martin and Lewis films, together with the way he was comporting himself around "The Colgate Comedy Hour," indicated that he was no longer the same humble Joey Levitch who, upon being introduced to Norman Taurog by Hal Wallis as the possible director of their next picture, got down on his knees on the pavement of the Paramount lot and begged, "Say you'll do a picture with us, Mr. Director. Say you'll do it."

Taurog not only did one Martin and Lewis film, he did the next six, including *The Stooge, Don't Give Up the Ship, Jumping Jacks, The Caddy,* and *Pardners*.

"In their early days, we had a lot of fun on the set during the pictures," recalls Taurog. "We all liked to come to work in the morning. There'd be lots of gags. Jerry once sneaked up in the catwalks and tied and gagged our head electrician. If he and Dean were good and didn't fool around, I'd give them lollipops as a gag bribe. They were like a couple of kids. And then when they became partners with Paramount and made pictures on their own, I had different cards made, like the idiot cards in TV, and I'd hold them up when they started fooling around. One such card said, 'It's your money.' Then Dean would say, 'Oh, Christ, yes, let's get going.'

"Dean was a very peculiar guy. He knew his words every morning when he came in. But he did it a la Crosby. He was a lousy rehearser. He'd just mumble his way through a scene until I turned the cameras on. Then he'd be fine. He wanted to get through the scene as quickly as possible so he could get onto the golf course."

Dino was a quick study, but, like most actors, every once in a great while a certain speech or pattern of dialogue would throw him. Taurog remembers an incident that occurred, unfortunately, when a group of Catholic priests from Italy was visiting the set. Knowing Dino was both Catholic and Italian, they'd come to the studio expressly to meet him and watch him shoot.

Dino played the part of a good Catholic. He welcomed the clerics warmly, shook their hands, then stepped before the cameras to do his scene. But he couldn't get through one particularly long and complicated speech. They tried seven takes, and Dino would go up in his lines in the exact spot every time.

Finally, he took Taurog aside and whispered, "I think the men in black are inhibiting me."

"Well, we can't throw them out," explained Taurog. "They've come all the way from Rome to see you perform."

"Do you mind if I get rid of them in a nice way?" asked Dino.

"Fine," said Taurog, "Go ahead. Let's just get on with the scene."

"OK," said Dino, "let's try another take."

At the same place in the scene where he had been blowing up before, Dino again forgot his lines. But this time he glanced heavenward and exclaimed loudly, "Don't look down on me, God. I told you to help me, not destroy me."

Taurog remembers hearing the patter of feet running off in all directions. When he turned around, there wasn't a Catholic priest in sight.

Dino wasn't always so conscientious. He once went through a period when he was always falling asleep in his dressing room and failing to show up for his scenes, usually because he was bored sitting around waiting for Jerry to tell the director what to do. To teach Dino a lesson, Taurog had his dressing room towed out onto the back lot the next time he caught him napping. When he woke up, Dino was three miles away.

Jerry had his moments of not wanting to settle down to business too.

"Every once in a while, he'd come to me and say, 'Gee, Norman, I'd like tomorrow off,' " says Taurog.

"If I could rearrange the schedule and we weren't behind, I'd try to accommodate him. But if the picture wasn't going well and there was no way of shooting around him, I'd have to say no. And I really believe he had every intention of cooperating with me. But the next day—suddenly he'd wind up with a terrible stomachache. And it would be genuine, and we'd have to send for his doctor, and I really would end up giving him the day off."

If the manifestation of Jerry's many neuroses could have been confined to just an occasional display of malingering, everyone would have been a lot happier.

"In the beginning, he was a doll," says Taurog. "He listened, did what I told him to do, and didn't bother anyone. Then one day I noticed him looking through the camera between takes and starting to make suggestions to Lyle Gregg, our cameraman, on things he had no business making suggestions about: how high a crane to put the camera on, for example, or what kind of a lens to use."

"The funny part of it is," recalls one cameraman who photographed a number of Martin and Lewis films but who wishes to keep his identity a secret, "the son of a bitch really did know about lenses."

"But that wasn't the point," adds Taurog. "I used to tell him, 'For God's sakes, Jerry, why do you want to waste your energy doing things other people are getting paid for? Nobody goes to a Martin and Lewis movie because you directed a scene or because you told the cameraman what to do. They go because it says on the marquee—Jerry Lewis in so and so; not Jerry Lewis, cameraman. Save your energy for acting.' "

As often as not, considerably more than Jerry's energy was lost by his meddling; much valuable time was also wasted. A scene, for example, would be all rehearsed and blocked out, and the actors would be in their places, waiting for the director to say, "Roll 'em." Suddenly Jerry would hold up his hand and shout, "Just a minute! I've got a funnier way of doing it."

Jerry's "way" might mean that the scene would have to be reblocked and rehearsed, and the lights would have to be reset. While Jerry and the production staff would be arguing the pros and cons of such a change, Dino (who would be most anxious to get the scene over so that he could go home or to the golf course) would look at his partner in complete disgust or slump down in a director's chair and bury his nose in a comic book or fall asleep until the director called him back for a "take"—sometimes as much as two hours later. By that time, Dino would be sick of the whole scene and would "walk through it" indifferently, which accounts partly for his reputation of not being conscientious about his work during the turbulent years of his and Jerry's waning partnership.

Another major area of conflict besides Jerry's constant meddling was Dean's and Jerry's widely differing concept of comedy.

In the early days of their nightclub success, their idea of comedy was "anything for a laugh"—from squirting seltzer in a customer's face to tackling the bandleader. Jerry not only had gone along with it but had been the major perpetrator.

According to Jerry, Dean was in favor of continuing that brand of wild unmotivated comedy in their pictures. But since the success of *That's My Boy*, which contained a story with pathos as well as slapstick, Jerry was opting for a more mature kind of comedy. He used to tell Dean, "I don't think you can sustain with a pie in the face as well as you can with a puppy on your lap." In Jerry's opinion, the best comedian was a man in trouble, a tragic figure, such as Charlie Chaplin's Little Tramp character or Jarring Jack Jackson's son.

Typical of what Jerry wanted to do—and did do—was a TV skit on "The Colgate Comedy Hour" in which he played a poor slob of a fellow who joined a "friendship club." He tried so hard to make friends that everybody went out to the refreshment stand and left him alone. For the blackout, Jerry ended up dancing with a mannequin. Dean hated that bit. He kept saying to Jerry, "Why don't you cut out this sad stuff and just be funny?"

Dean didn't like that kind of comedy, but Jerry was forcing him to swallow larger and larger doses of it in their pictures.

What Dino couldn't swallow in continuing doses was something more personal to him—the way Jerry would keep trying to cut Dino's song numbers out of their pictures. As long as Dean had three or four good song spots in each picture, he was able to overlook some of the inequities regarding the size of their respective roles. If the picture ran too long, however, the first thing Jerry suggested cutting was one of Dino's prized numbers.

"He wouldn't dare broach it to Dino directly," says Norman Taurog. "He'd go through Hal Wallis, who would call me up and say, 'You know that number of Dean's in the third reel. Well, I agree with Jerry. It doesn't really advance the plot. Can't we cut it?' "

Dean would hear about it and say to Taurog, "You can't cut my song. I won't have anything to do."

Then Taurog would have to say to Wallis, "Let's leave it in at least until after the preview. Then if it's too long, we'll cut it." But it was a struggle to keep the numbers in if Jerry wanted them out.

Jerry had another way of bugging Dino. If he liked a particular song in a score, he'd say to the composer, "Hey, I like that. Why don't you let me sing that one? Dino sings enough in the picture." Jerry actually believed he could sing as well as Dino, and he was always trying to prove it.

Although Jerry's co-workers acknowledge that Jerry had some talent in many specialties besides his own, it is the honest opinion of everyone but his merry band of stooges that out of ten ideas he created, one might be absolutely brilliant and the other nine either amateurishly unfunny or else in extremely bad taste.

In one of the pictures Jerry made without Dean Martin, the authors wrote a scene in which Jerry was supposed to meet a very old lady and give her a light kiss on the forehead.

Just before Taurog, the picture's director, was ready to start the cameras rolling, Jerry approached him and said, "You know, Norman, I've got a better idea. Instead of just kissing her, I think it would be funny if I grabbed her roughly, bent her over backward, and gave her a soul kiss."

"You've got to be kidding," exclaimed Taurog.

"No, I want to give her a real soul kiss," explained Jerry, "and then I want to watch her reaction."

"It won't work," said Taurog. "People will squirm in their seats if you treat an old white-haired lady that way."

"We need something funny here," insisted Jerry. "Let me try it."

"Jerry, for God's sakes," protested Taurog, "if you want to treat her respectfully and then have something funny happen, like maybe you sit on her glasses or a mouse runs across the floor, that's one thing. But sticking your tongue down her throat—forget it. I won't shoot it."

When Taurog refused to have anything to do with the gag, Jerry took over the direction and shot the scene himself.

"Well, it was so revolting I wanted to hide under my seat during the preview," recalls Taurog. "It just lay there, and I eventually cut it out. But Jerry was convinced it was the funniest thing he'd ever thought of. After I left him and he was making pictures completely on his own, he tried it again. Again it lay there like a rotten egg, and again it was cut out. He even tried it a third time, but that scene's never made it past the cutting room floor."

Conversely, Jerry would often allow his giant-sized ego to kill a good gag or comedy situation that somebody other than himself had conceived.

One day Taurog said to Dean and Jerry, "In your next picture, Jer, I'd like you to try a 'high and dizzy.' "

"What's that?" asked Jerry.

Taurog explained that in Hollywood parlance a "high and dizzy" was the kind of scene Harold Lloyd used to specialize in for milking laughs out of an audience and keeping them on the edge of their seats.

He was referring to the kind of situation in which Lloyd would either be hanging on for dear life to the hand of a steeple clock as it slowly revolved eight stories above the street or else be edging his way along a narrow ledge outside a skyscraper window trying to escape from the heavy, or perhaps he'd be hanging from a flagpole as his trousers started to fall off.

Dean was all for trying a "high and dizzy," but Jerry shook his head negatively at the suggestion. "I don't want to do that," he said.

"We wouldn't do the exact scene," explained Taurog. "We'll get the writers to come up with a brand new twist. The only similarity would be the height and you in danger of falling off."

"I couldn't do that," insisted Jerry.

"Why not? It'll be done in process. You won't really be in any danger."

"Because it's not Jerry Lewis being funny—it's the gag!" exclaimed Jerry.

So even though Dean wanted to try it, Martin and Lewis never made a "high and dizzy."

As Jerry's ego continued to expand, he stopped consulting with Dino altogether.

"Before that," states Dino, "if he made up a sketch or a joke, he asked if I thought it was funny because he knew I wouldn't con him. I had never broken up deliberately—you know, pretending to an audience that I thought he was funny when he wasn't. When he didn't get the kind of laughs from me that a second Chaplin should have had, he began to try his stuff out on six guys we had around as court followers. You might call them professional idiots. I could say, 'My father's got pneumonia,' and they'd guffaw.

"So Jerry didn't come to me any more for my opinion. He tried out his stuff on our idiot claque. He kept those six idiots after we broke up—only it got to be more like seven or ten idiots. That kind of thing builds. The bigger genius you are, the more guys you've got to have laughing at you."

A few of the people Jerry had hanging around whom he could count on to laugh it up, regardless of what Dino or anyone else thought, were Dick Stabile, his brother Joe Stabile, Irving Kaye, actor Tommy Farrell, Mack Gray, Jack Keller, his piano player Lou Brown, and Danny Arnold.

Although he's now a successful TV writer and producer, Arnold in those days was a struggling comic with a borscht-circuit background. He was a heavyset, slightly cherubic-looking fellow, with a large nose, a gift for comedy, and an even greater gift for buttering up Jerry Lewis.

He started with Martin and Lewis doing bit parts on "The Colgate Comedy Hour" shows and in a few of their movies, but, as their need for more material increased, he worked his way up to being one of their scriptwriters. He constantly had Jerry Lewis's ear, and it is said that one of the reasons Jerry liked him so much was his unswerving willingness to do anything Jerry asked of him.

One day during a story conference that writer Artie Phillips attended, Jerry got into an argument with Arnold over who was the best golfer. Golf was the one area in which Arnold felt superior to his boss, and when he voiced skepticism over Jerry's ability, Jerry said, "I'll bet I can hit a golf ball out of your mouth."

Jerry didn't have much golfing ability. In fact, the only reason he played was because Dean did, and he certainly couldn't be trusted to hit a golf ball off a human tee. Even a Jack Nicklaus will leave that kind of sport to the men who specialize in "trick" golf shooting.

But Arnold didn't have the courage to say no to Jerry. He dropped to the floor and let Jerry tee up in his mouth. Jerry then took a very professional-looking swing, missed the ball, and hit Arnold on the side of the neck with his club with such force that he knocked him out cold. When Arnold came to, he simply smiled groggily, got to his feet, and went on with the story conference.

Not satisfied with being a golf tee, Arnold sat down at a typewriter one day and, on a half page of paper, typed out an idea for a Martin and Lewis film.

All he had was a germ of a story. Jerry would play a caddy and, naturally, screw everything up. He called it *The Caddy* and handed it to Jerry, who flipped for the idea and gave it to Don Hartman, Paramount's production chief, saying, "This is our next picture. I want you to buy it for York Productions."

By that time—1952—MCA had negotiated a deal for Martin and Lewis with Paramount whereby they would, under their York Productions banner, make one independent picture a year for their own company in addition to the two they were tied down to do with Hal Wallis. Paramount would do most of the financing; Martin and Lewis would have a token salary and a percentage of the profits.

Paramount had final approval of any property Martin and Lewis chose to make. Since there was virtually nothing to Danny Arnold's story except the idea of Jerry Lewis playing a "funny" caddy and absolutely no part for Dean Martin, Hartman turned the property down.

This infuriated the volatile Jerry, who was just beginning to feel the power of his position as a star whose pictures were able to break box office records in an otherwise dwindling marketplace and whom Paramount needed more than Martin and Lewis needed Paramount.

So Jerry lashed back and said, "Either I make *The Caddy* or I won't make any more pictures for Paramount." He walked off the lot and remained incommunicado until Paramount changed its collective mind.

After two weeks elapsed, with no indication that Jerry was going to be reasonable about his ultimatum, Don Hartman called in two veteran writers he had under contract—Ed Hartmann and Hal Kanter—showed them Danny Arnold's half a page, and told them to see if they could whip up a feature-length film out of "this cockamamie idea."

Despite Danny Arnold's harassing remarks that they were ruining his "masterpiece," the two screenwriters finally managed to concoct an original story that could conceivably serve as the basis for a Martin and

Lewis picture. Paramount okayed it and told the writers to start work on the screenplay.

Since *The Caddy* was for Jerry's own company, Hartmann and Kanter had to deal mostly with Jerry during the nine weeks they were writing the screenplay.

Every day Jerry would burst into their office on the Paramount lot and make the same speech: "Don't worry about my comedy. I'll take care of that. What I've got to get is a great part for Dean Martin. I'm here to protect him."

He'd then sit down, read as much of the screenplay as they had completed up to that point, make several suggestions to build up his own part, and cut out something they'd written for Dean.

"Finally," says Hartmann, "Dean's part wound up as just a walk-on with about four songs."

Dean, meanwhile, never came around the studio to see just how his partner was "protecting him." Nobody ever saw him until the first day of shooting.

"By then Jerry was into everything, from telling the cameraman where to place his camera to giving Walter Scharf advice on what kind of orchestral arrangements to make," recollects songwriter Harry Warren, who'd been hired by Paramount to compose all of Dean's songs for the picture. "While Jerry was doing everything, Dean would just sit around and sulk."

One of the things Dino was sulking about during the making of *The Caddy* was the song "That's Amore," which Warren had composed for a certain spot in the picture that seemed to call for Dino to sing an Italian-type ballad.

Since Warren was not only one of America's top popular song writers (Double-A ASCAP and thrice a winner of Academy Award Oscars) but also an Italian, he had no trouble writing an Italian love song. He knocked off the little tune called "That's Amore" and proudly played it for Dino at the studio one day.

But Dino, who's never been crazy about learning anything new, told Warren he didn't like it. Besides, if he had to do a Neapolitan love song, why not go with his old standby, "Oh, Marie"? But the studio objected to that. After all, they weren't paying Harry Warren a bundle of money to write a score so that Dino could sing a standard he'd been doing since his Copa days with Jerry.

Under studio pressure, Dean agreed to sing "That's Amore" in *The Caddy*, but he stubbornly refused to record it for Capitol Records, feeling it wasn't worthy of his talents. Why Dino had such a lofty idea of his singing ability, nobody could quite understand. The critics still regarded him as just an ersatz Crosby, and he'd never made a hit platter, although he'd recorded plenty.

The studio wanted a record made of "That's Amore," however, for exploitation purposes, so they gave Capitol Records the right to take the platter directly off the picture sound track.

As proof of what a great judge of song material Dino was in those days, his recording of "That's Amore" was his first hit after seven years of trying. It sold more than 2 million records and was nominated for an Academy Award. "That's Amore" didn't win an Oscar in the final balloting, but it was responsible for making Dean Martin one of America's most popular singers, with an income completely independent of Jerry Lewis's and an identity all his own.

So despite his own poor judgment, he was, once again, Dean Martin, the solo performer—not the jerk who stood off to one side at the microphone and tried to get a line in every now and then if his partner would let him.

Jeanne and Dean Martin arriving at the Chinese Theater in Hollywood for the premiere of *West Side Story*, 1961. (*Wide World Photos*)

Dean, Jeanne, Patti, and Jerry arriving at a Hollywood party, May 1956. (*Wide World Photos*)

Jerry Lewis and wife Patti walk toward the Forum (not shown) from the Colosseum, during a brief vacation sightseeing tour in Rome, 1953. (*Wide World Photos*)

Jerry cautions his wife Patti not to forget her umbrella as he sees her off at La Guardia. (*Photo by Pictorial Parade*)

Jerry practicing his 16-mm. wizardry on subjects Ronnie, Patti, and Gary in the Lewis's Pacific Palisades backyard in the early 1950s. (*Photo by Pictorial Parade*)

Gary, Patti, Jerry, and Ronnie in their Pacific Palisades home. (*Photo by Pictorial Parade*)

Jerry and Patti with sons Ronnie, 5, and Gary, 10, arrive in New York by train from California, 1955. (*United Press International Photo*)

Jerry Lewis and family in 1965. First row, left to right: Scott Anthony, Christopher Joseph, baby Joseph Christopher, Patti, and Anthony Joseph. Second row, left to right: Ronnie, Jerry Lewis, and Gary. (*Wide World Photos*)

Jerry Lewis, 1965 national chairman of the Muscular Dystrophy Association, holds two-year-old Paul Hawkins, son of Mr. and Mrs. Robert Hawkins of Dillon, Montana, in Hollywood. Paul was named national poster child for the 1965 muscular dystrophy campaign. (*Wide World Photos*)

Fiftieth wedding anniversary party given in Hollywood in 1964 by Dean Martin for his parents, Mr. and Mrs. Guy Crocetti. Members of the Martin family are, back row, from left to right: son Craig, Jeanne, daughters Claudia and Deana, Mr. and Mrs. Crocetti, daughter Gail, Dean Martin, and son Dino. Front row: son Ricci and daughter Gina. (*Wide World Photos*)

Bing Crosby watches guest star Dean Martin's comedy antics in a scene from "Bing Crosby—Cooling It," on NBC-TV in 1970. (*Wide World Photos*)

Dean sports Afro wig in scene from "The Dean Martin Show," 1971. (*Wide World Photos*)

Dean Martin poses with new bride Catherine Mae Hawn at their wedding reception, Beverly Hills Hotel, 1973. (*Wide World Photos*)

Olivia Hussey and husband Dino Martin with Gina Martin at wedding reception for Dean and Cathy. (*Photo by Darlene Hammond*)

Left to right: Olivia Hussey, Nikki Mintz, Ricci Martin, and Dino Martin at reception. (*Photo by Darlene Hammond*)

Deana Martin with Mark
Landon at Dean's wedding.
(*Photo by Darlene
Hammond*)

Gail Martin with husband
Paul Polina at reception.
(*Photo by Darlene
Hammond*)

17

If Ever I Would Leave You

By the summer of 1954, newspaper feature writers and show business gossip columnists were spreading the word that all was not well within the Martin and Lewis entertainment factory.

Opinion was divided as to the exact nature of the trouble. Some said it was simply because Dino didn't want to work as hard as Jerry, and they cited several instances of Dino's being out on the golf course when he should have been in the television studio rehearsing.

Others were sure it was because their wives weren't getting along: A story in *The New York Enquirer* alluded to a Hollywood party at which the hostess remarked to Jeanne that Dean "would be nowhere if it weren't for Jerry." Patti seconded the motion, and Jeanne retaliated with some very salty aggressive language.

A magazine article reported that at another party when the Martins and Lewises were forced into each other's company, Dean had insulted Patti by uttering certain innuendos concerning Patti's morals *before* she had met Jerry. This exchange of insults allegedly ended up in fisticuffs between Dean and Jerry in front of a large group of Hollywood celebrities.

Of course, there was the most persistent rumor of all—that Dino simply resented Jerry's playing "big shot" on Dino's valuable time.

One thing is known for sure: Dino was fed up with being Jerry Lewis's partner and was beginning to have dreams of a free and independent life—a life in which he could make one picture a year, record a couple of songs, and spend the rest of his time on the golf course.

But Dino wouldn't have even dared to consider the idea of splitting with his dynamic partner if "That's Amore" hadn't turned into a Gold Platter recording.

Once "That's Amore" reached the top of the charts, however, well-meaning friends, heads of studios, and executives of rival record companies started filling Dean's ears with all kinds of fantasies.

"What do you need Jerry Lewis for?"

"You should be a leading man."

"You could be another Frank Sinatra or Perry Como without him."

"Get rid of Idiot Boy, and you'll be playing romantic leads in movies."

"You're good enough to have your own television show, where you'll be the boss, and you can sing all you want and what you want."

"You can concentrate on records. There's plenty more where 'That's Amore' came from."

Although Dean didn't take these siren songs too seriously at first, they did put him in a susceptible frame of mind and started him thinking that perhaps he *was* good enough to be a success on his own.

Basically, Dean is a very vain man; he wouldn't be an actor if he weren't. Not only isn't his nose his God-given one, but twice he's been operated on by a Beverly Hills plastic surgeon to have the bags under his eyes removed. He dyes his hair, and he pays Tom Stasinis, a Beverly Hills tailor, approximately $600 apiece to make his suits to order.

Jerry is no dummy, however. He was perfectly aware of what people were telling Dean behind his back and therefore couldn't be blamed if he wasn't overjoyed about Dean's sudden prominence as a solo performer. He viewed it as a very real threat to his own security. Even though he was pretty vain himself and regarded Jerry Lewis as the important one in the act, he still felt he needed Dino.

Despite his ambivalence, he was instinctively aware that there was a mysterious catalytic reaction at work when the two of them were performing together that made them a whole that was greater than the sum of its parts—therefore, the conciliatory, almost grandstanding gestures he made from time to time, such as telling their writers he was there "to protect Dean's part" and to keep in mind that they were "two comics" and not "a comic and a straight man."

Jerry had to remain "top dog" of the team in order to bolster his own security, however; for if Dean should slip out of his grasp, it was important for the world to know that it was Jerry Lewis who was the major talent and the one responsible for their huge success.

Because of Dean's and Jerry's many ambivalent feelings about each other and their respective careers—plus their many insecurities—they were not quite ready yet to go their separate ways.

Even if they chose to sever their partnership, they were constrained from doing so because all of Martin and Lewis's commitments with NBC,

Hal Wallis, and Paramount called for them to perform "together." If they split, they would be breaking up a combine capable of grossing $20 million a year for their various employers. No employer in his right mind was going to let them wiggle out of that just because they couldn't get along personally. After all, even Dean said in a story in *Time* about their difficulties, "What's the difference if we don't chum around? To me, this isn't a love affair. This is big business."

In some ways, their case could be likened to a husband and wife who hate each other but can't get a divorce because their finances and combined holdings are too intertwined. So they go on living together, but in misery—each secretly hoping to escape but not quite having the nerve or the know-how to take the initiative on his or her own.

Because they were miserable, Dino and Jerry started to vent their hatred for each other on one of the people responsible for keeping them together because he had them under contract—Hal Wallis.

Dean and Jerry had long been dissatisfied with their deal with Hal Wallis, even though he had raised their price from $50,000 to $75,000 per picture since he had originally signed them. But Wallis is a tough business man. He had no intention of bettering the terms. They were stuck with $75,000 a picture until the contract ran out.

While their next picture was still in the talking stage, Dean and Jerry sent their agent, Herman Citron, in to see Wallis to have another go at getting their deal improved. When Wallis remained adamant, Citron said that Dean and Jerry wouldn't report for work.

"They'll report or they'll go to jail," said Wallis, and he practically threw the agent out of his office.

Perhaps to pacify them, however, Wallis sent for Don McGuire to write the next Martin and Lewis picture. In addition to being one of Jerry's closest friends, McGuire had acquired quite a few screen credits since writing Jerry's first home movie, *How to Smuggle a Hernia Across the Border*. One of them was a Sinatra picture, *Meet Danny Wilson*, which Wallis had seen and liked.

When Wallis asked McGuire if he had any ideas for a Martin and Lewis picture, McGuire nodded and told him a notion he had that evolved from something he had read in the newspaper—that it was possible to study lion taming under the GI Bill of Rights.

The very idea of Jerry Lewis's studying lion taming under the GI Bill of Rights broke up the normally hard-to-please Wallis, and he immediately assigned McGuire to write a story around that premise.

McGuire spent several weeks developing the idea into a story, which he called *Three Ring Circus*. In it, Jerry would play a clown who wanted to be a lion tamer, and Dean would portray a sharpshooter-con man around The Big Top.

When it was completed, Wallis sent McGuire out to Jerry's house to check the story line with him before proceeding with his screenplay. As McGuire recalls it, the scene between him and Jerry went something like this:

"Jerry, I'm here to tell you the story for your next picture for Wallis," said McGuire.

"Why do you want to work for that schmuck?" asked Jerry, showing absolutely no interest in the idea at all.

"Because he's paying me good money," replied McGuire. "And it's a good job. And I'd like to write it for you, so don't be a putz."

"Well, we're not going to work for the old bastard anymore," Jerry informed him. "We're not going to show up."

When McGuire reported the results of his meeting to Wallis, the producer remained unruffled. "Just go ahead and write your screenplay," he told him. "They'll show up."

While McGuire was working on his screenplay, Jerry and Dean avoided any further contact with Hal Wallis. To show Wallis how they felt, however, they dropped into the studio from time to time and decorated the walls of the corridor outside Wallis's office with childlike graffiti. In dark crayon, they scribbled such memorable lines as "Hal Wallis is a putz" or "Hal Wallis is a cheapskate." Once they drew a large picture of Wallis sitting on a toilet and captioned it, "King Hal sitting on his throne."

On this promising note, Don McGuire finished his screenplay of *Three Ring Circus* and turned it in to Hal Wallis. Wallis approved and sent copies to Dean and Jerry.

Dean and Jerry phoned Wallis back several days later and said they weren't going to do *Three Ring Circus*. They were turning it down. It meant nothing to them that contractually they didn't have "script approval" privileges.

Wallis immediately sent for Herman Citron and asked him, "What's the trouble?"

"They just don't want to make it," replied Citron cagily.

During the next few weeks, there were a series of peace talks between Wallis and Citron, but both sides refused to compromise. Finally, Wallis stopped negotiating and went right ahead with his preparations to make the picture by hiring Joe Pevney to direct and Zsa Zsa Gabor and Elsa Lanchester to costar, having sets built, and selecting a location site, which was to be the winter headquarters of the Clyde Beatty Circus in Phoenix, Arizona.

On the day before the picture was scheduled to begin shooting in Phoenix, Wallis received a phone call from Dean and Jerry, saying they would like to come in and tell him what was wrong with the script. Wallis said, "Fine," and invited Herman Citron and Don McGuire to attend the meeting too.

(It's important to note here that McGuire had tried something unusual in the construction of *Three Ring Circus*—unusual, that is, for a Martin and Lewis picture. Instead of introducing them to the audience the first time in tandem, McGuire had devoted the first twenty pages to developing Jerry's character separately and the next twenty to developing Dean's character alone. The two characters met in the story for the first time on page forty.)

Promptly at the appointed hour, Dean and Jerry walked into Wallis's office with Herman Citron.

"OK, boys," demanded Wallis. "Tell me what you don't like about the script."

"We don't like it because we're not together soon enough," said Jerry.

"That's right, baby," echoed Dean. "We're supposed to be partners. We want to be together."

Here were two fellows who were barely speaking to each other, but in their mutual cause against Wallis they were now saying that the only reason they didn't want to do the picture was because they weren't together in it enough.

"You mean, you don't meet soon enough in the script—that's all that's holding up the thing?" asked Wallis.

"You bet your ass, baby," said Dino. "We don't meet until page forty."

"OK," said Wallis, picking up the script and riffling through the first twenty pages. "Here's twenty pages of Jerry doing his schtick, and here's twenty pages of Dean alone doing his schtick." In one quick movement, Wallis tore out the first forty pages of the script. "Now you've MET!" he roared at the two of them. "Be on the set tomorrow morning in Phoenix at 9:00 sharp."

"But—" protested Citron.

"That's it, Herman," yelled Wallis. "Otherwise I file suit."

Having failed in their gambit to break their contract, Dean and Jerry were stuck with each other, at least through the making of *Three Ring Circus*—but they didn't have to like it.

Between the meeting in Wallis's office and the first day of shooting, Don McGuire did some doctoring on his script to give Dean and Jerry entrances more to their liking. But that didn't cure their resentment of each other nor what was wrong with most Martin and Lewis scripts (at least from Dino's point of view); namely, that it was Jerry's part that usually carried the plot line, whereas Dino seemed to be around only to sing a few songs.

From the start there was trouble under The Big Top in Phoenix. Despite McGuire's doctoring of the script, there was hardly any work for Dino to do during the first two weeks in Phoenix.

As Dino later recalled, "There was no sense of me being in that picture at all. The picture was on thirty-five minutes before I sang one song. Then it was an old one, 'It's a Big, Wide, Wonderful World,' and I sang it to animals."

The director of the picture, Joe Pevney, had hired a couple hundred local townspeople to play the audience in the circus scenes. They were usually watching Jerry perform with the lions; Dino was generally waiting in the wings somewhere. One day, a scene called for Dean too. When he appeared, some of the extras in the bleachers made derisive comments to him:

"Hey, Dean, where have you been?"

"Say, you must have a big part in this picture."

"Are you still Jerry Lewis's partner?"

That evening, Dean was sitting in his motel room, thumbing through a magazine, when he came across a publicity picture taken during the filming of *Living It Up*, the previous Martin and Lewis movie. Dean remembered that the original photograph had shown the sexy blond bombshell, Sheree North, posed between Dean and Jerry. But the editors of the magazine had cropped Dean out of the picture altogether, and now it was just a shot of Jerry and Miss North.

A further blow to Dean's ego came the next afternoon, when he was out behind the circus tent between takes swinging his golf club. Practicing his golf swing was how he usually worked off nervous energy when he was waiting to go before the cameras. Paramount had even put a putting green on the studio lot for him.

Suddenly, a group of twelve-year-olds came running around the corner of the tent, spotted Dean, and ran up to him. "Hey, mister, where's Jerry Lewis?" asked one of the kids.

The mother of one of the child actors in the picture happened to be standing there at the time. She recalls that she's never seen such a disturbed look on anyone's face as she saw on Dino's when he was asked that question.

"Who the hell cares?" he muttered, looking as if he'd like to wrap his driver around the little darling's neck.

The climax of Dean's resentment came a couple of mornings later, when the embittered Italian strolled into Jerry's dressing room and found a still photographer taking a magazine layout of Jerry alone.

It was ulcer time in Dean Martin's stomach. "Hey, Jerry, what am I around here—a fifth wheel?" he muttered. "If I'm not important to the act anymore, just let me know."

Dean stormed out, and for nine days the two refused to speak to each other.

"I'm fed up with my partner's sensitivity," cried Jerry. "Everything I do is wrong. Anything happens to me he don't like, he blames it on me. He hates me. He's always got a chip on his shoulder."

When Joe Pevney tried to get them to make up, Dino would holler, "I'm sick and tired of playing stooge to that crazy mixed-up character," and he'd walk away and continue sulking.

Because they weren't speaking, the picture started to suffer. The people who had the largest stake in their careers—their agents, business managers, lawyers, and producers—became so worried that they called a truce conference after the *Three Ring Circus* company returned to Los Angeles to resume shooting on the Paramount lot.

The truce parley, at which the facts of Dean's and Jerry's financial life were once again explained to them, took place at the Beverly Hills branch of MCA on March 12, 1954. So many people attended the meeting that they didn't know whether to hold it at MCA or at the Los Angeles Coliseum.

As they say in Washington, the main thrust of that meeting was to inform Dean and Jerry that it would be suicidal to their careers to split up with so much money on the line. In addition to their obligation to make three more pictures for Hal Wallis, they were about to sign a new six-picture deal between Paramount and their own York Productions over the next five years, at the end of which they would each receive $2.5 million clear. Moreover, they still had three years to go with NBC, another year to go on their Colgate contract, and a further commitment still in the talking stage for York Productions to produce thirty-nine hourly Sunday TV shows, five of which they'd have to star in personally.

Dino and Jerry emerged from the meeting all smiles and issued a statement for the press that they were not going to split up. But, according to author Don McGuire, the two of them "walked through" the rest of the picture—"Dean with even more indifference than he usually did."

Close friends of both couples insist that another factor besides money figured in their strange détente, which was more like an armed truce.

At the height of Dean's and Jerry's discord, Patti Lewis's mother passed away. Patti and her mother had been extremely close. In fact, Mrs. Coloniko had been living with the Lewises in their Pacific Palisades home since the early days of their Hollywood success. When they were away, she took care of their kids. When she died, Patti was completely broken up. This affected Jerry emotionally too, and he found it difficult to work.

Despite past difficulties between the two women, Jeanne and Dean rallied to the Lewises' aid and spent a lot of time with them, giving them emotional support, until the Lewises recovered from their bereavement.

They even attended the unveiling of a statue in memory of Mrs. Coloniko in the Lewises' backyard.

"I couldn't have gone through it without Dean," Jerry confessed to a friend at the time. "Outside of my wonderful wife, Dean is the person I've been closest to in my whole life."

As far as the public knew, Dean and Jerry were bosom buddies again.

In a between-the-takes interview on the set of *Three Ring Circus* the last day of shooting, Dean told author Maurice Zolotow:

"Listen, I want to be honest with you. If people would only leave us alone, my partner and I wouldn't have any trouble. Sure, we had a blow-up in Phoenix. I guess you'd say it was kind of rough. But we've had them before. Do you know any two people who work together who don't have their arguments?

"If Jerry and I were in the hardware business or operating a hamburger-and-root-beer joint on Ventura Boulevard, nobody would be interested in any little argument we might have. But because we're two actors, I guess it's big news.

"Now, you write down this part word for word just like I say it. I know that individually, going it alone, we would not be as great as we are together. When we shook hands on our partnership, I said in my heart, this is forever, till death do us part. It still goes!"

Money makes strange bedfellows.

18

The Man Who Got Away

In the wake of their uneasy truce, Dean and Jerry appeared in four more pictures for Paramount and/or Hal Wallis in rapid succession: *Artists and Models,* in which Shirley MacLaine made her screen debut at the age of nineteen; *You're Never Too Young,* a remake of a Ginger Rogers film, *The Major and the Minor*; *Pardners,* a remake of *Rhythm on the Range,* an old Bing Crosby starrer; and last but least, *Hollywood or Bust,* which was more bust than Hollywood.

None of these films made motion picture history, for Dean's and Jerry's writers were coming up with fewer and fewer variations on the same theme—although they were successful after a fashion. There was a ready-made audience for most Martin and Lewis pictures, and if they were produced for a "price" ($500,000 or less), they could be counted upon to turn a healthy profit.

Artists and Models, however, wound up costing Hal Wallis $1.5 million. No Martin and Lewis movie could be profitable if it was brought in at those figures, least of all at a time when their popularity was slightly on the wane at movie box offices.

Wallis blamed most of the rise in production costs not on inflation but on Jerry Lewis's ever-increasing tendency (or was it a disease) to meddle in other people's departments. His suggestions held up production and threw the crew, director, and cast into constant turmoil.

Through all this, the rumors persisted that Dean and Jerry were again not getting along. And the rumors were correct. For, despite proclaiming their love for each other publicly, Dean and Jerry were barely speaking during the period it took them to sweat out their last four films for Paramount.

Periodically they made up—usually when they were off by themselves on the road making nightclub appearances and away from the disturbing influences of their wives, who were pushing not for a permanent settlement but for a split.

"Whether a woman wants to or not, she usually can cause more problems between two men than anything else," admits Jeanne Martin, who in that respect is willing to accept part of the responsibility for their feuding.

But, on the road, Dean and Jerry could thrash out their difficulties by themselves and return to their earlier close relationship.

In a period of eight months, Dean and Jerry finished two movies and also completed an arduous road trip involving nightclub and theater appearances. Jerry knocked himself out clowning madly from morning until night, trying to revive his old relationship with Dean.

But he was working too hard at it, and when they returned from the road in September 1954, Jerry collapsed from fatigue, wound up with a bad case of yellow jaundice, and had to be confined to his home for thirty-four days.

This resulted in Dean's and Jerry's having to cancel a television program, which cost NBC over $1 million in sponsor commitments. An engagement to play Ciro's was kept, but with Dino carrying on alone—well, almost alone.

When Dean heard that Jerry was seriously ill, with 104° temperature, he forgot their feud, rushed out to Jerry's bedside, took one look at Jerry, and said, "You stay right here. It will be all right—I hope."

That evening, Dean stood up at the mike in the celebrity-jammed Ciro's and, for the first time in many years, faced an audience all by himself.

"I wouldn't give this spot to the cleaners," he said, with a nervous but disarming grin.

But he didn't have to be nervous. The place was filled with some of the greatest names in show business—Jack Benny, Sammy Davis, Jr., George Burns, and Tony Martin—and they all had the greatest empathy for Dino's position. Everybody pitched in and did separate turns, substituting for the ailing Jerry.

Dino was such a smash that Jerry sent him a wire after the opening:

DO YOU KNOW HOW GREAT WE WERE LAST NIGHT? WE WERE WONDERFUL. THANK YOU. YOUR PARTNER. JERRY.

Tony Martin stayed on with Dino for the remainder of the engagement, and the two of them billed themselves as "Martin and Martin."

Tony Martin was no Jerry Lewis, however. By the end of the two-week engagement, Dino was very much aware that he still needed Jerry beside him at the mike.

Jerry was given an opportunity to repay Dean in full, and he did—by helping Dean and Jeanne get back together after they'd had the first serious rift of their marriage.

Jerry and Patti were about to take off for Hawaii when the phone rang. It was Dean, who said, "Jeanne and I have just split up. I'm in pretty bad shape."

Jerry didn't know what to do, but Patti solved the problem for him. "Go to your other wife," she said. "He needs you."

So the Lewises canceled their trip, and Jerry went to Carmel, California, with Dean.

Ironically, the breakup was over the Martin and Lewis partnership. Jeanne wanted to know how long Dino was going to go on letting Jerry run the partnership. She pressed her husband to make the break before it was too late. Didn't he have a mind of his own?

Dean reacted like the man who calls his own relatives all kinds of names but can't stand to hear anybody else say anything bad about them. He promptly took Jerry's side, claiming the "take-over" was as much his fault as it was Jerry's. After all, he'd been lazy about doing certain things, so he'd allowed Jerry to assume the responsibilities. Someone had to do it, and if it made Jerry happy, let him. It had just gotten a little out of hand. The upshot of this argument was that Dean lost his temper and walked out on Jeanne.

Eventually, Dean and Jeanne resolved their difficulties, and Dino credited Jerry with a big assist.

Another time that Jerry helped solidify the ailing partnership was on the occasion of the annual Share party.

Share, Inc., is an organization dedicated to the business of raising money for retarded children. It is run by the wives of important people in the film colony—Mrs. Billy Wilder, Mrs. Mike Franks, Mrs. Sammy Cahn—and every year they put on a benefit for the fund and charge a lot of money to get in, which people don't seem to mind paying because the quality of the entertainment is so good.

All the superstars in the business—Frank Sinatra, Danny Thomas, Barbra Streisand, Sammy Davis, Jr., in fact, whoever is in town—make their high-priced talents available for nothing to help out Share. The women in the organization contribute by performing in the chorus line, which over the years has included such names as Debbie Reynolds, Janet Leigh, Lucille Ball, and Rosalind Russell.

Jeanne was very active in the organization and, as a result, persuaded Dino to emcee the show one year. Dino was understandably frightened. Because of his long ordeal of working in Jerry's shadow, he still didn't have much confidence in his ability as a solo performer. He asked Jerry to emcee the benefit with him. Jerry agreed but pulled out a few hours before, when he learned that Abbey Greshler and his wife (who was also active in the Share organization) would be there. Jerry had never forgiven Greshler for getting him into his financial woes. Dino, however, can't hold a grudge for very long and was still on speaking terms with Greshler.

This was something Jerry couldn't understand, and it always led to sharp words between him and Dino. In the case of the Share party, the sharp words were simply, "I won't appear if that bum's going to be there."

Again a badly prepared Dino had to sweat through the ordeal of stepping up to the mike to face the large gathering of celebrities by himself. But just as Dino opened his mouth to speak, Jerry came dancing out of the wings to help him. The show went on and was a big hit.

This give-and-take relationship stopped at about the same time their partnership was running into serious obstacles.

Dino is not an uncharitable man. Although he would rather have been on the golf course or in a nightclub, Dino participated in many of Jerry's early telethons for muscular dystrophy. But as their relationship deteriorated, Dino demonstrated considerable reluctance to give up his personal life and appear for nothing every time Jerry felt like putting on another benefit for his "very own disease." Perhaps Dino felt, as many people were beginning to suspect, that although the cause itself was worthwhile, Jerry—the eternal ham—might have been using muscular dystrophy for his own personal aggrandizement, at least just a little.

Jerry personally took credit for raising the entire cost of a multimillion-dollar building for the Institute for Muscle Disease in New York City. He would travel anywhere, any time, to receive a scroll or a plaque from a charitable organization thanking him for his "unselfishness" in donating his time to the cause. At least once a year he took out a full-page ad in *Variety* and other publications—usually showing a large picture of Jerry Lewis with his arms around a crippled child in a wheelchair. Over this would be a banner caption in bold type reading,

THANKS, JERRY LEWIS

It was enough to bring tears to the eyes of everyone but Dino, who, more and more, refused to go along with anything Jerry was connected with—sometimes out of pure orneriness.

The final thing to which Dino registered strong objections was the world premier of *You're Never Too Young*, which was scheduled to take place in June 1955 at Brown's Hotel in the Catskills. It was the same Brown's where Jerry had got his start as a busboy, and he still had a soft spot in his heart for the place, even though his former bosses, Charles and Lillian Brown, had once fired him for wanting to quit toting dishes to go into show business with his record act.

You're Never Too Young was one of the pictures Jerry and Dino had made for Paramount under their independent setup, York Productions.

Usually Paramount favored lavish out-of-town premieres for Martin and Lewis films, with the stars themselves making personal appearances. But because *You're Never Too Young* had gone considerably over budget —the final figure on that one was about $2.5 million—Paramount had become slightly chintzy about where to hold the premiere. They were in favor of holding it someplace close, like in Ralph's Market.

When Charlie and Lillian Brown offered to pick up the tab for the whole press junket if *You're Never Too Young* premiered at their resort, Paramount jumped at the idea and started making elaborate preparations. Not only would it be an excellent publicity gimmick to premiere at the place where "Jerry Lewis got his start," but it would save money for the studio.

Being highly sentimental, Jerry fell in love with the idea. It's never been clearly established whether it was Jerry's idea to begin with. Circumstances rather suggest that it was. From the way Dino reacted, however, it was obvious that he thought Jerry had put Paramount or the Browns up to the idea, and he immediately objected on the grounds that he, as a full partner in York Productions, should have been consulted about where the opening was to take place.

Jerry told Dino that he thought Paramount had cleared the idea with him; Dino replied that they had not. Jerry, who had suddenly turned astute businessman, then informed Dino that holding the premiere at Brown's Hotel was a great way to save money for their own company. Dino's reply was, "When our company spends $2.5 million on a picture—which I think is too much—you don't have to pinch for a premiere."

Suspecting that Dino's feelings were hurt, the sensitive Jerry offered to hold the premiere in Dean's home town—Steubenville, Ohio. Dean replied that he didn't want to go to Steubenville either. "Let's take it to a nice neutral place—like we did last year," he suggested. "There are plenty of neutral places to go."

When Jerry refused to compromise, Dean blew up and said he didn't care where they held the premiere. He was too tired to go on a publicity junket anyway. Instead, he was taking Jeanne to Honolulu for a long overdue vacation as soon as they finished the picture.

Nobody, including Jerry, believed the normally tractable Dino would stick to his word. But when the time came for Jerry and Patti and all their kids to board the train taking them, the press corps, the cast, and the studio executives east, Dino was on a plane bound for Honolulu with his wife.

The opening ceremonies—played against the dramatic backdrop of Brown's Hotel in the Catskills on a summer evening—found a bereft and misty-eyed Jerry Lewis carrying on the burden of the entertainment alone, but bravely, in front of a large gathering of hotel guests, Paramount brass, and the nation's press.

At one point he broke down and wept real tears and had to ask Patti to step to the mike and sing a song with him because he wasn't used to "going it by myself."

The audience listened to his schmaltzy closing remarks, punctuated with enough platitudes to keep a political convention supplied for the next century. In hushed silence, he spoke haltingly of his "problem," of his "heavy heart," and of his tremendous "cross to bear." All he needed to make the scene complete was to have beside him a crippled child in a wheelchair, kissing the hem of his $400 Sy Devore dinner jacket.

In all fairness to Jerry, he missed Dean's support and suffered true anxiety when he was jilted by him. During the junket to Brown's, Jerry rarely spoke of anything except how he felt that Dean had let him down. And his talk was tinged with unaccustomed bitterness that didn't bode too well for the survival of the team.

But when *You're Never Too Young*, which was written by Sidney Sheldon—an Oscar-winning screenwriter—turned out to be one of the funniest pictures they had ever made, even in the opinion of the critics, there was renewed optimism about the team's future. After all, Dean and Jerry had been on the verge of a split before and made up, so, in light of the success of their latest picture, everybody was confident that, after they cooled off separately in different parts of the globe, they would get back together again, if only to fill their mutual needs.

But when the feuding pair returned to Hollywood, the situation seemed to have worsened. Dean was going around telling all his friends that he'd rather work for $100 a week in a two-bit nightclub than have to go back to being Jerry Lewis's partner; and he wasn't speaking to Jerry at all, and vice versa. The only communicating the two of them were doing was through their various agents and business managers or by letter through their attorneys.

Then, just when it looked as if the relationship really was kaput, Jerry received a letter from Dean. It was a legal letter, written in the cold formal phrasing one invariably finds in the language of attorneys. The gist of it was that since they were bound by contract to make another film for Paramount, Mr. Martin would obey the terms of the contract. It closed, "Sincerely yours, Dean Martin."

Evidently the harsh realities of how much it was costing Dino to live on the grand scale he and Jeanne had grown accustomed to had changed his mind about working in some gin mill in preference to being Jerry Lewis's partner.

It wasn't so much that he didn't have confidence in his ability to carry on as a single. After all, he'd just come up with a second hit record, "Memories Are Made of This," which sold another million platters for Capitol. In addition, Joe Pasternak, who produced many of MGM's most important musicals, had made tentative inquiries as to Dino's availability to appear by himself in a new film called *Ten Thousand Bedrooms*.

But Dino had tremendous financial obligations that even a couple of hit records and a possible job at MGM couldn't reduce.

Dino was still in hock to the government, although MCA and a new business manager were assisting him in slowly clearing up his debts.

He and Jeanne had just purchased their first home—a beautiful English house on an estate-sized lot, containing a swimming pool and tennis court, which was located on Mountain Drive in Beverly Hills. This cost them well over $200,000, but of course it was heavily mortgaged.

Dino was also supporting Mama and Papa Crocetti, who had retired and were living, as were many other people, on their generous son's income.

Through all his troubles with Jerry and his many business obligations away from home, Dino had not lost the knack of being one of the most prolific begetters of children in the entertainment business. In the first five years of his marriage to Jeanne, he was belting out the bambinos with the same regularity that he did in his first marriage.

In 1951, it was Dino, Jr., a blond-haired, blue-eyed boy; in 1953, Ricci, a brown-haired, blue-eyed brother for Dino, Jr.; and in 1956, Gina, a beautiful little girl.

In addition, the Martins were soon to inherit the children from Dean's first marriage to Betty—Craig, who was now thirteen; Claudia, eleven; Gail, ten; and Deana, seven.

At the time of the divorce in 1949, Betty, of course, got complete custody of the children. Good mother that she was, however, she wanted them to be able to see their father as much as possible while they were growing up.

This was made practicable because the second house Dean and Jeanne had rented, a French colonial in western Los Angeles, was just a couple of blocks from Betty's Holmby Hills residence. But, according to Betty, Dean showed very little inclination during the early part of his second marriage to spend any time with his children. This was not because he didn't love them, but probably because, like many men who have divorced and remarried, he just wanted to have as little contact with his first wife as possible, and being around her children was bound to evoke unpleasant memories and reawaken old guilts.

Betty recalls one Christmas when Jeanne sent the chauffeur to pick the children up. Within an hour, all four had returned. Each of the girls had received a dress (all three were alike), and Craig, then about eleven, was given a game suitable for a six-year-old.

Despite Dino's indifference, as the kids grew into their teens and became old enough to know their own preferences, they started to gravitate toward their father, who was—let's face it—a more glamorous figure. He also could give them more in the way of physical luxuries—allowances, cars, clothing, and everything else needed to make children of the rich happy.

Dean was paying Betty good alimony, but she was a bad manager of her money. She spent entirely too much on food, liquor, and her own pleasures and not as much on her children as they felt they deserved.

As a result, the children were not entirely happy living with Betty and without a father. Betty had had a succession of boyfriends after she and Dean separated, but because of her Catholicism she had vowed never to remarry, and she never has.

Perhaps feeling they needed the guidance of a man, the four children started dropping into Dean's and Jeanne's Mountain Drive home after school in the afternoons and on weekends and vacations—using the pool and tennis court and very often staying to dinner if they could wangle an invitation from Jeanne.

When things reached the point where Craig, Claudia, Gail, and Deana were starting to spend more time in their father's home than in their mother's, Jeanne and Dean felt it was time to change the rules of the game. So even though she wasn't anxious to have four more children who weren't her own underfoot to worry about, Jeanne agreed with Dean that it would be a smart move to take official custody of them. If nothing else, it would save Dean $1,000 a month in child-support payments.

On November 17, 1957, Dean shocked Hollywood by filing suit in Santa Monica Superior Court, asking for custody of his four children with Betty and charging that she was an "unfit mother."

His suit alleged that the four children had been neglected and that no financial provision had been made for their futures. He further charged that Betty had failed to provide a proper home and that she had set aside no funds or property for the children, despite Dean's paying her $100,000 in child support and $250,000 in alimony since the divorce.

Betty Martin didn't contest the case, and, on December 10, 1957, the Superior Court granted custody of the children to Dean.

Subsequently, Betty has denied vehemently that she relinquished custody of the children because she was "an unfit mother," as Dean's lawyer had charged. Betty maintains that she gave them up because she couldn't afford them.

"You see," she says, "at the time of the divorce, I was so hurt I wasn't thinking clearly. Instead of saying, 'OK, I'll take a percentage of your income,' I took straight alimony plus child support. Well, I knew nothing about taxes—and, after a few years, the government came in and told me I owed them close to $100,000. It seemed unreal. Anyway, I lost everything. I had a ranch for the kids in Nevada, and that went.

"I was getting $250 for each child—but they went to private school, and they also had lessons in dancing, piano, swimming, and just about everything you can name. Suddenly I was left with nothing but the fact that I'd be paying heavy taxes for years to catch up. So I did the realistic thing. Dean had all the money and that big house, so I felt they'd be better off with him."

But Dean's and Jeanne's new house, while luxurious and spacious, wasn't large enough to accommodate four more children without everyone doubling up. Four, plus three of their own, plus themselves added up to a household of nine, and sometimes ten if Jeanne's mother was visiting, not counting the servants.

As a result, Dean's first four kids were packed off to boarding school before they'd even spent a week in Dean's and Jeanne's new house. Craig was so unhappy about the situation that he ran away.

Eventually, Dean built separate quarters onto the house for the four additional children, enabling them to live home, and that helped their morale considerably.

Jeanne took on the extra burden with a cheerful smile and showered as much love and attention on Craig, Claudia, Gail, and Deana as she did on her own three—well, almost as much. A close friend of Jeanne's, who doesn't wish to be identified, claims that there were times when having so many children underfoot became just too much for the young mother.

"Those kids of *his*," Jeanne once exploded, shortly after getting up one noon and finding all four of Betty's kids sitting at the foot of the stairs, waiting for her to come down to breakfast. "They sit around like vultures and wait for handouts!"

All in all, however, Jeanne was a good mother, considering the situation. It's not always easy for a young bride, running her own household for the first time and with a husband who's rarely around, to take on another mother's four nearly grown kids and always be civil to them.

At any rate, she put up with them because she loved Dean and she knew it pleased him to have all his brood under one roof.

Add up all those expenses, plus what it cost the hedonistic Dean to enjoy himself gambling at the rate of $5,000 a round of golf at the Riviera Country Club, buying expensive automobiles and $600 suits, and eating in the finest restaurants, and it's easy to see why he changed his mind about returning to work as Jerry's partner.

As distasteful as the idea may have been, there was a certain amount of security and comfort in knowing that he and Jerry were good for a couple of million dollars a year if they kept their noses to the movie, TV, and nightclub grindstones. Not even Frank Sinatra could be sure that every song he recorded would be a hit; indeed, in 1953, the Voice was broke, in debt to Uncle Sam, and unemployable.

The vicissitudes of show business were enough to make even an arrogant Italian like Dino swallow his pride and adopt the realistic philosophy that he had already espoused to *Time*: "What's the difference if we don't chum around? To me, this isn't a love affair. This is big business."

So although the coolness remained, the show went on. Through it all, Jerry remained determined to make the marriage work and was even thinking creatively once again.

Shortly after they had temporarily patched things up, Dean and Jerry were playing an engagement at the Sands Hotel in Las Vegas. Their nightclub act was a smoothly polished vehicle now, and they still seemed to get a kick out of working together, which strongly belied the rumors that they were splitting up. The yaks were big and plentiful, and, as usual, business was good.

Don McGuire came to Las Vegas for the weekend, and, one evening between shows, he and Jerry bumped into each other in the casino at the Sands. They hadn't seen each other since the troubled days of *Three Ring Circus*, but the bitterness was forgotten as Jerry put an arm around the writer and said, "I have an idea for a movie for Dean and me. Would you like to write it?"

"Of course," answered McGuire.

"Don't you even want to hear it?" asked Jerry.

"What's the difference?" said McGuire.

"But the story's—"

"What's the difference, Jerry? You pay. I write it. Nobody looks at 'em anyway."

McGuire, who has an acerbic sense of humor, was, of course, kidding Jerry. But Jerry, who, like most professional funny men, has very little sense of humor about himself, was dead serious.

"But I got to tell you the idea," he protested, and he sat McGuire down in the cocktail lounge and said, "I just want to lay two words on you— Damon and Pythias."

"What about 'em?" asked McGuire.

"Well . . . you know . . . the relationship."

"Do *you* know?" asked McGuire, still kidding him.

"Seriously, what do you think?"

"Jerry, what's the difference? It's a picture. You make it. You hope to make some money."

"But it's got a theme about friendship," said Jerry. "And Dean and I would like to get together and be as close as people because he doesn't understand."

It was obvious that Jerry had picked up a few bits and pieces of the Damon and Pythias relationship somewhere in his travels—certainly not in a book—and he thought if he and Dean made a picture on the subject, it might help cement their partnership.

There was something pathetic about Jerry's desire to bring back the old camaraderie of the Club 500 days.

"OK," agreed the cynical McGuire. "What do you want me to do?"

"Come and see me and tell me how you can work it out," said the grateful Jerry.

"So I went home and thought up an idea, and when Jerry came back to town, I went to his office at the studio and told him what I had," recounts McGuire. "I said, 'Jerry, here's what I'd like to do. Dean plays a cop, and you play a kid who's dumb . . . an apprentice janitor who'd like to be a cop more than anything else in the world. Now you look up to Dean, who takes you by the hand and tries to carry you through so you can be a cop. And you live in a tough neighborhood, and you're a dummy, but you and Dean have a close relationship.' "

"That's sensational," exclaimed Jerry. "Put it down on paper in a couple of pages. I'll get Frank Freeman to approve it, and we're in business."

"Don't you want me to tell Dean the idea first?" asked McGuire.

"No, no—I'll tell him. Don't worry about that," said Jerry.

On that note, McGuire made a deal with the studio to write a screenplay, which was eventually called *The Delicate Delinquent*, and to direct the picture.

But knowing that the Martin and Lewis relationship was a bit strained, McGuire took the precaution one day of seeking out Dean Martin on his own and telling him the idea of *The Delicate Delinquent* so that it wouldn't come as a total surprise on the first day of shooting.

After listening to the bare bones of the story, Dino drawled, "That's all right, man, you know . . . a cop, and everything else . . . it's all been done, anyway."

He gave McGuire the impression that he couldn't have cared less. He was just going to take the money and run.

"During this period, the rumors persisted that they were breaking up," relates McGuire, "but I kept on writing and writing because I know that Y. Frank Freeman is a man of his word and that I'm going to get paid regardless. But I figure they can't actually break up until they make this picture, which is all I'm really worried about. And why they're going to break up is a mystery to me, except that people are saying to Dean, 'You should be a leading man—you're another Rudolph Valentino,' and people are telling Jerry, 'You're better than Charlie Chaplin.'

"Meanwhile, both camps are having battle meetings. Jerry and his agent, Dean and his agent, and there are all kinds of secretive phone calls behind each other's backs. I'd be at Jerry's house, and he'd be on the phone saying to somebody at MCA, 'Dean's trying to get out of it.' Another time, Mack Gray comes to me and says, 'Isn't there something we can do to save this thing? These guys belong together.' "

Even though Mack Grey was just a "go-for" for the two of them, he had a large stake in the outcome too. If they broke up, they might not be able to afford to keep paying him for whatever it was he was supposed to be doing.

Writing the best he could under the circumstances, McGuire finished the script, and the studio approved it and sent copies to both stars.

Like all Martin and Lewis scripts, the bulk of the comedy was thrown to Jerry, whereas Dean played straight and carried what little love story there was. But the ratio of comedy to straight was no different from what it had been in any of their pictures.

"That's the way I wrote for them," states McGuire. "I didn't think that Dean Martin was the act. Jerry was the guy who made him a hit, made him funny. So I wasn't going to be writing a picture that I was going to direct and not give the comedy to Jerry. I'd be a schmuck to do it any other way. Dean was a terrible actor. He could barely talk."

But Dean did plenty of talking after he read the script. Boiling mad, he sought out Jerry and asked, "You mean, I'm gonna play a cop in uniform?"

"That's it," said Jerry. "A cop."

"I don't want to play a cop," said Dino.

"Then we'll have to get somebody else," said Jerry loftily.

"Start looking, boy," said Dino, and he stormed out of the office, phoned Herman Citron, and instructed the agent to tell Y. Frank Freeman that he was through making pictures with Jerry Lewis.

"It wasn't actually the cop thing," recalls McGuire, who was caught in the middle of the fracas, since he was working for both Martin and Lewis. "Dino simply thought I had written him out. At the same time, I was hearing from Jerry that I'd given Dean too much. But what it really amounted to was that Dino had finally made up his mind that he just didn't want to work with Jerry anymore—he couldn't stand him, even if he starved to death—and he was using my script as the excuse to make the break. It was a terrible situation. The studio had to make a decision: whether to force the guys to work together against their wills or to break up the team and let Jerry make the picture alone."

At the height of the crisis, Y. Frank Freeman called a meeting in his office and invited everyone concerned with the breakup to be present—Jack Karp, his assistant; Dean; Jerry; Herman Citron; and Don McGuire.

After everyone was present, Freeman turned to McGuire and said in his southern accent, "Don, do you think this picture should be made with the boys or not?"

Motivated by pure selfishness (he would lose his director's fee if the picture were shelved), rather than any altruistic desire to reunite America's greatest mismatched couple, McGuire jumped to his feet and made an impassioned plea in favor of the two of them doing his story. In his speech, McGuire pointed out that his script was "a helluva Martin and Lewis vehicle," that "both Dean's and Jerry's parts are equally good—just different," and that *The Delicate Delinquent* was liable to be "the boys' biggest money-maker to date."

His remarks were punctuated from time to time with pithy observations from those two great humanitarians—Y. Frank Freeman and Herman Citron—who said such things as, "Fellows, you really shouldn't let your personal differences get in the way of your picture," and "Weber and Fields never got along and neither did Gilbert and Sullivan, so why do you have to?"

Dean listened in moody silence until everyone voiced an opinion. Then, as all eyes turned to him for an answer, he dismissed his entire ten-year partnership with Jerry Lewis with one earthy word: "BULLSHIT!"

Following that, Dino stood up and walked out of the room and out of Jerry Lewis's life—forever, except for one brief stand the two of them were committed to make together at the Copacabana later in the summer.

19

All God's Chillun Got Rhythm

Perhaps because it was the last time they would ever work together, Martin and Lewis's final stand at the Copa in July 1956 did a record-breaking business.

Although Dean and Jerry had never been funnier, the bitterness of the impending divorce was apparent.

During a roughhouse clowning routine at the chic bistro one night, Dean brought his left heel down on Jerry's foot with the force of a pile driver. Jerry let out a shriek that could be heard as far away as Staten Island.

Dean claimed there was absolutely no vindictiveness involved. "It was only an accident," he told reporters smilingly.

Accident or not, Jerry suffered two fractured toes, wound up under the treatment of an orthopedist, Dr. Edgar Bick, and had to play out the remainder of their engagement at the Copa wearing soft velvet slippers and limping quite noticeably.

This infighting, however, didn't prevent them from putting on a "schmaltzy" closing-night performance, climaxed by their singing "Pardners" (from their next to last picture together) and embracing and kissing affectionately for the benefit of all their misty-eyed well-wishers who were urging them to remain together.

But once the phony sentimentality of the occasion had faded away into the past along with the cigarette smoke and the body odor of the prancing Copa Girls, Jerry was suddenly overcome with grave doubts about his ability to face the future without Dean. He expressed his feelings later in a feature article in *Look*:

When we finished the last show together, I went back to my dressing room. I was numb with fright and shaking all over, my clothes were drenched with perspiration. I sat in my dressing room, crying. I thought I'd never be able to get up before an audience again. I thought it would be impossible for me to work without Dean.

After I finished crying in my dressing room, I phoned Patti in California. I said to her, "It's all over." She said, "Don't be afraid. I'm your friend"—and I cracked up completely. Then Dean came in and we both cried. We shook hands and wished each other luck.

That night Jerry had to sleep under sedation.

Jerry remained in the same uncertain frame of mind until August 2, when he and Patti went to Las Vegas for a long overdue vacation *together*.

But Jerry wasn't enjoying it or any of the things Las Vegas had to offer —the sun, the golf, the shows, or the gambling. Perhaps there were too many memories of the great times he and Dino had spent there together all flooding back to spoil the present. For four days, Jerry just sat around the Sands Hotel brooding.

Finally, on August 6, Jerry decided he and Patti ought to go home. There was no use wasting money having a rotten time.

At 6:45 in the evening, Jerry and Patti were in their suite packing when something happened that caused Jerry to recover his old confidence. Ironically, it was somebody else's misfortune.

The phone rang just as they closed their suitcases. It was Sid Luft, Judy Garland's husband, with a request for Jerry to go on in Judy's place at the New Frontier Hotel. Judy had a strep throat and couldn't sing, and all the other entertainers in town were busy doing their own shows.

Jerry froze at the thought. How could he possibly fill the great Judy Garland's shoes? He didn't even have an act yet that he could do without Dino.

"You go on for Judy and you'll be fine," Patti reassured him. "God will take care of you."

Jerry hurriedly put on a dark suit, borrowed Patti's St. Anthony medal, and checked his wallet to make sure that his kids' pictures were in it.

When Jerry goes on stage, he carries nothing in his pockets except pictures of his family. Twice in his career he forgot the pictures, and both times he had bad luck. The first time, in 1949, at the Roxy Theater in New York, he fell into the orchestra pit and broke his collarbone. Six years later, in Minneapolis, he fell and almost broke his spine.

Jerry isn't superstitious about anything else, but he is sure that pictures of his family are talismans. When he gave Patti a pink Thunderbird for her birthday, he had the radio removed from the dashboard and replaced it with five fluorescent-lighted picture frames that contained photographs of himself and his family.

Little wonder he checked his pockets before filling in for Judy Garland at the New Frontier.

As he walked on the stage, Jerry still didn't know what he was going to do for a whole hour. And neither did the all-male chorus who backed up Judy and sang her introduction. They sang it as usual, "Introducing— Miss Judy Garland."

A ripple of laughter went through the audience when Jerry Lewis appeared in Judy's place. He faced the audience nervously and then said the first thing that came into his mind. "I don't look much like Judy, do I?"

The audience was with Jerry from that moment on, and for an hour and six minutes he put on an impromptu performance that was reminiscent of the best of Martin and Lewis in their early Copa days. He joked, danced, led the orchestra, kidded the audience, did routines from his pictures, and even tackled the band leader. His performance brought tears to the eyes of his biggest rooter—Patti.

That night Jerry could do anything—except one thing. He didn't know how to get off. Finally, he turned to Judy, who was sitting in a chair on stage, and asked, "What do you sing in your act?"

"Come Rain or Come Shine," she whispered in his ear.

Jerry than announced to the audience, "You're now going to hear Judy by proxy."

Then, with Judy whispering the lyrics into Jerry's ear, he dropped down on one knee and belted out the song as he remembered Al Jolson, his boyhood idol, used to do.

Jerry doesn't have a bad voice; he doesn't have a good one either. About the best that can be said about his singing is that he's enthusiastic and that he can carry a tune, even if the delivery is a little nasal.

At any rate, his first serious attempt to sing in front of an audience brought rousing applause. This so encouraged him that he promptly sang another one of Judy's numbers, "Rock-a-bye Your Baby."

At the end of the show, the audience gave Jerry a standing ovation, and, for the first time since July 24, Jerry believed in himself once again. So to Judy Garland must go the credit for helping Jerry shake off his depression. On the negative side, she must be blamed for causing Jerry to believe he was a singer.

A few weeks later, Jerry recorded "Rock-a-bye Your Baby" as a single for Decca Records—the first of many such attempts to convince the world that he could sing as well as Dean Martin.

Not only had Jerry regained his lost confidence, but, by the time he returned to Hollywood and Paramount, he was actually feeling cocky enough to start feeling sorry for his ex-partner.

Meeting Walter Seltzer, Hal Wallis's assistant, on the Paramount lot one day, Jerry put his arms around him and said, "Promise me, Walter, that if Dean and I don't get back together, you and Hal will take care of him. I know he can't take care of himself."

Actually, Dean's future was a source of puzzlement to the Paramount brass. According to the hastily drawn terms of Dean's and Jerry's not very amicable divorce, Dean and Jerry would finish out their commitments with Hal Wallis and Paramount working separately.

"At least we'll try it for one picture," Y. Frank Freeman announced to *The New York Times*, "and we'll see how it works out."

It worked out better for Paramount than it did for MGM, which, once it learned Martin and Lewis were separating, firmed up its offer to costar Dean with Anna Maria Alberghetti in Joe Pasternak's *Ten Thousand Bedrooms*, slated to go before the cameras that fall.

Since no producer on the Paramount lot was dying to go ahead with Dino alone nor did any of them have a vehicle suitable for a man of his questionable talents, Y. Frank Freeman gladly gave him permission to hang out his crooner's shingle in Culver City for a while.

Retaining what everyone considered to be the better half of the team, Paramount then decided to go ahead with *The Delicate Delinquent* and told McGuire to start preparations to shoot the picture with someone else playing the role of the policeman. McGuire looked over a long list of available young leading men and gave Dean's part to Darren McGavin, a newcomer he had discovered while on a trip to New York.

Before proceeding with the picture, however, he first renegotiated his own deal. "I figured that if I was going to get mixed up in this kind of madness, I might as well share in the profits, just in case it turned out well by accident," says McGuire. "So I offered to direct the picture at Guild minimum scale in return for 6 percent of the gross 'after break-even,' and Freeman gave it to me."

McGuire then rewrote the entire script so that it could be shot for under $500,000. It had originally been budgeted at $1.2 million, but, with an unknown playing Dean Martin's part, he had to do something to protect his percentage position. As little respect as he had for Dean Martin as a performer, McGuire realized that the team had a certain amount of charisma and audience appeal that he wasn't sure Jerry had by himself or with Darren McGavin. But if he made *The Delicate Delinquent* economically, there was a chance he could stave off total disaster and possibly even realize a profit for himself and come out looking like a hero to Paramount.

While the picture was in the preproduction stages, Jerry, fully recovered now from the shock of being left at the altar by his "Italian lover," started thinking of himself as the Man of All Talents again.

One day, he came to McGuire and asked that he be allowed to sing three songs in the picture, even though his part as a janitor's apprentice didn't call for it.

"Sing? You mean that fourth-rate imitation of Jolson you do?" asked McGuire. "Why?"

"Because Dean's singing in *his* new picture."

"Dean's a singer," pointed out McGuire. "When you sing, you're lucky they don't shoot you from the balcony with a Mauser."

"I've got a good voice," said Jerry.

"Well, you're not going to ruin my picture with it," insisted McGuire. "There's no spot for you to sing in the picture. You're playing a janitor's apprentice who's only sixteen years old. How in hell are we going to motivate a sixteen-year-old janitor's apprentice suddenly to go into an imitation of Jolson? Forget it. It'll just slow up the action."

All during the preparation stages, Jerry kept after McGuire to let him sing at least "one number" in the picture. McGuire remained just as adamant that he was a rotten singer and that he stick to being a straight comedian.

"It was just my luck," recalls McGuire, "that, in the midst of all this, Jerry's record of 'Rock-a-bye Your Baby' turned into a hit. It sold over 1 million records, so what choice did I have? I had to let him sing. It was bloody awful too, the low spot of the picture at our first preview. But since Jerry was the producer, he had last say as to the final cut, so his number stayed in."

On the first day of shooting, Jerry began to push his producer weight around again.

"He walked on the set in the middle of a rehearsal and started giving instructions to everybody," says McGuire. "I finally said to him, 'Jerry, there's no use my being here—I'm only the director. So I'm turning the whole thing over to you.' Jerry apologized, and, from that moment on, he was fine—except I had to listen to his rotten singing."

McGuire remembers one positive aspect of Jerry's behavior during the making of *The Delicate Delinquent*, and that was his total dedication to the muse of comedy.

There was a scene, for example, in which Jerry was supposed to be repairing a light fixture in the ceiling. By mistake he stuck his finger in a hot socket, and the electric shock sent his head through the ceiling and into the room above, where a man was sleeping.

"Now a normal person," states McGuire, "would have said to the director, 'Hey, wait a minute. How are we going to shoot that without cracking my skull open?' But to show you the insanity of Jerry, when I broached the gag to him, he just said, 'Fine, let's do it.' He gave no thought at all to what it might do to him to have his head go through a plaster ceiling.

"Of course, we weren't using hard plaster for the gag. The prop man just put a thin coating of wet plaster on the ceiling. But it took too long to light the set, and, by the time I shot it, the plaster had hardened. When Jerry's head went through the ceiling, his scalp split open and started to bleed profusely. But do you think Jerry noticed? He just kept right on with the scene. All that mattered to him was that it 'should be funny.' "

Because Jerry behaved himself and wasn't feuding with Dean Martin, McGuire was able to bring *The Delicate Delinquent* in for a record $460,000. This feat so astounded Hal Wallis, whose misfortune it was not to have been connected with this picture, that he sent for a print of *The Delicate Delinquent* and ran it in his private projection room. Then he summoned Don McGuire.

When McGuire strolled into Hal Wallis's office, the producer had all the production figures from *The Delicate Delinquent* laid out before him on long production budget sheets on his desk.

"I don't understand these figures," he told McGuire, shaking his head. "Four hundred sixty thousand dollars! The last picture I made with that little so and so cost me a million-two. You must be juggling the books."

"It's very simple," explained McGuire. "Jerry didn't fool around in this picture. He was trying to prove something."

What Jerry was trying to prove was that he could be a success without Dino.

When the grosses and reviews of his and Dean's respective pictures started coming in, Jerry seemed to have proved his point.

The reviews on *The Delicate Delinquent*, although not all that enthusiastic about the screenplay, verified that Jerry Lewis was perfectly capable of getting along without Dean Martin. More astonishingly, *The Delicate Delinquent* grossed $7 million before it was through, despite Jerry's singing. Jerry did a twenty-six-city promotional tour, which certainly did not hurt.

Jerry sold his percentage of the picture back to Paramount for a $2.5 million capital gain. This got Jerry out of all his personal debts and made him a rich man for the first time since he had achieved stardom.

But Jerry's success as a single did not stop with *The Delicate Delinquent*. Following its release, Jerry decided to try out his solo wings in the live-entertainment arena and signed to do four weeks on the stage of New York's famed Palace Theater, starting February 8, 1957.

This took more than Jerry's usual amount of courage, for, at the time, the owners of the Palace were trying to revive its glorious past by bringing big-time vaudeville back to New York's main stem.

Prior to Jerry's engagement, the blockbusters of show business had all played there and broken records—Betty Hutton, Danny Kaye, Alan King, and Judy Garland. The New York critics ascribed "perfection" and "magic" to Judy Garland's performance, and, as a result, she held forth at the Palace for fifteen weeks prior to Jerry Lewis's opening.

It was a tough act to follow, and it isn't surprising that Jerry had opening-night jitters—especially since half the audience was wondering if he could possibly go it alone on stage without Dean Martin. But with the help of his great energy and a walletful of family pictures in his hip pocket, Jerry met the challenge and faced the audience of sophisticated first-nighters with a gutsy smile.

"I used to double," he said, "but"—gesturing to the Aristocrats, an octet of young male singers and dancers who backed him up—"now I've cut it down to eight."

That broke the ice. The audience screamed its approval, and Jerry leaped vigorously into his familiar zany act. He imitated Jolson, he danced, he cavorted, he did the monkey bit, he slipped in his false buck teeth and went into an imitation of a Japanese tourist. Then he climaxed the evening by coaxing the audience into joining him in an old-fashioned "community sing." When one diffident gentleman in a box refused to join in, Jerry clambered up the proscenium, vaulted into the man's box, and started tickling him in the ribs. This persuaded the recalcitrant to conform, and, before Jerry was through, the man was belting out "Shine on Harvest Moon" with the enthusiasm of Kate Smith.

Although Jerry refrained from squirting seltzer into the audience during the act, he did forget himself and lapsed into some questionable material in several spots during his performance. This resulted in one of the critics the next morning writing that Jerry's act was more suitable for a nightclub than for the Palace. But the majority of the reviews were favorable.

Writing in *Variety*, editor Abel Green said,

> Ninety minutes of Jerry Lewis, with his great versatility, makes this Palace excursion very worthwhile. That Lewis had first-night jitters is incidental, because despite the somewhat uphill struggle, it cannot be denied that he has nothing but talent and is as potent a comic as there is to be found in front of a mike—electronic, saloon, or podium. *Vaudeville is not dead.*

That Abel Green was right was conceded four weeks later at the finish of Jerry's run.

His first week at the Palace hit a new high, bringing in $61,500 at the box office. There was such a demand for tickets that he could have easily gone on past the fifteen weeks Judy Garland had stayed. But Hal Wallis was beckoning him from Hollywood to come back and start making pictures again, so Jerry could only stay at the Palace a few days past his original booking. But, in his first four weeks, Jerry's appearance grossed more than $275,000. Chalk up another record for Jerry Lewis.

On his closing night, March 13, Jerry was given two more awards to be hung alongside his many others in the Gar-Ron Playhouse in the Pacific Palisades.

On stage Sol Schwartz, the manager of the Palace, presented Jerry with a silver tray, engraved with an etching of the front of the Palace, which was in appreciation of his efforts to keep the much revered Palace out of the hands of the receivers. And on behalf of Decca Records, Steve Allen gave him a gold platter of his "Rock-a-bye Your Baby" recording, honoring its sale of over 1 million records. This, amazingly, was more than Al Jolson's original recording of the number had chalked up.

While Jerry was making a bum out of Jolson and outgrossing all the other Paramount stars at motion picture box offices, everyone's worst fears about Dean Martin's future were confirmed with the release of *Ten Thousand Bedrooms* early in 1957.

Reviewing the picture in *The New York Times*, Bosley Crowther wrote,

> More than a couple of vacancies are clearly apparent in the musical film *Ten Thousand Bedrooms*, which came to Loew's State yesterday.
>
> One is the emptiness alongside Dean Martin, who here plays the lead without his old partner, Jerry Lewis. And that's an emptiness, indeed! Mr. Martin is a personable actor with a nice enough singing style, but he's just another nice-looking crooner without his comical pal. Together, the two made a mutually complementary team. Apart, Mr. Martin is a fellow with little humor and a modicum of charm.

Ten Thousand Bedrooms was a total disaster at the box office.

To add salt to the open wounds, Dean Martin hadn't had a hit record in a couple of years, while his former sidekick not only was the recipient of a gold record but had also recorded a twelve-song long-playing album titled "Jerry Lewis Just Sings," which was also climbing to the top of the charts.

If that proved anything, besides the abominably bad musical taste of the American public, it was that Dean Martin's Italian luck had finally run out on him.

20

Who's the Greatest Star?
(I Am by Far)

What must have hurt Dean even more was how incredibly well Jerry appeared to be doing without him. (Could all those gloomy predictions have been right? Should he have swallowed his pride and taken all of Jerry's nonsense?)

In his first solo flight at the Sands in Las Vegas, Jerry again proved he didn't need Dino. *Variety* didn't give him an all-out rave. It credited him with being extremely funny when he was funny, but it panned him for being overly long (his opening show ran nearly two hours) and for frequent lapses into bad taste (particularly his takeoff of a homosexual, which it said went beyond the laugh stage and got to the shock point!). Finally, it suggested that if he wanted to sing, he might get better results if he'd latch onto some new material and stop doing a shopworn imitation of Al Jolson.

But audiences liked what Jerry had to offer, and he was a hit not only at the Sands but in nightclubs all over the country.

But nightclubs were just a sideline with Jerry. By 1958, he was back on the air again with his own weekly TV variety show over NBC. This show, although not as funny as the Martin and Lewis Colgate comedy programs, remained high in the ratings until the early 1960s and netted him somewhere in the neighborhood of $2.5 million over the next four years.

During the same general period—it was actually the spring of 1959— Jerry signed a new contract between Paramount and his own newly formed film production company, Jerry Lewis Productions. This contract, negotiated by Herman Citron, MCA, and Jerry's attorney, Joe Ross, represented what was for those days the biggest single transaction in film history for the exclusive services of one star. Jerry was to get a payment of $10 million to star in fourteen films over a seven-year period—seven for Jerry Lewis Productions, which he would produce, and seven for Paramount.

The idiot from Irvington, New Jersey, had finally gotten his wish: He was not just a performer, he was a genuine movie mogul with a suite of offices encompassing some 65,000 square feet in the new Paramount Building; a number of secretaries to get past if a person wanted to see him; his own golf cart, with his name on it in lights, for use in scooting around the Paramount lot; about forty flunkies to laugh at his jokes; complete autonomy, productionwise (except when he was making *The Sad Sack* and *Boeing Boeing*, which finished off his unfulfilled commitments with Hal Wallis); and an enormous executive-style desk and a swivel chair.

Jerry's office was filled with memorabilia. "Two of everything," recalls Don McGuire; "two baseballs autographed by the Dodger team, two footballs autographed by the Rams, two solid-gold fountain pens, two pictures of himself and the president, and all kinds of plaques and trophies."

Out of this impressive setup poured forth such a flood of Jerry Lewis comedies over the next five years that it's impossible today or tonight to turn on your TV set without seeing at least one of them on some channel. At the rate of two a year (one in winter and one in summer), they came off the Jerry Lewis assembly line with a regularity that could only be accomplished by using Serutan.

In addition to *The Delicate Delinquent*, there were *The Ladies Man*, *The Errand Boy*, *Rock-a-bye Baby*, *The Sad Sack*, *The Geisha Boy*, *Don't Give Up the Ship*, *Cinderfella*, *The Bellboy*, *Visit to a Small Planet*, *It's Only Money*, and *Boeing Boeing*.

Besides starring in them, Jerry wrote, produced, and directed many of these pictures. The rest he just appeared in and produced. But the Jerry Lewis stamp was on all of them—plenty of slapstick and hokum, very little story, occasional lapses into bad taste, and liberal doses of his rotten singing.

Kids flocked to see Jerry's movies in such numbers that Leo McCarey, one of the all-time greats of comedy directing, once commented, "He's the Pied Piper of the business, the heir to the mantle of Charlie Chaplin and Harold Lloyd. He can do no wrong."

Explaining why he was so popular with children, Jerry told a reporter, "I get paid for doing what children are punished for . . . I'm constantly impersonating a child. I always feel sorry for him. I think of the character as him! I take him on stage with me. He's a sensitive, kind, tender kid who's always getting belted around for some reason."

A fourteen-year-old fan put it another way: "Jerry Lewis is just a nice big kid who makes us laugh. He's also generous. Kids love him because he's really one of us."

Unlike Sid Caesar, Danny Kaye, or Groucho Marx, Jerry Lewis was never a pet of the intellectuals nor did he ever enjoy the reputation of being a comedian's comedian. In reviewing his TV show at the time, *TV Guide* called Jerry "an unfunny Milton Berle" and accused him of vulgarity because he took a wad of gum out of his mouth and dropped it into a stooge's hand. Jerry was deeply hurt and didn't understand what was vulgar about it. He explained that he had copied the bit from his two-year-old son, Scottie, who had done it to a friend.

Critics, for the most part, hated Jerry Lewis films. Not to be outdone, Jerry Lewis hated most critics. As a result, there was generally a running battle between Jerry and the critics going on somewhere in the nation's press at all times.

The following *Newsweek* review of *The Geisha Boy* is typical of the kind of criticism Jerry's films were beginning to evoke (or is it "provoke"?) in the nation's press. *The Geisha Boy* was written and directed by the late Frank Tashlin, who was a very talented writer of children's books, and it costarred those two giants of the American theater, Suzanne Pleshette and Marie McDonald.

> Jerry Lewis's *The Geisha Boy*, still another in what appears to be an endless series of film farces presenting the comic as a manic boob, features him this time as a magician whose act is so bad he can't even land a job in daytime TV. He ends up with a USO troupe in Japan.
>
> As in all Lewis movies, the trouble with this one is that the star seems not to know when to stop. Instead of building a bit of funny dialogue to a climax and then leaving it there to simmer, too often he messily lets the pot boil over. He does not allow himself a simple artful double take; he has to make it a triple take or even a quadruple take.

Jerry's rebuttal in the same issue of *Newsweek* follows:

> I don't care about critical acclaim. I could do the damnedest satire on Noel Coward you ever saw, and you critics would love it. But then I'd have an audience of only 250 critics, and I'd have lost the audience of 40 million people I have now.
>
> So I don't listen to the critics. I listen to the milkman I bump into on my way to work in the morning (movie producer Lewis arrives at his studio office at 6 A.M.) because he represents 200,000 other milkmen, and if he says he didn't like something in my last movie, I make damned sure to change it the next time.

I make movies for Mr. and Mrs. Two and One-Half Room Flat. They've been married for thirty-seven years, see, and they're not going to make any changes. They're stuck with their lives. So when they decide to get out of their flat and go to a movie, they ask only two questions: What's the movie about and is it in color? Well, if it's a *Marty* or *On the Waterfront*, they don't want it. It's no escape for them. But if it's an hour and a half of laughs and silly stuff and color like in my movies, they'll buy it.

I say that's the way the majority of people see movies, no matter *what* the critics think. And I say that's the market I'm playing to, not the sophisticates. . . . Don't get me wrong. *Marty* and *Waterfront* were great movies with great acting. But those two and most of the movies that producers are making today are made for their friends at the Friar's Club, not for Mr. and Mrs. Two and One-Half Room Flat. That's why the movie business is suffering. I don't care about impressing anybody. What I do care about is that I've never made a flop picture. . . . When the sophisticates take over the country, that's when I'll change my stuff. But you know what? It'll never happen.

For some reason, a number of critics across the Atlantic in France read something meaningful into Jerry's films to which American critics were blind. Several important cinema magazines—*Posit* and *Cinéma Paris*—published long articles analyzing Jerry's comedy, and two publications, *Premier plan* and *Cinéma d'aujourd'hui*—devoted their entire issues to Jerry Lewis. They saw in Jerry's "little guy" character something terribly symbolic and remindful of the "oppressed Jew" who down through the ages has been beaten, pushed around, and forced to flee from one country to another.

But even though for a brief time Jerry Lewis enjoyed enormous popularity among the French intellectuals, this did little to assuage his outrage against the press for mistreating him in his own country.

However, from a strictly business viewpoint, it wasn't terribly important that Jerry didn't turn out sophisticated movies or that his creative feelings were hurt by critical sniping. There was one thing nobody could argue with: His pictures *did* make money, and that was why Jerry was something of a hero to the people who ran Paramount Studios, to the managers of the drive-in and multiple-run theaters where his pictures generally did the best, and to the chocolate bar, bubble gum, and orthodontics set who loyally flocked to see every Jerry Lewis comedy that came out.

In the same issue as the review above, *Newsweek* broke down Jerry's annual gross income as $3 million from movies, $1 million from his hour-long TV show, and a few extra hundred thousand dollars from nightclub appearances.

With so much wealth at Jerry's fingertips, it was inevitable that the money would start burning holes in the pockets of his made-to-order Sy

Devore blue jeans. Although he and Patti had stoutly maintained through the years that they would never leave their little twelve-room shack in the Pacific Palisades, because it had everything any two human beings could possibly want to make them happy ("and what it doesn't have, we can add on"), Jerry started looking around in 1958 for a house more befitting a movie mogul and his rapidly expanding family.

By 1959, it seemed that Jerry was trying to compete with Dino in the bedroom as well as in front of the cameras.

There had been three more additions to the family since the Lewises had adopted Ronnie in 1950, and all of them were their own: Scottie, three; Christopher, two; and Anthony, an infant. Whatever the medical problem was that had prevented Patti from having more children after the birth of the Lewises' first child, it had been corrected by expert gynecological help plus a good deal of faith in God.

One of the greatest ambitions in Jerry's life, aside from achieving material success, was to have a large family, consisting of not less than five children. He also wanted to have a daughter. But a daughter seemed to be the one gift God didn't wish to grant the Lewises. The indomitable Jerry, however, refused to accept that verdict, and during Patti's fourth pregnancy he decided to enlist the aid of "positive thinking."

Early in Patti's pregnancy, Jerry selected the name "Katherine" for the new offspring, and all during the months she was carrying the child, he kept dashing out to stores and buying expensive dresses for his "daughter."

Jerry had his heart so set on a girl that when the baby was born at St. John's Hospital on October 9 and *she* turned out to be a "Christopher" instead of a "Katherine," Patti was afraid to tell Jerry. She was still worrying how he would take it even when they were wheeling her out of the delivery room and down the corridor toward her private room.

Suddenly, Jerry's head appeared above hers.

"Are you disappointed?" she asked apprehensively.

"No, Mommy," replied Jerry, "but I don't think this kid's going to like being called 'Katherine.' "

Jerry was able to bounce back from his disappointment and even wax philosophical about it by the time Patti was out of the hospital.

"You know," he told Patti one night when they were sitting around in their cozy little den in the Pacific Palisades home, "everything is planned by God. We were meant to have a boy, I guess, because we were meant to have a big family. We're going to try to have a kid who'll answer to the name of Katherine. If we'd had her this time, we might have decided that our family was complete. But this way we'll have more babies—until we get our girl. And maybe that will give us a family of a dozen, until we get that someone who'll be able to wear those dresses I bought."

The next two to come along were Anthony, in 1959, and Joseph, in 1960. Obviously, someone "up there" wasn't paying attention. Or else He's a male chauvinist.

Regardless, the Lewises had an awfully full house, so Jerry decided he wanted more space and also a place that was slightly closer to the studio. With the density of suburban building and the resultant increase in traffic on Sunset Boulevard, the Pacific Palisades was no longer a quiet haven just a twenty-minute ride from Paramount Studios. It was closer to forty minutes, even with all of Jerry's bells and sirens clanging on his Lincoln Continental. That was too much time for a busy movie mogul to have to waste in a car, even though the car had a phone and he could make all the calls he wanted from the front seat.

Accordingly, Jerry and Patti went house hunting again and found just what they were looking for in a section of Los Angeles known as Bel Air.

Perhaps it's just a coincidence, but the house that Jerry bought and into which he moved his family had formerly belonged to Louis B. Mayer, the movie mogul of all movie moguls.

Mayer's former residence, for which Jerry reportedly paid $350,000, was more than a house—it was an estate fit for any Hollywood potentate. It was a squarely built two-story bastard colonial on two rolling acres in Bel Air's most costly neighborhood. The Lewises' new home had thirty-one rooms, seventeen baths, a swimming pool and a tennis court, a recreation area for ping pong, pinball machines, and lounging chairs for just sunning oneself.

Before Jerry was through, the new house could boast a number of additions that even Louis B. Mayer didn't have before they carted him out.

Among the new features were the following:

1. A den that Jerry used for a combination office, retreat from the family, and private apartment within a home. This room contained many shelves of different-colored leather-bound volumes, each with gold lettering detailing the contents—scripts of Lewis films beginning with *My Friend Irma* right up to the present; glass cabinets overflowing with awards, plaques, and gold and silver cups that spilled out onto shelves and tables in the room; books of photographs of his career with and without Dean Martin, as well as volumes of photos of Patti and the children and assorted relatives. On one wall was a large framed painting of Jerry dressed as Emmett Kelly, the clown. Another side of the room held a large sliding glass door that looked out on the garden area. Facing each other at opposite ends of this area were statues of St. Anthony and Moses.

And on a little table in front of the sliding glass lay a silver-covered copy of the Old Testament in Hebrew, a copy of the complete Bible, and a leather-bound autographed script of Cecil B. DeMille's *The Ten Commandments*.

2. A stereo room—L-shaped for best acoustics—containing five professional tape recorders, complete 16-mm movie camera equipment, a hookup with an FM radio station in which Jerry held a percentage of ownership, tape and record albums (all neatly catalogued), three large powerful speakers, and an intercom system that connected with every room in the house.

3. A living room that contained a Cinemascope screen that could be lowered by pressing a button.

4. A projection room (behind the living room) that contained two of the latest 35mm movie projectors. Next to the projectors were cans of films containing landmark movies, including a print of Charlie Chaplin's *Modern Times*.

5. A film-editing room complete with movieola, where Jerry sometimes cut and worked on his own pictures.

For security purposes, the grounds are completely encircled by tall shrubbery and a chain-link fence complete with electronic gate that can be controlled from either house or car. An asphalt driveway leads from the house down to St. Cloud Road, along which a never-ending stream of tourists flows past in automobiles bearing license plates from various states of the union.

Occasionally they stop and a tourist will hop out and take a picture of the house or of his family standing in front of the gate. On the gate and along the driveway, signs are posted warning trespassers to "Keep Out" and tradesmen to "Drive Carefully—Children at Play."

Jerry had to staff his new house with a full complement of servants, including a cook, a butler, a governess for the children, a full-time gardener, and a private policeman to patrol the grounds twenty-four hours a day.

The twenty-four-hour guard became necessary as a result of Jerry's generosity and compassion for a fellow human being in trouble.

On one of his many trips around the country, Jerry met an ex-vaudevillian whom he had known slightly during his years of struggling in New York. Now their positions were reversed. The man was down and out and, in addition, needed a couple of operations. Jerry felt sorry for the man, paid for his trip to the West Coast, and financed the operations. When the man recovered, Jerry gave him a job as a gagman. The stuff the man turned out was not usable, but Jerry kept him on the payroll anyway.

The untalented gagman evidently resented his material's never getting on the show. One day, when Jerry was on the set at Paramount, the gagman rushed over to him, grabbed him by the throat, and started choking him. It took four of the crew to pull him off Jerry, and a studio cop had to be called to kick him off the lot. As he was dragged away, the man screamed at Jerry, his benefactor, "I'll get your kids—I'll kill your kids!"

Ever since that day, Jerry hasn't felt safe without a guard patrolling his estate.

Besides living in Louis B. Mayer's home, there was a further manifestation of Jerry's new position in the film industry.

Late in 1958, after working all day on his newest movie, *Don't Give Up the Ship*, Jerry developed severe abdominal pains during the night, and Patti had to call in their physician, Marvin Levy, who, after examining him, rushed him to Mt. Sinai Hospital in Hollywood. Levy diagnosed his condition as a perforated bleeding ulcer complicated by a slight heart condition.

The heart condition was more psychosomatic than physical, according to Jerry's statement to the press at the time. "I have what they call an aggravated heart. My doctor says I'll die twenty years earlier than I would if I took it easy, but I'd rather die earlier living the way I do and having done what I've done."

But the perforated bleeding ulcer was quite definitely physical. Following his release from the hospital, Jerry was ordered to bed for two weeks and advised to work only four hours a day when he returned to the studio.

Back in his studio office, behind his huge desk, Jerry analyzed his physical condition with typical Jerry Lewis modesty. "I'm an overnight success," he told his staff. "As a producer I've got in two pictures what it took Zanuck and DeMille twenty years to get."

Jerry not only got ulcers and all the other related diseases, physical and otherwise, that stem from overwork, exhaustion, and bad living habits, such as not eating and sleeping, but also probably caused a few with his eccentric, egomaniacal, and sometimes just thoughtless behavior.

His work habits alone were enough to drive his employees up a wall. Being Jerry's personal secretary was one of the hardest jobs on his staff. Some women managed to last with Jerry a few weeks, some only a few hours. Janie Thompson, a pretty twenty-five-year-old blond, with what must have been the disposition of a saint, stuck it out for two years.

The hours Jerry kept when he was getting a picture ready for production or preparing a TV show were back-breaking. People had to marvel at his stamina, if not his talent as a producer.

Except for the janitors, the gate men, or the night watchman, Jerry was probably the first one on the studio lot in the morning. Generally he drove his big car through the "DeMille Gate" no later than 6:00, and he insisted that his secretary be there not long afterward so he could start making calls to writers and other associates to spring ideas on them. Often he'd be frustrated because some people kept more sensible hours in their own offices than he did.

One morning at 6:00, he placed a call to a producer at MGM. When Miss Thompson informed Jerry that the producer wouldn't be in his office until 10:00, Jerry snapped, "What's the matter, doesn't he like his work?"

Frequently Jerry would work round the clock with his writing staff, preparing a TV show for the air. Often a script needed this much work; but, just as often, he was driven by insecurity. As the critical sniping became worse, it became more and more difficult for the writers to please Jerry.

Sometimes he kept everybody working out of pure loneliness. This was particularly true if Jerry was out of town and Patti and the children were in Los Angeles.

One time, Jerry was playing a week in Las Vegas but had taken his entire staff along with him to work on his next TV show. Patti and the children had stayed with him the whole week, but on Sunday night they flew home because of school the next day.

That night Jerry kept the staff up until daybreak. At 6:00 he let everybody go to their rooms. At 7:00 Miss Thompson was wearily climbing into bed when the telephone rang. "Get everybody here right away," screamed Jerry. When the staff, in various stages of undress, arrived in Jerry's suite, he meekly explained, "I couldn't sleep and I didn't want to eat breakfast alone."

A thing like that isn't pure egomania. Jerry has a real fear of eating meals alone. If he walks into a restaurant by himself and doesn't see anyone he can join, he'll walk right out again and skip that meal rather than eat by himself.

There could be no other explanation for much of Jerry's behavior around the studio, however, than that he was on a giant ego trip. Under the desk in his office, for example, was a clear plastic shield designed to protect the plush white carpet from the rollers of his swivel chair. Under the plastic shield, face up, were a number of 8″ x 10″ photos of Jerry Lewis in all different poses. "I wouldn't have believed it if I hadn't seen it," reported Charlie Isaacs after emerging from a story conference with Jerry.

Unlike most actors, who make a point of keeping strangers off the set, Jerry insisted that things be just the reverse when he was working. Over the entrance of every sound stage where a Jerry Lewis film was being shot was a large sign reading:

THIS IS NOT A CLOSED SET. COME ON IN.
YOU'RE MOST WELCOME.

Another Jerry Lewis innovation was having a man on the sound stage to play electronic mood music between takes and a special fanfare for Jerry's first entrance every morning. For example, when Jerry, the picture of a Hollywood fashion plate, strode jauntily onto the set in his $100-a-pair Sy Devore slacks and a tan windbreaker, drums sounded, and Jerry walked in to their beat.

As time went on and his pictures continued to be successful, Jerry graduated from straight egomania and started to take on a Napoleonic complex. This is reflected in Jerry's treatment of two of the writers whose talent did much to enhance his picture career—Don McGuire and Cy Howard.

Following the success of *The Delicate Delinquent,* Jerry wrote Don McGuire a letter thanking him for "the swell job" he had done writing and directing the picture and hired him to go to work immediately on another project.

McGuire came up with a story called *The Baby Doctor.* Jerry liked it and hired him to write the screenplay and to direct it. After he read the final draft, Jerry came to McGuire and said, "There are no songs in here."

"That's right, Jerry," said McGuire. "There's no spot for one."

"I want to sing six songs in it," Jerry told him.

"Look, Jerry," said McGuire, "There's no place in this picture for songs. It'll spoil the picture."

"OK," said Jerry, and ostensibly he forgot about it.

A few weeks passed, during which Jerry never mentioned his singing. But when McGuire called the production department to clear a "start date" to begin shooting the new picture, the answer he received was evasive. He was told to check with Jerry. But when McGuire tried to contact Jerry, he couldn't reach him.

A couple of days later, Herman Citron dropped into McGuire's office, closed the door, and said, "I think I should tell you Jerry's not going to go ahead with your movie. I hate to be the one to have to give you the news, but Jerry won't tell you himself. You'll get paid, of course, for the script."

"I don't understand," said McGuire.

"He's changed his mind about the story, and he's hired Frank Tashlin to write and direct another one."

"I guess Tashlin's going to let him sing six songs in it," speculated McGuire dryly.

"No, eight," answered Citron quickly.

McGuire was shocked, but he wouldn't be satisfied until he heard it from Jerry's own lips, so he confronted Jerry in his office and asked him if it was true.

"You're going to get paid," said Jerry, as if that explained it.

"I know I'm going to get paid," said McGuire. "That's not the point. But how could you let me go ahead with all the preparations, getting a start date, having sets built, and not have the decency to tell me you were not going to go ahead with the picture?"

But Jerry looked the other way and wouldn't answer him. McGuire left, and the two didn't speak for years.

The incident that ended Cy Howard's relationship with Jerry was even more humiliating.

After doing three of Jerry's most successful pictures, Howard wrote an original screenplay on spec for Jerry. When Jerry heard about it, he asked Howard to send the script right over. Howard did, but then didn't hear from Jerry for weeks. Finally he received a call from Jerry's secretary setting up a meeting at the studio to discuss the new script.

When Howard walked into Jerry's office, the comic was sitting at his desk surrounded by a number of his flunkies. Howard's script was on the desk.

"Well, what'd you think of the script?" asked Howard.

In reply, Jerry threw Howard's script on the floor. "I don't need this to be funny. All I need is a table and some chairs."

"Fine," retorted Howard icily. "From now on, you can be a Jewish waiter."

And he, too, walked from the office and out of Jerry's life forever.

Meanwhile, as Jerry became increasingly impressed with his own position, his practical jokes took on a flavor that was more sadistic than funny.

One of his tricks was to creep up behind Janie Thompson when she was talking on the phone or working at the typewriter and bind her to her desk with Scotch tape. If he were feeling particularly puckish, he might even tape her lips shut.

In his ingenious use of the tape recorder to get a laugh, Jerry was light-years ahead of Watergate. For instance, he liked to bug his office or living room at home and record intimate conversations unbeknown to the participants. Then he'd play the tapes back to them in front of others, usually to everybody's mutual discomfort.

Sometimes the items Jerry picked up with his tape recorder were a good deal more intimate than just a private conversation. He went through one phase where he used to bug the Ladies' Room the women in his office used. This was good for a lot of laughs.

Say a woman excused herself to "powder her nose," as his personal secretary did one afternoon during a story conference that was attended by a number of important people at the studio. When she returned to the conference room, Jerry played back the tape on which he had recorded all her toilet sounds. When the poor woman realized what they were all listening to and laughing at, her face flushed a crimson color, and she nearly fainted from humiliation. She quit the job on the spot.

Jerry's TV writers frequently had to run another kind of gauntlet. When he was in the mood to have a little sport with his minions, Jerry would line up half a dozen of his gag writers about five feet apart on the studio street. Then he would hop on his bicycle and weave his way through them at breakneck speed, trying to frighten them by coming as close as possible without actually knocking them down.

Sometimes his aim was less than perfect, but how could one complain? He was the boss of Jerry Lewis Productions, and the pay was good.

Were it not that Jerry's and Cecil B. DeMille's pictures were about the only product keeping Paramount solvent in those days, he'd never have gotten away with many of his cute tricks on the studio lot. But as it does in most businesses, money breeds power. Hence, nobody was immune to Jerry Lewis's pranks and madness—not even two of the most revered men in the history of Paramount Studios—Cecil B. DeMille and Adolph Zukor.

In the Paramount commissary, just above Cecil B. DeMille's personal corner of the room, was a large color mural of a scene from one of his most famous pictures—*Samson and Delilah*. The mural depicted Samson holding up a stone pillar, and DeMille was very proud of it.

One night, Jerry hired a studio art director to paint out the original Samson and supplant him with Jerry Lewis holding up the enormous pillar instead. When DeMille saw it at lunch the next day, he nearly keeled over with a heart attack and threatened to commit mayhem on whoever had perpetrated such heresy against what he considered his personal property—the Holy Bible.

Because in his youth Jerry was skinny and uncoordinated and didn't have many opportunities to engage in sports, he tried to turn himself into an athlete after he became rich and had the time, or even if he didn't have the time.

For example, when he was shooting a picture on location, he would take a bat and ball along and hit flies to his flunkies between takes. During the football season he would walk around the studio, carrying a football, in case he wanted to have a quick catch with someone.

One of his favorite gags was to send an aide out for "a short pass"; then, when the man turned around to catch what he thought would be a gently thrown ball, Jerry would hurl it at him with all his might, usually knocking the wind out of the double-crossed pass receiver.

Nobody was safe from this brand of fraternity house humor.

One noon Jerry, carrying his football, walked into the commissary with his entourage just as Adolph Zukor was coming in for lunch. Adolph Zukor had founded Paramount Studios back in Hollywood's halcyon days. But now Zukor was nearing his ninetieth birthday, and he was a doddering old man who could hardly walk without assistance.

Spotting Zukor, Jerry suddenly yelled to him loudly from about ten feet away, "Go out for a short one, Adolph!" and he hurled the pigskin at the aged film maker as hard as he could throw it.

As the football whizzed toward the startled Zukor with the speed of a bazooka shell, a look of sheer terror crossed his face. Miraculously, the ball just grazed the old man's ear and caromed off—probably into somebody's soup.

People around who saw the incident—particularly those in Jerry's retinue—laughed their heads off. Why shouldn't they? Everything the Pied Piper of Comedy did in those days was funny—even the bit he did at a B'nai B'rith dinner he emceed, when he went through the audience afterward, passing the hat for poor Dino. The inference, of course, was that Dino was surely going to need some charitable contributions to keep from starving on his way to the poorhouse.

21

With a Little Bit of Luck

As he faced 1957 without Jerry Lewis, Dino had to be feeling much the same way. He had seven kids to support, a back-breaking alimony load to shoulder, and a flop picture to live down. It was fun to play golf, but caddies and golf balls were as expensive as girls were. Of course, he hadn't hit bottom yet.

Herman Citron had come up with a commitment for Dino to play the Sands Hotel in Las Vegas by himself in April. But, despite his outward lack of concern, he wasn't any more sanguine about succeeding as a solo nightclub entertainer than Jerry had been before he had substituted for Judy Garland.

Although he felt more at home in nightclubs than he did making movies by himself, Dino's overall confidence in himself as a performer had been badly shaken by the abysmal failure of *Ten Thousand Bedrooms* to attract customers. Moreover, he couldn't forget the many newspaper reviews pointing out the noticeable void at his side.

In addition, Dino had no act without Jerry, and he seemed to be at a loss as to how to put one together.

In short, Dino was in deep trouble, and everybody recognized it and wanted to help out—which is one of the major differences between Martin and Lewis. When Jerry is in trouble, most people say, "That's good—couldn't happen to a nicer guy." But when Dean is in trouble, friends inexplicably come running to his rescue.

But Dean was in such a strange moody frame of mind that he was refusing help. It was almost as if he hated the entire world. He wasn't even getting along with Jeanne. At one point he became so difficult that

she took her children and moved to Palm Springs. She stayed there until
Dean became "halfway bearable" once again.

A close friend of Dino's—songwriter Sammy Cahn—who specialized in
writing nightclub material (notably for Frank Sinatra) was one who tried
to come to Dino's aid. At every opportunity, he bolstered his morale by
pounding into him the notion that he sang well enough to make it on his
own and that he had nothing to fear but fear itself.

For a time Sammy Cahn even worked with Dino to put an act together
consisting of jokes and special material. But Cahn's stuff was too flip, and
Dino didn't feel comfortable doing straight "stand up" routines. So, after
a few weeks of fruitless collaboration, Dino thanked the composer for his
efforts but said he didn't need any creative help. He told Cahn that he'd
just sing for the customers at the Sands and perhaps do a little "fooling
around" if he was in the mood. And if that wasn't good enough, "screw
'em."

Like most performers, Dino has perpetuated the myth that he wrote
the act with which he opened at the Sands.

In a *Look* article published in 1959, Jeanne Martin is quoted as saying,

> Whatever he's accomplished, good or bad, he's done it himself.
> When he went out on his own, he had seven children to support and
> tremendous alimony to pay, and I imagine it was a frightening six
> months, until he could break in his new act. But he was determined to
> have no help. He even wrote the act himself, so whatever it was, it
> was his.

As romantic as that may sound, it's far from the truth. His first act was
written and staged by a writer whom Martin and Lewis had once fired
from the Colgate show—Ed Simmons.

Ironically, the writing team of Ed Simmons and Norman Lear had
broken up at approximately the same time that Martin and Lewis had
kissed each other good-bye. Simmons had always equated himself with
Dino, believing that each was the "quiet half" of his respective team. Now
that he too had been left without a partner and also had no job, Simmons
could feel a great deal of empathy for Dino's position. He certainly felt
no bitterness toward Dino, for in the intervening years he had learned
that it was actually Jerry who had been instrumental in getting him and
Lear fired from "The Colgate Comedy Hour" and that Dean had actually
opposed their dismissal but didn't have the courage to stand up to Jerry.

Consequently, when Simmons heard that Dino was scheduled to open
at the Sands in less than two months and that he hadn't the slightest
semblance of an act, he decided that what the two of them needed at the
moment was each other. So he took a chance, phoned Dino, and set up a

date for the two of them to meet over a drink at the Polo Lounge in the Beverly Hills Hotel that same night.

In the murky ambience of Beverly Hill's most chic gin mill, Simmons wasted no time in acquainting Dino with some very sobering facts.

"Dean," he started out, "they're laying eight to five you'll be singing at Larry Potter's in the Valley in a year. Let me write your act for you. I've got something to prove; you've got something to prove."

"I'm not gonna do an act," replied Dino stoically, "I'm just gonna sing."

"It won't work," said Simmons. "Audiences today expect more."

"What else am I gonna do?" asked Dino plaintively. "Here I am alone —I'm doing it by myself. I'll manage."

"Look, I'll make a deal with you," said Simmons, who suspected that the main reason Dino was stalling was because he didn't have the money to pay a writer. "For a necktie, I'll write you a whole nightclub act."

Dino shook his head stubbornly. His attitude was almost suicidal, as if he realized he was heading for oblivion and he wanted to get there as soon as possible, and without any detours.

"OK, have it your way," said Simmons, scribbling his name and phone number on a scrap of paper and standing up. "Here's my phone number, Dean. Call me if you want me."

Simmons wrote Dino off as just another spoiled egomaniacal performer who believed he didn't need writers. With such an attitude he would undoubtedly fall by the wayside.

But the gods were watching out for Dean Martin again at this very important juncture in his career. Or perhaps he had just read how well Jerry was doing. At any rate, ten days before Dean was to open at the Sands, the phone rang in Ed Simmons's apartment. Dino was on the other end of the line.

"Ed, baby," drawled Dean, sounding just a bit worried. "How would you like to earn a necktie?"

"Give me your address, and I'll be right over," replied Simmons.

When the two of them finally got together at the Martins' baronial home on Mountain Drive, Simmons found a badly frightened Dino thrashing around in a pool of his own creative ineptitude. He was no closer to having an act than he had been two months previously. He didn't even have any good new jokes.

But he did have a "concept" for a character he could play that might be the basis of some humor. In a moment of truth with himself, Dino had realized that a character of his own was something he'd never been able to develop when he was working with Jerry, which was why he always came off in the movies as such a colorless individual.

A character of some sort was something every performer needed badly if he hoped to get anywhere in show business. Everybody who was anybody had one—for example, Jack Benny, "the Tightwad"; Frank Sinatra, "the Swinger"; Phil Silvers, "the Conniver"; Lucille Ball, "the Bumbler"; and let's not forget Jerry Lewis, "the Idiot."

Recognizing this, Dino suggested to Simmons that he try writing him as the booze-sodden drunk character that had been so successful for Phil Harris and Joe E. Lewis. "No one is doing the drunk anymore since they quit," Dino pointed out.

The idea appealed to Simmons, who realized that the "drunk" would not only add some color to Dean's nonexistent character, but it "was also a marvelous cover-up for any goofs he might make in the act." It also enabled him to kid himself, which is a surefire way to ingratiate a performer with his audience.

Crooning in his inimitable Crosby style would, of course, still make up a large part of Dino's new act, but Simmons loaded the in-between patter with a liberal assortment of jokes kidding Dino's legendary fondness for alcohol.

"Drink up—the drunker you get, the better I sound."

"I don't drink any less, but I don't drink any more."

"I will now sing a song from my new album—'Ballads for B-Girls.' "

The day before Dino's opening at the Sands, Simmons went to Las Vegas with him and helped him rehearse his act.

Dino was backed up with the usual assortment of Jack Entratter's leggy, bosomy showgirls, but, except for them, Dino was virtually doing a one-man show.

"I sat with him in his dressing room Thursday night, the night of the opening," recalls Simmons, "and it may be the only time in show business history when the writer was drinking in the dressing room and Dean wasn't. Dino had had a light gray Sy Devore tuxedo made just for the opening and a light pearl-gray tie. He put the new tuxedo on, but he was so nervous as he was tying his tie that he finally said to me, 'I can't wear this . . . I've gotta go back to a regular tuxedo.' So he ripped it off and put on his old tux."

He had good reason to be nervous, for he had a celebrity-laden audience: Jack Benny, Lucille Ball, Desi Arnaz, Frank Sinatra, Dino's agents, his managers, his wife—in fact, just about everyone who meant anything in show business was there, except Jerry Lewis. But they were all pulling for him as he stepped nervously to the mike and faced them for the first time.

"Don't think I'm gonna do anything different," began Dino with a boozy smile. "The only thing is, I'm going to be standing here instead of here." And he stepped about a yard to the side where he usually stood when Jerry Lewis was hogging the mike.

"Oh, that's great!" exclaimed Jack Benny from his ringside table.

The rest of the audience also appreciated it, as a wave of laughter resounded through the huge room.

"From that moment on," says Simmons, in true appreciation for the man he was writing for, "Dean had total control. I will, of course, give credit to the material. But his own head was working with it. He did ten minutes of introducing celebrities from the audience for which I hadn't written one word, and it was hilarious."

Between shows, Simmons visited Dean in his dressing room to make some cuts and minor changes in the act.

"He had wall-to-wall celebrities in there, slapping him on the back and congratulating him on how great his show was. But when I said to him I wanted to make a few changes, he told his friends that they had to go because 'I've gotta talk to my writer.'

"Everybody left. We sat and did the changes. Then he went on and did the second show. It was perfect. Dino added things. He was marvelous."

One of Dean's additions that pleases audiences to this day is the way he will start to sing a straight ballad, and then, when he has the audience listening in engrossed silence, switch the sentimental lyric into some kind of a joke.

While pleasing audiences, this habit usually annoys the songwriters, who, historically, are known to possess little sense of humor when a performer is deviating from their lyrics.

On one occasion, he changed a Sammy Cahn lyric from "My darling, if I hurt you, forgive me" to "My darling, if I marry you, forgive me."

Sammy Cahn rushed backstage after the show and confronted him with this bit of heresy. "Why? Why?" asked Cahn. "Didn't you hear how quiet they were when you were singing my lyrics the way I wrote it?"

"Sure," Dino replied, "but did you hear that laugh?"

Dino just couldn't take himself seriously. "Perhaps," Cahn says, "because he distrusts his own talent."

He didn't have to distrust it any more after his smash opening at the Sands. In contrast to Jerry's review at the Sands, Dino drew a rave from *Variety*'s Joe Schoenfeld:

> Dean Martin's opening as a single at Jack Entratter's desert playground established at least one other important precedent besides that of his solo flight. For the first time since the Las Vegas casinos began importing big-name shows, a production got on and off in sixty minutes, which surprised the croupiers to such an extent they were caught with their sticks down.
>
> The credit, and its only one of many, goes to Martin, who kept his entire turn, including a beg-off speech and the introduction of a number of celebs in the audience, to thirty-eight minutes. This is in sharp contrast to the average Vegas headliner, who appears to make a con-

test of who can outwait the other. (Jerry's opening ran almost two hours.) Besides that, Martin is a big click, delivering expertly as a nitery performer with a winning personality that's a relaxed admixture of Schenley and Crosby.

Martin's way with a song is surefire. Like Joe E. Lewis, he makes a point of kidding a love of the grape and the grain and obviously has the knack to sell this type of comedy for big laughs. If audience reaction is any criterion, Martin will be around long and strong as a single entertainer and headliner. Opening night he could have heeded the customers' demands and remained on much longer. He wisely quit way ahead.

As for Ed Simmons, "I left Las Vegas the day after the opening," he relates without any rancor. "I never worked for Dean again. I never got the necktie. I never got a penny. I never got one word of acknowledgment. I've seen him a couple of times since—when I've had him as a guest star on shows I've produced. And I rib him unmercifully about the tie I never got. I tell him, 'Hey, Dean, I'm wearing a lot of brown now, so if you were thinking about getting me a blue tie, I'd rather have a brown one.' But he reacts as if he never heard me."

As his confidence in his own ability grew, Dino polished and embellished his act without any help. Sometimes the jokes were at Jerry's expense.

"See these muscles," Dino would say, flexing his large biceps, "I got them carrying Jerry all these years."

Audiences ate up that kind of humor, which was OK with Dino. He'd always wanted to be a comedian, and if he could get laughs kidding Jerry, all the better.

Dean's nightclub career as a "single" may have been reborn with his successful opening in Las Vegas, but in New York and Hollywood, where the miasma of *Ten Thousand Bedrooms* was causing people to reach for their gas masks, the prognosticators of doom were counting him out as a motion picture star.

Then from out of nowhere came an unexpected break. Twentieth Century-Fox was about to make a major motion picture out of Irwin Shaw's best-selling novel *The Young Lions*. The script contained three important male roles: a sensitive Jewish young man, a Nazi zealot soldier, and a Broadway singing star who wants no part of soldiering and who pulls all kinds of strings to avoid serving his country.

Montgomery Clift and Marlon Brando were cast as the Jew and the Nazi respectively, but what self-respecting male star would accept the role of a draft dodger, even if it was only make-believe?

Twentieth combed most of the Broadway and Hollywood agencies and casting offices for an actor who could sing, who had an acceptable "name," and who wouldn't ask for too much money. Brando and Clift were each getting $100,000, but the studio was hoping to pay less for the draft-dodger role, which was the least important of the three. Sinatra, of course, would have been perfect, but, after his Academy Award-winning performance in *From Here to Eternity*, he no longer had to accept short money or unheroic parts.

When Herman Citron suggested his client, Dean Martin, there was considerable hesitation on the part of the studio. Edward Dmytryk, who was going to direct *The Young Lions*, wasn't sure Dean Martin could handle straight dramatic acting. Besides, he wasn't very hot after that last "turkey" he'd been in. Still, it was an interesting idea if he'd work cheap enough.

They finally offered $35,000. Dean, of course, could make that much in a few weeks of working in nightclubs. "But I'd have done it for nothing," Dean later confessed. "I needed a good, strong, meaty part to get going. You remember how Sinatra got his break in *From Here to Eternity*? Only Frank did that for ten grand."

Dean and Jeanne were in Pittsburgh, where Dean was picking up a few bucks trying out his new act in a nightclub, when Citron phoned him from Hollywood and said he had the part. The call came through while the Martins were together in their hotel room. They were completely overwhelmed that hardhearted Hollywood was going to give Dean a second chance.

"Jeanne and I sat down and had a real nice cry—with real tears," says the guy who many have accused of being "a very cold fish."

The Young Lions, released in the Spring of 1958, turned out to be an Academy Award contender; all the reviews were excellent; and Dean Martin proved to be a better straight actor than anyone had suspected.

Variety wrote, "Dean Martin does a remarkable dramatic job. It is not just the case of a singer doing a surprisingly good acting job; it is honest and penetrating emoting by any rule."

The Los Angeles Mirror News had this to say: "Marlon Brando, Montgomery Clift, and Dean Martin are all excellent in subtly under-played performances. Biggest surprise of the trio is Dean Martin, who holds his own with the other two as the braggart draft dodger."

And from *The Los Angeles Examiner* came this comment: "Few will deny the surprise Dean Martin contributes through his mature and beautifully shaded performance."

After that, things began to roll for Dean Martin, "the Serious Actor." Hal Wallis, who had been unable to find a suitable vehicle for Dean after he and Jerry had split, quickly came up with three vehicles in a row for Jerry Lewis's former doormat.

When Martin and Lewis had split, they still owed Hal Wallis four pictures by the terms of their last contract. When they broke up, they *each* owed him four. So Hal Wallis got himself eight pictures for the price of four—a real bargain—and Wallis is a man who likes bargains.

As Dean's success grew, Herman Citron thought Wallis should pay Dean more. But Wallis insisted on sticking to the terms of the last Martin and Lewis contract of $75,000 a picture for the team, or $37,500 each.

Dino thought Wallis was taking advantage of him. Every time he was ready to do a new picture for Wallis, he'd say, "How about a $75,000 bonus, Hal?" But Wallis would dismiss this request with, "Don't be crazy."

Finally, after the old contract ran out, Wallis asked Dean to make an extra picture for him.

"Herman and I came up with a new price tag—$475,000 for my services," says Dino. "When Wallis's eyeballs stopped spinning, he asked, 'How did you reach that figure?' And Herman said, 'We figured $250,000 for the picture, then we added three of those $75,000 bonuses you didn't give us.' "

Needless to say, Dino didn't do the picture, his success in *The Young Lions* notwithstanding.

Although *The Young Lions* was instrumental in sending Dino along the comeback trail, it was *Some Came Running* that secured him a permanent place in Hollywood as an important marquee name and top money earner. And like everything else in his career, *Some Came Running* came to him in more or less an accidental manner.

The film was based upon the best-selling novel of the same name by James Jones. Two of the three main roles were already cast when Dino first heard about the picture: Frank Sinatra as the returning GI and Shirley MacLaine as the hooker with the heart of gold (a role that eventually made her). But a third part, that of a drifter called Bama, a blackjack dealer who spoke with a lazy southern drawl, had yet to be filled.

There was considerable speculation in the trades as to who would get that plum. For some reason, none of the people at Twentieth Century-Fox had thought of giving it to Dean Martin.

During this period, Dean and Jeanne attended an important Hollywood party, celebrating the premiere of *Kings Go Forth*, Frank Sinatra's previous picture.

At the party Dean bumped into Sinatra, whom he knew only casually. They had originally met at Skinny D'Amato's 500 Club in Atlantic City, and they'd said hello to each other a few times around the Copa and at Hollywood parties. But they weren't really close.

But, at this affair, Dino walked right up to Sinatra as if he was his closest pal. "You bum!" he greeted him.

"What have I done now?" asked Sinatra.

"You're hunting for a man for your next picture who smokes, drinks, and can talk real Southern. You're looking at him."

Sinatra gave Dean a long stare. "Well, what do you know!" he exclaimed.

"All I want is a hundred and fifty thou, and when and where do I report?" said Dino.

"Next week in Indiana," said Sinatra, without batting an eye.

"And that's the way I got that role," relates Dino. "It was the happiest picture I've ever been in. A part like that will never come my way again. Being with Shirley MacLaine and Frank—I don't know, it was just happy."

Indeed it was. *Some Came Running* was a huge success, both critically and at the box office. Dean Martin got excellent personal reviews. And through that association with Sinatra, a close and financially rewarding friendship between the two singing paisanos came into being.

When they were doing their location shooting in Indiana and Kentucky, the two of them constantly palled around together in their off hours. They drank together, they indulged in their favorite sport—girl watching—together, and they shot craps at the gaming tables in Covington, Kentucky, together.

Because they had so much in common, they were more like Damon and Pythias than Dean and Jerry had ever dreamed of being.

They followed *Some Came Running* with *Ocean's Eleven*, the story of five GIs who decide to knock over a Las Vegas gambling casino. This film was produced by Sinatra's own company, and, of course, the boss cast Dean Martin in one of the main roles. The others in the cast were Sammy Davis, Jr., Peter Lawford, and Joey Bishop.

Since the picture was to be filmed in Las Vegas, using the facilities of the Sands Hotel and casino, Jack Entratter got the brilliant notion to capitalize on Sinatra's blockbuster cast by having them perform in his showroom in the evening. In return for this, the hotel would give Sinatra's company a break in the use of the hotel for location shooting.

The five entertainers agreed, since they were all in for a "piece" of the picture profits. As a result, the world-renowned summit meeting of the Rat Pack was held.

With Sinatra, Martin, Davis, Bishop, and Lawford all holding forth on the Sands stage in one exciting show, customers from every part of the United States started heading for Las Vegas in such numbers that one native commented, "You'd think it was the gold rush all over again."

With the success of the summit meeting, Dean Martin had suddenly turned into one of America's superstars—making superstar money.

By 1961, he was getting from $250,000 to $300,000 per picture and was booked for as many films in advance as he cared to take on. He was earning $50,000 a week for his Vegas appearances, and he owned a piece of the Sands Hotel, which he had been given as a bonus for signing. As a crooner of popular songs, Dino was selling millions of records and recording at least two long-playing albums a year for Capitol. He was only doing TV sporadically, because he didn't want to work that hard, but when he did appear on a special, he received no less than $50,000 for an appearance.

In addition to everything else, he owned a restaurant on Hollywood's Sunset Strip called "Dino's."

All in all, he was good for approximately $2 million a year—or enough to enable him to climb out of debt at last and to start building a personal and well-deserved fortune.

So much success on his own did something for Dean Martin as a human being. Suddenly he wasn't bitter about Jerry Lewis anymore. He even had a sense of humor about his old partner.

Although in the years since their split-up there had been occasions when they both were on the Paramount lot or in the NBC Building simultaneously, neither Dean nor Jerry actually bumped into each other until Jerry was doing a guest-shot on "The Eddie Fisher Show."

In one of the comedy routines on this program, Jerry was supposed to insist that he be allowed to sing, while Fisher was to insist just as strongly that he didn't.

"*I'm* the singer—you're just supposed to be funny," Eddie Fisher was to tell his guest.

Just as Jerry and Fisher were doing this routine on the air, Dean Martin and Bing Crosby happened to be walking down the corridor outside the studio. When someone tipped Dean off that Jerry was on the Fisher show, he tiptoed into the studio, stuck his head through a curtain in full camera range, and shouted to his ex-partner, "Don't sing—just don't sing!"

The audience roared. Jerry appeared stunned, then recovered his composure, and started running after Dino, shouting, "Come back! Come back!"

People in the business and also loyal Martin and Lewis fans figured this was a prearranged stunt and that it augured a reunion of Martin and Lewis. But this was not so. Dino did not come back. Of course, he never would. And the two reverted to the coolness of their former relationship.

That they couldn't even be friends was more Jerry's fault than Dino's. Jerry still thought of himself as the jilted lover. He couldn't get over Dean's having left him, and he would never forgive him for it—even though they were both doing better independently than they had ever done together.

When he was making *All in a Night's Work* for Hal Wallis, Dean used to see Jerry driving around the lot on his golf cart, and he was hopeful that they'd finally come face to face so they could make up. But every time Jerry spotted Dean coming, he'd quickly drive his cart around a corner to avoid a confrontation—even a friendly one—with his former partner.

After Jerry did that to him three or four times, Dino walked over to Jerry Lewis Productions, barged his way through about twenty secretaries, and ended up in Jerry's private office, where Jerry was sitting at his desk.

"You little so and so—why are you ducking me?" asked Dino. "What's the matter with you, anyhow?"

"I didn't mean it like that," answered Jerry.

"What do you mean? You saw me just now, and you darted around a corner. Why did you do it?"

Jerry squirmed uneasily. "I didn't feel right," he said.

Dean got him to come out from behind his desk. "Come up to my room," he said. "There are no bells or secretaries there. Anybody can walk right in. Anybody at all."

Upstairs in his own bailiwick, Dean ordered Jerry to "sit down and have a drink."

Jerry declined the drink but listened while Dean talked to him in a very brotherly fashion for fifteen minutes about how silly it was for them not even to be on speaking terms. Gradually, Jerry warmed up and admitted he had been acting like a child.

"Now, isn't this better than ducking me?" Dean finally asked.

"Yep," grinned Jerry. And they shook hands on it, and he left.

"I felt pretty good about it," recalls Dino. "But the next time Jerry saw me he ducked around a corner again."

After that, Dean quit trying.

Despite Jerry's infantile attitude, Dean refused to revert to their former bitterness. As was often the case after the breakup, some heckler in the audience would interrupt Dean's nightclub act at the Sands by shouting up to him, "Hey, Dean, where's Jerry?"

It was the perfect spot for Dean to say something nasty about Jerry if he wanted to keep the feud going. Instead, he would reply suavely, "I don't know where he is, but wherever he is, he must be doing just fine, because he has bundles of talent and he's a wonderful guy."

Following the applause, which would always be thunderous, Dino would add one final fillip, "How do you feel now, you jerk?"

As Dean's confidence in his own ability grew, not only could he afford to be more tolerant of Jerry, but his relationship with Jeanne was also improving. In the past, there had been many critical moments in Dean's

and Jeanne's marriage, leading to heated quarreling and frequent separa-
tions. Always there would be passionate reconciliations and avowals that
it would never happen again.

Contrary to the rumors, so widespread over the years, that Dean is an
incurable "girl chaser," little of the trouble between Dean and Jeanne
during the first half of their marriage had anything to do with other
women—except trouble caused by his first wife. But not "woman trouble"
in the more sexual meaning of the term.

"My husband's not comfortable with women," Jeanne was once quoted
as saying. "He's not even comfortable with me. He'd much rather play
cards with the boys than face an evening trying to make small talk with
the girls."

Most of the difficulties in the marriage in its first ten years stemmed
from Dean's unhappiness and discontent with himself, and that feeling
grew directly out of the Jerry Lewis situation. Afraid to make the break
for many years, Dino could be moody and irritable at home. Around
Jeanne, who enjoyed the high life, he wasn't always the gay caballero he
appeared to be in public. And this moodiness and irritability led to frequent
battling and emotional door-slamming exits.

"There was a time when Dean was always coming over to my house
and spending the night," remembers Cy Howard, who befriended Dino
during his many periods of separation.

But by 1960, when Dean's success without Jerry seemed virtually
assured, he became easier to live with, and a period of tranquillity settled
over the Martin hermitage in Beverly Hills.

"You never saw a happier, jollier, gayer house than ours," Dean told
Pete Martin in an interview with *The Saturday Evening Post.* "My wife
Jeanne and I make it happy. We tell the others, 'There's going to be
happiness in this house, see!' and we do everything we know how to make
it happy. We have a tennis court. We have friends over every Saturday
and Sunday. There are tennis games going on with the kids playing.
Jeanne plays too. And we have a big pool in which everybody swims."

On the subject of Jeanne, Dean said enthusiastically, "Jeanne's got the
kind of sense of humor that breaks me up constantly. If we have an argument, two or three hours later one of us will say a line kidding the
argument we've had; then we're smiling again. We never go to sleep at
night angry or without speaking to each other. We always kiss each other
good night. It's terrible if you don't. I used to get angry and freeze up
until she made me start talking. Once you start talking, you feel better.
And before they go to school, our kids march in and kiss us. Even if we're
sound asleep, they still kiss us good morning. Those are some of the
reasons why I call it a happy house."

The Martin marriage was rolling along so smoothly that, in September

1960, Dean threw a big bash for all his friends at his restaurant on Sunset Boulevard.

"What's the occasion?" asked director George Sidney as Dean met him at the door of "Dino's" with a drink in his hand.

"It's my twentieth wedding anniversary," replied Dean.

"But you and Jeanne have only been married ten years," Sidney reminded him.

Dean grinned and said, "Ten years to that first broad—ten years to Jeanne. That makes twenty."

22

By Myself

In the race between Martin and Lewis to see who could survive best without the other, the pony from New Jersey was leading by a nose over the Italian stallion as they made the turn into the backstretch. But the Jersey pony was pushing himself mercilessly, even going to the whip, to keep from being overtaken, whereas the Italian stallion was taking long, easy, loping strides and showing a lot more class.

Coming into the homestretch, Jerry must have felt Dean's hot breath on his flank, for the harder he tried to look better than Dean, the more he stumbled. Evidently, Jerry had not yet learned the lesson that Dean's pal Frank Sinatra had made so famous in song: "Nice and Easy Does It Every Time."

Because Dino owned a restaurant on Sunset Strip called "Dino's," Jerry had to have one called "Jerry Lewis's." Like virtually every nonshow business enterprise with which Jerry has been associated, it was a dismal failure, both as a place to have a good meal and as a tourist attraction. Eventually Jerry gave up ownership, the place changed its name to The Classic Cat, and in the metamorphosis became a joint featuring "amateur topless and bottomless" entertainment.

As a golfer, Jerry didn't stand a chance of becoming Dean's equal, but there was a period when he took his game as seriously as did Arnold Palmer. He bought hundreds of dollars' worth of equipment and clothing, joined a country club, took lessons, and had grosses of personalized golf balls made up with his name and a caricature of Jerry Lewis's face printed on them.

Everywhere Jerry went he took his golf clubs and personalized golf balls and practiced—even when he went aboard a United States battleship to shoot location scenes for *Don't Give Up the Ship*, which Norman Taurog directed. To the crew's bewilderment, Jerry clambered up the gangplank followed by a flunky carrying an enormous bag of golf clubs and a couple of grosses of golf balls. Who but some kind of a nut (or Jerry Lewis) would think of using a battleship at sea for a driving range?

But to Jerry it was the most natural thing in the world. Between takes, he pulled out his golfing equipment, stepped to the fantail of the ship, and started socking hundreds of brand new golf balls into the ocean. Lined up behind him watching were hundreds of shocked gobs—shocked at such a brazen disregard for money.

Taurog finally had to take his star aside and say, "Jesus, Jerry, look behind you. Those poor gobs are making seventy bucks a month, and you're hitting more than that into the ocean every twenty minutes. Some of them might even play golf on their days off, probably with cheap drug store golf balls. Did you ever stop to think how they must feel watching you waste all those?"

The next day Jerry showed up with a whole crate of his golf balls and distributed them to the crew.

In the early 1960s, Norman Blackburn was producing a TV show called "Celebrity Golf" on which Sam Snead played nine holes against a different celebrity every week, with the celebrity playing to his regular handicap. The celebrity didn't receive a salary, but he was given $100 for every par he carded, $300 for every birdie, and $1,000 if he beat Snead. Whatever the celebrity won, he was supposed to donate to his favorite charity.

Blackburn approached Jerry about appearing on "Celebrity Golf," and Jerry said, "Sure, I'll do it. I'll give what I win to muscular dystrophy."

The match was played at the Bel Air Country Club. Jerry showed up at the first tee the very picture of a golfing fashion plate, in about $500 worth of Sy Devore clothing. Playing to a twelve handicap, Jerry figured he could beat Snead handily as he teed up his ball and prepared to do or die for good old muscular dystrophy. .

Jerry drove his first shot about 180 yards, but he hooked the ball into deep rough and behind some trees. It took Jerry four shots with a three iron to get out of the rough and eight before he was in the hole.

This exposure to the world of what a golfing hacker he really was completely devastated Jerry. For the remaining eight holes his game continued to fall apart. He carded nothing but a series of bogeys, double bogeys, and triple bogeys. Snead, of course, whipped him soundly.

After nine holes it was customary for Snead to give his celebrity guest an on-camera lesson in whatever part of his game he felt needed the most work. When this portion of the show arrived, Snead looked at Jerry and said, "I guess you need a lesson in how to get out of the rough with a three iron."

Snead dropped a ball into the same rough that had given Jerry so much trouble, took out his own three iron, and belted a shot about 250 yards into the center of the fairway near the green. He then handed his three iron to Jerry, showed him how to grip the club properly, and told him to try it.

To the crowd's astonishment, Jerry swung and drove the ball out of the rough almost as far as Snead's shot. Jerry tried it again, with the same result. When it happened a third time, Jerry turned to Snead and said, "I've gotta have that club."

"Don't be silly," drawled Snead. "That's my club."

"I've gotta have it," insisted Jerry. "I've got the feel with it. I'll give you $100 for it."

"I don't want $100," said Snead. "That's my favorite three iron. Use your own."

"Two hundred!" said Jerry.

"Forget it," said Snead.

"Three hundred," bid Jerry.

"Don't be ridiculous," replied Snead. "I'm not gonna sell you that club for $300."

"God damn it, I've gotta have that club," screamed Jerry. "I'll give you $500 for it!"

Jerry created such a scene in front of the shocked spectators that Snead finally relented. So Jerry got his three iron, and Snead got $500. But muscular dystrophy failed to make the cut.

Not content with making one lucky gold-platter recording of "Rock-a-bye Your Baby," Jerry decided to compete with Dean by featuring his own singing on his TV shows.

When Dean did one of his infrequent specials, he very sensibly hired a comedian to handle the main comedy chores. But on Jerry's TV shows, the star not only wrote, produced, directed, and did the comedy, but also hired a fellow named Jerry Lewis to be the vocalist.

One of Jerry's favorite crowd-pleasers was the Arthur Schwartz–Howard Dietz song "By Myself":

> I'll go my way by myself;
> I'll build a world of my own.
> Nobody knows better than I myself;
> I'm by myself, alone.

It isn't difficult to get the not very subtle message of those lyrics as they applied to him and Dean. But Jerry Lewis fans ate up his blatant appeal for sympathy. What did they care if he didn't have a very good voice? That he could carry a tune at all impressed a lot of people—so much so that Jerry was able to talk NBC into letting him star in "The Jazz Singer" on TV.

"The Jazz Singer" was a former Broadway musical.about a cantor who wanted to be in show business. Thirty years earlier, Warner Brothers– First National had put Al Jolson in it and made motion picture history by turning it into the first "talkie."

By contemporary standards, the story was old-fashioned and full of bathos, and, besides, Jerry Lewis was no Al Jolson. Nevertheless, Jerry wanted to play "The Jazz Singer" as much as the cantor wanted to go into show business. And whatever Jerry wanted in those days, Jerry generally got.

According to public and critical response, Jerry should have let "The Jazz Singer" remain buried in the La Brea tar pits. Jerry, playing the part of a singing rabbi, was enough to convert the most dedicated Jew to another religion, and the critics were so vitriolic about his performance that all Jerry could think of to say in response was that they were "caustic, rude, unkind, and sinister."

Despite the failure of "The Jazz Singer" to convince anybody that Jerry was a serious actor or that he could sing as well as Jolson (or even Dean Martin), the entertainment industry conferred an unexpected honor on Jerry Lewis that year.

The Academy of Motion Picture Arts and Sciences chose Jerry to emcee the nationally televised Oscar awards ceremony, which up until that year had been Bob Hope's private domain.

Replacing Bob Hope on the Oscar telecast was almost as difficult as following Judy Garland at the Palace, but Jerry accepted the challenge with his usual enthusiasm. Unfortunately, he turned the evening into a Jerry Lewis comedy show, pulling out all his surefire schtick, including leading the orchestra. Jerry may have gotten a few laughs, but in doing so he failed to realize it was not *his* night; it belonged to all the people in the movie industry who were there to receive Oscars.

Most people resented Jerry's attempts to be funny, and, in *The New York Times* the following morning, TV critic Jack Gould panned him by calling his performance "a tour de force of uncompromising ineptitude."

It was enough to turn a guy into a complete paranoid. Jerry was beginning to anticipate horrible reviews even before he went on the air.

On May 20, 1960, the day of his first TV appearance of the season, Jerry gave out the following interview to United Press International as he drove through Hollywood in a huge convertible, dressed in a black leather jacket, corduroy trousers, and cowboy boots:

> I can write the reviews for my show before we ever go on. They hit the show for one reason or another, saying, "He's too busy and antagonistic," or "He's trying to sing." They'll drive you crazy if you listen to them.
>
> The critic who belts my show does me a favor. They create a bond between myself and the fans I know are watching.
>
> I don't need a critic. I know when I've done a good show or a bad one. Don't tell me when I've made a flop. Just let me crawl into a corner and lick my wounds.
>
> Look at all the shows the critics liked that aren't even on the air anymore. I don't think critics have got enough strength to keep anyone on the air, but they can plant a seed that'll get a guy off.
>
> As for my show, I've had very few good reviews, but I'm still on.

Jerry summed it all up by saying, "I do the best I know how. Nobody has a right to expect a man to give more than that."

Despite this bravado, Jerry was beginning to get fed up with TV. He felt that because it was a medium where people didn't have to pay to get in but simply sat at home and twirled a dial, they were often more critical than they had a right to be. Besides that, his ratings hadn't been especially good, so when his deal with NBC ran out after the 1960–1961 season, Jerry took a two-year sabbatical from TV, to concentrate his energies on making pictures. Jerry Lewis films were still big favorites with the kids.

Despite the critics, who hadn't been any kinder to his movies, Jerry still hadn't lost his enthusiasm for film making. If anything, he was more intense about it than ever and was still turning out films at the rate of two a year—one to be released in December and the other in July.

Paramount didn't like to deviate from that release schedule because December and July were the months kids were on vacation. School-aged children constituted the bulk of Jerry's audience, and the studio dared not lose them.

In 1960, Jerry made *Cinderfella*, a modern spoof of the fairy tale but with a switch in gender of the main character so Jerry could take the part of the orphaned waif, Cinderfella. Get it?

In accordance with the Paramount release schedule, it was to open in July. Jerry wanted to hold it for the Christmas season, however, feeling a fantasy was a better bet for the holidays. Paramount wouldn't hear of it because they had no Jerry Lewis film to put into the July slot.

Things remained at an impasse until Jerry, on his way to Florida to play the Fontainebleau that spring, got an idea and stopped off in New York City to talk over his problem with Barney Balaban, the current lord high chancellor of Paramount.

When Balaban reiterated Paramount's desire for a July release, Jerry told him he could have one but it wouldn't be *Cinderfella*; it would be a different one. "But we don't have another Jerry Lewis film in the can," Balaban reminded him.

Jerry promised him that they would have something to release by July, and he promptly started to ad-lib an outline for a Jerry Lewis picture that had occurred to him on the plane. In the proposed film, there wouldn't be much of a plot, just a series of funny sketches in which Jerry would play a bellboy who couldn't do anything right, at a resort hotel in Florida. They wouldn't have to build any sets because they could use the facilities of the Fontainebleau.

As for a cast, that wouldn't be any problem. Jerry would play the title role—*The Bellboy*—and he would write cameo parts for whatever celebrities happened to be visiting Miami at the time. They would play guests of the hotel. In addition to writing and starring, Jerry would direct, which wouldn't make this picture any different from any other Lewis picture except that *he* would get the directing credit instead of someone else.

Finally, since Jerry's nightclub act only took a few hours of his time in the evening, there'd be no problem about shooting. Jerry would shoot the picture during the day instead of lounging around the pool, which bored him anyway.

After listening to a couple of the sketch ideas, Balaban gave Jerry the go-ahead and started to make the physical arrangements, which included getting permission from the Fontainebleau to shoot the picture there. The management gladly cooperated because it was a good promotional stunt for the hotel.

In Florida, Jerry wrote each scene the night before he shot it—for whomever was in town. Not many stars came to Florida that spring. The biggest name Jerry was able to snag for a cameo was Milton Berle. But what difference did that make? It was basically a Jerry Lewis picture— with one new twist: Although everyone else in the cast had speaking parts, Jerry played the part of the bellboy completely in pantomime, no doubt borrowing this technique from Charlie Chaplin's *Modern Times*.

The Bellboy was far from a *Modern Times*, but, considering the shoestring circumstances under which it had to be made, it was a remarkably able tour de force, and it contained some brilliant visual comedy bits, which even the critics acknowledged were amusing.

In one sequence, Jerry found himself at the controls of a runaway jet liner. After accidentally making a perfect landing, he walked out of the plane with the nonchalance of a husband just returning from the grocery store in the family car.

One of Jerry's chores at the hotel was to walk the dogs of the guests in the morning. He had about twenty of them on leashes when a cat crossed

his path. The dogs, of course, took off after the inconsiderate feline, dragging Jerry through the lobby of the Fontainebleau and along its elegant
marble floors like a riderless aquaplane.

Another unforgettable moment resulted when a guest pulled up in front
of the hotel in a Volkswagen and said to Jerry, "Empty my trunk, boy, and
bring it up to the room." DISSOLVE, and we find Jerry walking along the
hotel corridor carrying a Volkswagen engine, which he presents to the guest
at his door.

Writing and performing by night and shooting by day, Jerry managed
to finish his first directorial assignment in four weeks, in plenty of time to
make the July release date.

Eight sketches in search of a plot weren't quite enough to satisfy the
critics. Although admitting that *The Bellboy* was funny, *The New York
Times* criticized Jerry and the picture for having "no point of view," for
trying to emulate the old master Chaplin not only by working in panto-
mime and by shooting in "black and white" but also by trying to do
everything himself, and, lastly, for having no plot.

"My pictures don't need plots," was Jerry's waspish answer to that final
criticism. "That way a mother can bring her kid into the theater at any
point in the show and still know what's going on."

Jerry must have had a pretty good idea of what it took to please the
average Jerry Lewis fan. *The Bellboy* cost $900,000 to make (cheap for a
picture shot entirely on location) and wound up grossing nearly $8
million.

Despite its Christmas release, *Cinderfella*, with a supporting cast including Ed Wynn as the fairy godfather and Judith Anderson as the wicked
stepmother, was a bit of a bomb at the box office. Although the spirit of
Christmas was in the air, the critics were not very generous to their old
adversary, Jerry Lewis.

The New York Times was particularly vicious (and also funny). The
following are excerpts from its review:

> Judging by *Cinderfella*, one of the dullest comedies of the season—
> if not the year—Jerry Lewis by now has become fascinated with the
> sound of his own breathing. . . . We'll bet good money that even the
> kids will be bored. . . . Mr. Lewis, sounding like a parched parrot,
> croaks three tunes. He's also the producer, and, believe us, no one
> should doubt it.

A final slap in the face was that Cy Howard sued Jerry for plagiarism,
claiming that he had once told Jerry and Hal Wallis the idea for
Cinderfella when he had been working with the two of them. Jerry denied
stealing the story but wound up settling with Howard for $30,000.

What did $30,000 mean to a fellow who was about to spend $3.1 million of Paramount's money on his next picture—*The Ladies Man*, which he also wrote, directed, and produced. For *The Ladies Man* Jerry came up with an entirely new concept of picture-making—realism without going on location.

The Ladies Man was the story of a young fellow who got himself a job at the Hollywood Studio Club, the elegant boarding house the YWCA has long operated as a domicile for aspiring young actresses. Working in such an establishment provided Jerry with plenty of scope to run amok among several dozen toothsome exemplars of female pulchritude.

Rather than shoot at the Studio Club, which was just down the street from the Paramount lot, Jerry talked the studio into building him a replica of the establishment on Stage Fourteen. But this wasn't an ordinary studio set. It was a virtually complete steel-framed forty-room building three and a half stories high. The structure was 177 feet long, 154 feet wide, and several rooms deep. The rooms not only were completely furnished but also contained built-in individual lighting and sound systems to facilitate camera work at any point.

The only difference between Jerry's studio club and the real thing was that the outside wall of his building was cut away to provide a sort of X-ray view of the inner doings.

According to Jerry's way of thinking, this would enable him to capture *The Grand Hotel* atmosphere of simultaneous interrelated action without having to stop the cameras, relight the scenes, and shoot them individually, as was the usual custom. Without stopping except to reload the cameras, he could also shoot the picture faster and therefore save the studio money.

In an interview at the time, Jerry explained that his scenic innovation reflected his conviction that the movies needed a return to "hugeness." It also would engender "spontaneity of comedy," which "audiences were crying for to offset the recent crop of depressing psychological dramas."

This so-called "spontaneity of comedy" lost most of its spontaneity when it was discovered after viewing the first day's dailies that comedy scenes can't be photographed only in long shots from a crane. Comedy requires reaction shots, and these need close-ups, and close-ups require individual lighting for the person or persons reacting. As a result, there had to be the usual stops between takes and the usual delays.

So Jerry's $500,000 play house turned out to be just that. *The Ladies Man* could just as easily have been shot on a regular set, and the studio wouldn't have had to worry about what to do with a complete life-sized replica of the Studio Club after the shooting was completed. (After all, they couldn't rent rooms out to aspiring actresses. What beautiful young starlet would feel safe living on a studio lot?)

Nevertheless, Jerry got an "A" for effort from at least a couple of critics. *The New York Times* summed up everyone's feelings about *The Ladies Man* when it wrote, "It's a setup for a Jerry Lewis film that's different, but after a half hour it dies on its feet."

Not that Jerry gave a damn about what the critics said, as long as his pictures made money. Unfortunately, a Jerry Lewis film couldn't make money at a cost of $3.1 million. It would be lucky to break even—especially in a period when movie comedies were getting such stiff competition from the dozens of situation comedies on TV, not to mention all the old movies.

In his frenetic strivings to do something "different" (and perhaps even please the critics, for in the long run it was better to have them with you than to suffer their invective), Jerry, in his last series of pictures for Paramount, started to veer away from playing the character that made him famous—the bumbling schnook in tennis sneakers who got rousted about by life.

Jerry followed *The Ladies Man* with *The Nutty Professor*, a satirical version of *Dr. Jekyll and Mr. Hyde.* Jerry played the professor with the dual personality, and the results were disastrous.

Critics across the nation were unanimous in their hostility toward this Jerry Lewis offering. Jerry's feelings were hurt, but that didn't stop his eternal jousting with critical windmills.

In Boston, while on a promotional tour for the picture with an entourage of fifteen, Jerry barred all TV writers and trade press from interviewing him. Only Jerry would have the *chutzpa* to try to win friends and influence critics in such an ungracious fashion.

Naturally both Boston papers panned *The Nutty Professor*. Marjorie Adams writing in *The Boston Globe* said,

> It isn't our lovable Lewis as we ever knew him before. I would just as soon not know him again in this kind of dual role . . . I don't know what Lewis has in mind when he makes his final remarks indicating that there's an important moral hidden under the zany doings of *The Nutty Professor.*
>
> It has something to do with valuing yourself high if you want other people to do so. But it doesn't mean very much considering the clumsy language in which it is delivered. Jerry Lewis can do better than this in making people laugh. Next time around I am sure he will.

The following September, Jerry was back on network television again but in a different kind of format—at least for him. It was a two-hour talk show.

The idea for the new program came about when Jerry took over for Jack Paar as host on "The Tonight Show" for two weeks the previous winter, 1962.

Jerry surprised network officials, sponsors, critics, and fans of "The Tonight Show" by being a host par excellence. He was funny, his ad-libbing was in good taste, he was adept at interviewing guests, and he could sell the sponsor's product. He was such a marvelous host, in fact, that there was considerable speculation in the trade at the time that Jerry Lewis would be the one to replace Paar when the latter retired, as he was soon about to do.

When Johnny Carson got the nod instead, however, ABC wooed Jerry away from the only network he'd ever been associated with by offering him a contract to do a show similar in format except that it would only go on once a week, on Saturday nights, from 9:30 to 11:30. Jerry signed for forty weeks, in a deal that was reported to involve millions of dollars.

"The Jerry Lewis Show," which was to have a Jack Paar format, was to be the most costly of its ilk ever attempted. It was budgeted at some $200,000 a show (half as much as the first Martin and Lewis picture); guests would get top money, not just "scale," as they do on most talk shows; and Jerry's compensation would be comparable with the $10-million-and-up deals other TV giants like Gleason and Berle had made with the networks.

In addition, the network completely refurbished, at a cost of over $1 million, the El Capitan Theater in Hollywood to suit Jerry's personal tastes and entertainment requirements.

Prior to the ABC venture, Jerry had never been completely happy working in television because he found its time requirements too restrictive to his uninhibited ad-libbing. He also did not like network officials' or sponsors' dictating to him about what he could and could not do in the way of comedy.

But in the new show, Jerry promised, all that would be changed, because it would be a "free form" show that would permit him to employ the gamut of his multiple talents and to do so spontaneously so that audiences wouldn't know what was coming next.

"I'll be in complete control," Jerry told the press when he made the announcement concerning his agreement with ABC. "It'll be something I've never done before. It'll be what people want—strictly entertainment. No song and dance stuff. No working under pressure with people who are frightened.

"This is going to be what this infantile medium should be—live. I'm going to play it loose. I'll be what I am. I suppose I'll have guests. If they're hostile, I'll be hostile. If they're warm, I'll be warm. If they're zany, I'll be zany."

Although Jerry was "in complete control," he had Perry Cross as a producer and his long-time associate Ernie Glucksman, who was also vice-president of Jerry Lewis Productions, as executive producer.

The show's announcer and straight man was an amiable fellow named Del Moore, who collapsed at every one of Jerry's lines, funny or otherwise —something Dean Martin would never do.

On the show's opener September 21, 1963, Jerry's guests were Mort Sahl, Steve Allen, Jimmy Durante, Jack Jones, Kay Stevens, and Harry James. Another important scheduled guest, Clifton Fadiman, was left standing in the wings, and finally departed in a huff without making an appearance because there wasn't any time for him.

In addition to his "host" chores, Jerry took part in an "improvised" sketch and introduced a massive Adonis as "the winner of the Jerry Lewis look-alike contest."

Then, borrowing a little from Eddie Cantor, he made Patti and five of their kids, who were in the audience, stand up and take a bow, after which he got cute and sang a number called "Think Pink," in which he hoped the next Lewis offspring would be a girl.

Cecil Smith, in *The Los Angeles Times*, called the show "amiable dash," admitted the sketch was "hilarious," but summed it all up by writing, "At one point, Lewis said, 'We're just having fun here—for a fortune.' It looked that way."

But, for the most part, critics around the nation were either outright hostile or indifferent; and many of the viewers resented Mort Sahl's criticism of the then-current administration and his poking fun at racial strife. "We're celebrating the centennial of the Civil War by having another one," quipped Sahl at one point. Another time he said, "Ole Miss is either a university or the president's legislative program."

Funny stuff, but in those days network officials and sponsors preferred their highly paid TV stars to stay out of politics for fear they would chase away many of the viewers who might have differing opinions on political subjects. In addition, it became evident by the second show that Jerry could not handle two hours of ad-libbing every week and still maintain an entertainment level that would hold an audience.

As the ratings, which started out high, began to plummet, ABC expressed a desire to have some control over the show. The network insisted on a "set" format, with everything laid out beforehand in script form. This touched off a running battle between Jerry and ABC and the sponsors that culminated on November 19 with the network's announcing that the Jerry Lewis weekly two-hour live television show would be discontinued on December 14, after only thirteen of its scheduled forty performances.

The story in *The Los Angeles Times* said,

> Despite a firm forty-week commitment, the network has granted Lewis's request to withdraw the show due to extreme differences of opinion regarding its format.

Lewis said today that since the differences of opinion had little chance of being solved in the immediate future, it is much better to call a halt to the show and make a fresh start some time in the future.

A spokesman from the Lewis camp said,

If he were to accede to the network's concepts, the resultant work load, added to his regular movie, personal-appearance, and other commitments would be too heavy.

Both statements were face-savers. The real trouble was simply that no one was interested in watching Jerry Lewis on television any more.

Having failed on television for the second time without Dean Martin, Jerry quickly retreated to the safety and security of Paramount. There, in rapid succession, he produced and appeared in a quintet of Jerry Lewis movies that were distinguished only by their mediocrity: *Who's Minding the Store?*, *The Patsy*, *The Disorderly Orderly*, *The Family Jewels*, and *Boeing Boeing*. All of these films contained some flashes of the Jerry Lewis that had made millions laugh, but the magic was gone, and Jerry's film career, too, started its long toboggan slide downward.

In show business, there are several theories on the reason that Jerry Lewis never fulfilled his early promise of becoming the successor to Charles Chaplin.

One theory, as expressed by his former director Norman Taurog, is, "Jerry never should have stopped playing the 'Little Guy' character—the guy who wore the sneakers and was shy with women and got shoved around by everybody. He should have kept on with it, just as Chaplin did with his Little Tramp. I knew Jerry was in trouble once he started playing the swinger and having his blue jeans made by Sy Devore and he became aggressive with girls, because with that fellow he lost all sympathy on the screen."

An opposing theory avers that it would have been impossible for Jerry to continue playing the exophthalmic Idiot as he grew older and more gross looking. Chaplin's Little Tramp character was ageless—perhaps because the real Chaplin was hidden by his costume and mustache. But Jerry couldn't disguise the ravages of time behind a tramp costume. Now that he was approaching forty, he was beginning to resemble the owner of a moderately prosperous delicatessen. This man could no longer get away with the same things on the screen that he could get by with when he was a thin crewcut innocent-looking kid fresh out of Irvington, New Jersey. As time went on, his zany behavior and facial contortions seemed more frenetic than funny.

But what character could Jerry play? He wasn't a very good straight actor. His characterization in *The Nutty Professor* was funny, but not in the way it was intended. His interpretation of the swinging airline pilot with a girl in every port that he played in *Boeing Boeing* wasn't much more believable, nor was the old man he portrayed in *The Family Jewels*.

Sad as it was to believe, perhaps there was no role in films for a mature Jerry Lewis.

A third theory is that Jerry's downfall was brought about by his inexorable determination to surround himself with mediocre talent.

First-class writers who refused to buckle down to him or who expressed dissatisfaction over the way he ran roughshod through their material generally got fired—Simmons and Lear, Don McGuire, Bud Yorkin.

Jerry rarely rehearsed a scene. According to the late Frank Tashlin, who wrote and directed five Jerry Lewis films, Jerry never looked at his dialogue until he walked on the set and "then he never stuck to the lines anyway."

Many top directors who'd heard of his reputation wouldn't touch a Jerry Lewis picture at all; those who did rarely went back for seconds—either through choice or because Jerry drummed them out of his unit for insubordination. A couple of good directors, namely Norman Taurog and Frank Tashlin, were able to put up with Jerry's antics for more than one picture, but they had saintly patience and dispositions.

The same was true for Ernie Glucksman, who'd been associated with Jerry in one way or another since "The Colgate Comedy Hour." Although the exact nature of his chores wasn't always clear, he usually wound up with executive producer credit on Jerry's movies and TV shows. By his own admission, Glucksman has more gold watches with Jerry's thanks engraved on them than does anybody else in the business. "A trunkful," admits Glucksman. But, after twenty years of loyal service, Glucksman was fired by Jerry in a dispute over "policy," and he was forced to sue the comic for breaking what was a "handshake" contract.

The creators who lasted with Jerry were the exceptions. Usually only the unemployable made good with Jerry over the long haul. These people couldn't afford to talk back to the Pied Piper of the business; they had nowhere else to go.

At one point, Jerry's importance in the business was so great that even the top brass at Paramount were afraid not to capitulate to his whims for fear he wouldn't report for work (which had happened with *It's Only Money*) or would leave and go to another studio. Only Hal Wallis insisted on complete autonomy, and when the time finally came when he couldn't control Jerry, he too severed their relationship.

When Y. Frank Freeman retired in 1960 and his assistant, Jack Karp, took over the studio, the new boss swiftly came to the realization that Jerry could not keep on traveling the same headstrong path for very long without breaking the studio. Karp decided there was something wrong with what Jerry was doing. Perhaps they ought to go back to the old Jerry Lewis formula—the schnook caught up in a bigger-than-life situation —that was so successful for Don McGuire when he was writing and directing for Jerry.

At the time Jack Karp took over Paramount's leadership, the studio was going through an economy wave. One day, Karp was looking over the studio's backlog of shelved properties to see what could be salvaged when he came across Don McGuire's original screenplay of *The Baby Doctor*—the picture Jerry had refused to make because McGuire wouldn't let him sing in it.

A quick rereading of *The Baby Doctor* confirmed Karp's suspicions that Jerry never should have withdrawn from the film in the first place; it was a perfect vehicle for him. He immediately contacted Jerry and urged him to make it as his next film for Paramount. Jerry, who was more malleable now that he was enjoying less success, agreed to star in it.

Karp then went after McGuire to direct it. McGuire was an important part of the package, because his original deal had specified that he, and no one else, was to get the directorial assignment. He was to receive $50,000 for the directing chore, which Karp figured any creative man would be glad to get. But when the studio head and McGuire sat down at Paramount to talk about it, McGuire was indifferent.

"I don't have the time," said McGuire, who by then was writing novels and doing very well at it.

"But this can be a helluva Jerry Lewis picture."

"Jerry doesn't need my script," said McGuire. "With his talent he can write one himself, and direct it, and produce it, and cut it, and be the parking lot attendant at the opening. He's crazy about cars."

"But he needs a good picture," said Karp. "And Paramount needs a good picture from him."

"What for?" said McGuire, who like everyone else in the business believed the propaganda Jerry had been feeding the press. "According to Jerry, he's never made a picture that hasn't done well at the box office."

Karp smiled grimly and said, "Jerry's last five pictures have all lost money!"

When McGuire expressed disbelief, Karp threw open the books on the last five Jerry Lewis pictures and proved it to him in black and white and also a lot of red.

"Now do you believe me?" said Karp. "Jerry Lewis needs a good picture or he's through. So how about it? Do we have a deal?"

"You know how much I like money?" said McGuire.

Karp nodded.

"Well, let me tell you this," said McGuire. "If I had my choice of Jerry Lewis or the gas chamber, Jerry would lose out."

And he got up and left.

A few months later, Jerry Lewis was also out of Paramount—he claims because Paramount promised to send a print of one of his films to a home for orphaned boys and then, on the day it was to be delivered, reneged. "I walked out of Paramount and never went back," Jerry stated to the press.

What Paramount was saying, by innuendo, was that it could no longer afford to indulge Jerry in all his little extravagances—like building $500,000 sets for what should be a low-budget comedy. If they had really wanted him around, they would gladly have swallowed the $200 cost of a print of film.

23

Nice and Easy Does It Every Time

If there was ever any truth to Jerry's accusations that Dean didn't take his work seriously, it was certainly belied by the impressive list of films he appeared in following his successes in *The Young Lions* and *Some Came Running*.

While an incurable case of megalomania was killing Jerry's career prematurely, his ex-partner was fattening his bank account and also increasing his stature in the movie business by starring or costarring in a series of "A" pictures that included *What a Way to Go!* (with Shirley MacLaine), *Kiss Me, Stupid* (written, directed, and produced by Billy Wilder), *Durango, Five Card Stud, Marriage on the Rocks* (with Frank Sinatra and Deborah Kerr), *The Silencers* (the first of the Matt Helm detective series), *Toys in the Attic* (from the Lillian Hellman Broadway hit), *Bells Are Ringing* (with Judy Holliday), *The Wrecking Crew* (the second of the Matt Helm series), *Robin and the Seven Hoods* (with Sinatra and the *Ocean's Eleven* gang), *Who Was That Lady?* (from the Norman Krasna Broadway hit), *Come Blow Your Horn* (from Neil Simon's first play), and, finally, *Airport* (produced by Ross Hunter and directed by Academy Award winner George Seaton, with an all-star cast, including Helen Hayes and Burt Lancaster).

His inclusion in the cast of *Airport* proved once again the wisdom of the adage, "It's better to be born lucky than smart"—at least as it applies to Dean Martin's career.

When Ross Hunter originally offered him the role of the pilot of the distressed airliner, Dean turned him down on the grounds that the picture didn't fit him. Who would believe a booze-sotted Italian crooner landing a troubled airliner in a snowed-in airport? But when Ross Hunter sweet-

249

ened his offer with a percentage-of-the-profits deal, Dean was persuaded to sacrifice his artistic integrity, and he accepted the role.

Dean's agent got his client 10 percent of the gross after the break-even point. To date, *Airport* has grossed over $50 million, and Dean's share of the pie is well into the millions.

In addition to his motion picture work, Dean was committed to at least eight weeks a year of doing his nightclub act at the Sands in Las Vegas, to as many guest shots on other stars' television shows (such as Danny Thomas and Lucille Ball) as his busy schedule would permit, and to record-album recording dates for Reprise, the company Frank Sinatra formed and later sold to Warner Brothers.

The only thing Dean didn't have going for him in the early 1960s was his own weekly television show, and that was of his own choosing. Having had four years of steady television as Jerry's partner, Dean was reluctant to commit himself to such a back-breaking grind again. Of course, he wouldn't have to contend with Jerry. Still, live TV put a heavier burden on a performer than did any other medium, first, because it's such a voracious consumer of material and, second, because most producers don't feel comfortable without at least four days of rehearsal. Dean refused to rehearse that diligently.

Typical of Dean's television attitude is a statement he made in 1972: "I say to guys like Andy Williams and Glen Campbell, who are my buddies, 'Why do you waste four days shooting an hour show?' I can't see it. You know the Lucille Ball show. It's a half hour, right? They wanted me there three days to rehearse. 'Why three days?' I asked. 'So we can learn everything without the cue cards,' they said. I say, if cue cards are there, why not use them? But nobody wants to do things simple."

Since nobody wanted to do things "simple," Dean assiduously avoided having his own TV show until the fall of 1965.

In what has to be the strangest bit of irony of all in the entire Martin and Lewis saga, Jerry was the person indirectly responsible for Dean's getting his own show on NBC, which is the step in his career that finally catapulted the "Italian stallion" into the millionaire class, along with Seabiscuit and Secretariat.

When ABC yanked the Jerry Lewis fiasco off the air in the middle of the TV season, it was stuck with two hours of blank prime time to fill on Saturday night. Having no stars of any real magnitude to fill the vacancy —most "names" who meant anything already had their own shows—the network brass hastily threw together a potpourri called "The Hollywood Palace," which emanated from the stage of the remodeled El Capitan Theater on a Saturday night soon after Jerry's demise. "The Hollywood

Palace" was a combination of "The Ed Sullivan Show" and old-time vaudeville of the kind that killed it in the first place.

The show was to be hosted by a different star each week, but because most real entertainers weren't interested in trying to emulate Ed Sullivan, it was next to impossible to attract important names for the show in the beginning. As a result, the feeling in television was that "The Hollywood Palace" wouldn't be any more successful in the Saturday night time slot than was Jerry Lewis. But it had a few things on the plus side.

It was a brassy show, with lots of girls in scanty costumes, lively music, and the overall feeling that the average stay-at-home on Saturday night didn't have to strain his brain to enjoy it. Besides, anything was better than the Jerry Lewis bomb, so ABC decided to try it for a season.

"The Hollywood Palace" caught on almost from its inception, and, after the first season, it was attracting bigger and bigger names as guest "hosts": Danny Thomas, Milton Berle, Groucho Marx, and others of their stature.

After Bing Crosby, the laziest crooner of all in show business, took a turn on the stage of "The Hollywood Palace" one Saturday night, even Dean Martin consented to take a crack at being host, with the proviso that he didn't have to rehearse for more than one day.

Nick Van Off, the show's producer, agreed because Dean was "hot" and everyone wanted to use him, and he immediately put his two writers, Jay Burton and Joe Bigelow, to work preparing a monologue for Dino.

Their monologue was well stocked with jokes about Dean's legendary drinking habits—so well larded, in fact, that when the two writers went up to Dean's house one evening to let him look over the material they'd written, Jay Burton nervously asked, "Do you think we've got too many drinking jokes?"

"Can't have too many, baby," replied Dean. "How do you think I got this big house?"

Dean came in on a Friday and rehearsed for one afternoon. On Saturday night, he did the show, reading everything, including song lyrics, off cue cards.

Dean's performance on "The Hollywood Palace" boards was "a rollicking success," in the words of one reviewer. He sang his repertoire of old favorites, including "That's Amore" and "Oh, Marie," and he kidded around with the chorus girls. Whenever he was in trouble, he reached into his bag and pulled out another one of his seemingly inexhaustible supply of drinking jokes.

"My doctor told me to take a little drink before I go to bed," Dino told the audience at one point. "Do you know I find myself going to bed nine or ten times a night?"

Afterward, exhilarated by his success as host of "The Hollywood

Palace," Dino remarked to his agent that he wouldn't mind having a TV show of his own "if they could all be that easy."

That set the wheels in motion. Hal Kemp, a producer at NBC, heard about it and proposed to the network brass that Dean Martin be given a variety show of his own to host every week and "sing a few songs."

At first, the NBC executives were hesitant about giving Dean Martin a regular weekly assignment. They expressed concern about his "drinking habits" and his reputation for not wanting to rehearse. Kemp explained to them that his "drinking" and "laziness" were just part of the character Dean Martin had built for himself and that the truth of the matter was that he actually worked very hard at making hard work look easy.

Eventually Kemp talked them into giving Dean a chance on the network, and he was authorized to make Dean an offer. Dean's response to NBC's offer wasn't very reassuring: "Yeah, I'll do a show if I don't have to work too hard."

The first Dean Martin show was aired on September 16, 1965, at 10:00 on a Thursday night. Despite Dean's charm, wit, able crooning, and male chauvinist appeal to most women of all ages, "The Dean Martin Show" was not a runaway hit its first season on the air. Part of the trouble was that Dean wasn't participating in many of the comedy sketches. He was just sticking to his thing—singing and introducing the acts. As one Hollywood writer described him, "He's an Italian Ed Sullivan."

The other problem was that there was considerable friction between Dean and Bill Colloran, the show's producer. Colloran expected Dean to rehearse along with the other actors, which was against Dean's code of How to Be a Successful Performer Without Really Trying.

Whatever the reason, Neilsen ratings on "The Dean Martin Show" ran the gamut from "fair" to "poor," and there was considerable speculation that NBC would drop the show at the end of the season.

The show's cancellation seemed a certainty after Bill Colloran quit because he couldn't tolerate Dean's laissez-faire attitude. But when Greg Garrison, the show's director, said that he could handle Dean, the producing reins were turned over to him, and NBC decided to stay the executioner's axe for another season.

In its second season, "The Dean Martin Show" climbed into the top ten in the Neilsens and remained in the higher strata for a long time.

If anyone had ever predicted that Dean Martin could discipline himself well enough to remain on the air through nine seasons, Dean would have been the first to bet that he couldn't. That he could is due largely to the efforts of Greg Garrison, who foresaw a lot of gold in those Italian hills, if only he could figure out a way of mining it simply.

When Garrison took over the show, there was immediate rapport between him and Dean—mainly because Garrison bent over backward to accommodate Dean's wishes not to work too hard instead of fighting him as Bill Colloran had.

One of the criticisms of the show in its first season had been that its star was merely "walking through it" and not participating in any of the comedy sketches with the guests. Garrison recognized that. Unfortunately, comedy sketches require rehearsing to come off successfully, no matter how well written they are. Rehearsing was the one thing Dean refused to do.

To solve that hang-up, Garrison invented what is known as "The Dean Martin Rehearsal Caper Plan"—a plan that enabled Dean to be on the golf course or even as far away as Las Vegas during the first four days the show was in rehearsal. The Garrison plan worked in the following way.

A standby actor was hired to play Dean's part in rehearsals. Not until the day of the show's taping did Dean show up. Then he would go straight to his dressing room and, while lying on a couch, watch a run-through of the show through a monitor.

Having sopped up the rudiments of his part through this vicarious procedure, Dean would emerge from his dressing room about five minutes before the final rehearsal, stroll onto the set, and say to Garrison, "Which way do you want to point the Italian?"

With Garrison guiding him, Dean would then walk through all the sketches and musical routines, reading his part off cue cards. Frequently, he read his song lyrics off the cue cards too.

Dean's carefree method of doing his show evoked plenty of grumbling, not only from his high-priced guest stars but also from the show's regulars, such as Paul Lynde and Dom De Luise, all of whom felt, and rightly so, that their own performances were hurt by the lack of contact with Dean.

Many of the women singers who did his show—such as Eydie Gorme and Diahann Carroll—stated privately that they hated doing numbers unrehearsed with Dean. "With no rehearsal, you never know where he's going to stand or when he's going to put his arm around you," complained one important female singer. "In fact, you never know what to expect, so you wind up just looking stupid."

Writers also didn't care for Dean's rehearsal schedule because of how it made their material look. Garrison hired a host of good writers—there were at least eight names on the crawl each week—and he paid them well. Over the years, the writing staff included Charlie Isaacs, Rod Parker (now the producer of "Maude"), Jay Burton, Hal Goodman, George Bloom, Al Gordon, and Harry Crane. But except for Harry Crane, who acted as "head writer," the turnover was constant.

Crane had started out with Martin and Lewis on "The Colgate Comedy

Hour" and had elected to stay with Jerry for a while after the split. But as Jerry started to slip and Dean grew bigger, Crane deserted Jerry and went with the Italian.

Because of his long association with Dean, Crane was about the only one of the writers in whom Dean ever had any confidence. As a result, Crane was the go-between. Someone had to be, for another one of Dino's idiosyncrasies was that he refused to sit around a conference table with the writers, as other comedians like Jack Benny and Bob Hope do, and punch up lines or analyze what's wrong with a script.

"Dean never saw a script or knew what he was going to have to do on the show until the afternoon of the taping," laments Al Gordon, who stayed with the show for a couple of seasons. "At a run-through, he'd read all the wrong lines and forget what business he was supposed to do. In fact, he couldn't care less. He just wanted to get the show over with so he could leave."

Frequently the show had that look—almost as if it had been thrown together by a bunch of drunks—but audiences didn't seem to care. They loved Dean's casual approach to entertaining, his outrageous double entendre quips to the toothsome Ding-a-Ling Sisters, and his parodying the lyrics of popular songs:

> How I love the kisses of Dolores,
> Since she uses Lavoris.

They also loved his jokes kidding himself, as in the following routine with Steve Lawrence:

DEAN: I'll never forget . . .
LAWRENCE: Never forget who?
DEAN: I'll let you know as soon as they flip the card.

Added to the whole mélange was the overall good feeling that sex was fun and not to be taken too seriously. There were bosom jokes galore; also plenty of bosoms to bounce them off.

Dean and Paul Lynde, while doing a body-painting routine with a gorgeous bountifully built near-nude model, bantered the following:

DEAN: (looking at her cleavage) Now I know what they mean by *Beyond the Valley of the Dolls.*
LYNDE: Dab some green on her, and we'll have the Jolly Green Giants.

A sketch in an airliner between Dean and Steve Lawrence brought forth this dialogue:

DEAN: (glancing out the plane window at the ground) What's
               that down there—mountains?
LAWRENCE: No, Raquel Welch lying on her back.

So what if the jokes sometimes smacked of burlesque or the Folies
Bergère? People wanted to laugh. The country was in a depressed mood
because of the Vietnam war. Watching Dean Martin, nobody had to
think. They could sit back with a beer, enjoy the jokes and the pretty girls
and for an hour forget the kids dying in the rice paddies.

As the show became increasingly risqué, there were plenty of complaints from prudish listeners, who felt sex was serious business and not
to be lampooned. Later on, the more militant of the women's liberation
movement complained that the show's heavy emphasis on women as sex
objects was ruining their image and making it impossible for them to get
jobs as truck drivers and baseball umpires and jockeys. Two seasons ago,
in fact, a large group of them picketed outside NBC's main studio in
Burbank in an effort to force network officials to silence Dean's lecherous
remarks and demeaning treatment of women.

But, after several weeks of fruitless picketing, they went back to driving
trucks and weight lifting, for nobody can stop America's chief hedonist
from doing exactly what he wants—and getting away with it. The following season, in fact, "The Dean Martin Show" countered by giving
Dean a sexy girl in a tiger's outfit to be his personal "pet."

After the second year of the show, Dean and Greg Garrison formed
their own television production company. Thereafter, they produced "The
Dean Martin Show" in partnership with NBC. The show had a
staggeringly large budget—$200,000.

Dean personally was making $50,000 a program, plus receiving an
undisclosed amount of RCA stock, in a deal that Herman Citron, who is
still his agent, made for him.

In view of all that money—plus the show's enormous popularity—was
it any wonder that Dean felt it foolish for other entertainers to waste so
much of their time meeting with writers and rehearsing? He'd figured out
a way to beat the system, and his fans couldn't care less.

After the show's final "sign-off," Dean would turn politely to the audience and say, "Good night, folks. I gotta go pee." Then he'd head for his
dressing room, never to be seen again by any of his staff until the following
Friday when they taped the next show.

After finishing a taping, Dean would, according to associates, jump into
his Cadillac by himself and drive straight to Stefanino's, a chic Italian
bistro just inside Beverly Hills, on Sunset Strip.

Since Dino was friendly with the management, he was allowed to park
his car in the owner's spot and enter the restaurant through the rear door.

On his way to the dining section, he would have to pass through the kitchen. There a cook or a waiter would automatically hand him a large plate of pasta, which he'd grab without slackening his pace as he walked to his special table in the Venetian ambience of Stefanino's main room.

Where Dino would go after devouring his pasta and perhaps a dish of sausage and peppers, washing it all down with a few glasses of vino, nobody could ever say with certainty. Sometimes he'd go straight home to Jeanne, sometimes to a poker game at Billy Wilder's, and sometimes out on the town with Frank Sinatra.

His proclivity for the latter almost got Dean in some very serious trouble one Friday night in June 1966, when Sinatra and Jilly, the New York nightclub operator, threw an impromptu party for him in the Polo Lounge of the Beverly Hills Hotel. The trio was celebrating Dean's forty-ninth birthday, which was just a few days off, and getting pretty noisy about it —"obnoxiously so," one witness volunteered.

Sitting in the booth next to the Sinatra party was Frederick N. Weisman, a prominent Beverly Hills businessman and brother-in-law of millionaire philanthropist Norton Simon. With Weisman was his future son-in-law, whom he was entertaining for the first time and trying to impress.

When the birthday celebrants in the neighboring booth became a little too noisy for Weisman, he yelled to them to "quiet down." According to his son-in-law, this evoked some kind of an anti-Semitic remark from one of the people in the Sinatra party—but not Dean Martin. Weisman demanded an apology.

According to the police report, Sinatra then walked over to Weisman's table and told the man, "You shouldn't be talking like that while you're sitting down and wearing glasses."

According to Sinatra, Weisman, who'd been drinking heavily, then stood up, lunged at him, and struck him below the eye.

Whoever struck whom first, Weisman ended up unconscious on the floor with a broken ashtray beside him. When he didn't recover consciousness, he was taken to the Beverly Hills Emergency Hospital, and when the doctors there couldn't revive him, he was taken to Mt. Sinai Hospital, where he underwent cranial surgery the next day for two and a half hours.

When Police Chief Anderson questioned the "birthday boy" about the incident, Dean, who had been sitting there through the whole fracas, steadfastly maintained that he "hadn't seen a thing." When the Beverly Hills police tried to get hold of him the next day for "further questioning," Dean, for no apparent reason, turned up at Lake Tahoe, where he made himself unavailable for comment.

Dean remained at Lake Tahoe until the whole mess blew over—which it eventually did when Weisman's family, including his son-in-law, mysteriously failed to press their original charges that the "thin singer" had slugged the businessman with something blunt.

But a large cloud of doubt has remained over the case ever since. Weisman himself has never been able to shed any light on what really happened because he suffered a partial loss of memory as a result of the blow and has never fully recovered his health. The only person who might have been able to clear up the mystery was Dean, and he elected not to see it and to take a powder rather than to say anything that might get his pal in trouble. As a result, Dean has often been criticized for his role in the Weisman affair.

But there is something inside Dean that won't permit him to "become involved." He just wants to go through the remainder of his life minding his own business, volunteering nothing, and hoping other people will leave him alone to his favorite pursuits.

It was this attitude—more than his appetite for other women—that led to the eventual crack-up of his marriage to Jeanne. Not that Dean didn't enjoy the company of beautiful women.

When someone once accused him of looking as if he were having a little "too good a time" kidding around with the pretty young ladies on his television show, Dean is reported to have replied, "Sure, I've got lots of beautiful girls working on my show, and I enjoy having them around. Why not? I'm a man."

Jeanne, who was still in her thirties, with honey-blond hair and a face and figure that were every bit as exquisite as when she was the Florida Orange Bowl Queen, still had the equipment to contend with competition from other women.

The competition she feared, and that eventually dashed the marriage on the rocks, was Dean's work. For along with his success as an individual performer came a transition in his character. Gone was the happy-go-lucky paisano who was only interested in wine, women, and song. He'd been replaced by a man fraught with as much ambition as was Jerry Lewis.

Suddenly Dean was accepting every job that came his way. If he wasn't doing his own TV show, he'd be guesting on someone else's. If he wasn't in Hollywood filming a picture, he'd be shooting on location in Mexico or Italy or any other exotic port of call the script demanded. If he wasn't on location, he'd be in Las Vegas or Lake Tahoe playing to nightclub audiences.

He couldn't stop running. When a friend asked Dean why he was driving himself to the point of exhaustion, Dean replied, "Sure, I work hard. But I remember times when I didn't bring in enough to feed my wife and kids. You don't forget things like that. Now it's all coming my way, and I want to take advantage of every opportunity."

But was it only money? He just about acknowledged that it wasn't the day he walked on a hot dusty outdoor location set in Arizona, where he was shooting *Durango*, took one look at the God-forsaken desiccated surroundings, glanced skyward at the blistering sun, and exclaimed loudly, "What the hell am I doing here? I've got $26 million!"

If money wasn't his sole motivation, perhaps then he was trying to deny, by accepting all that work, that Father Time was slowing him down. At fifty he was no longer the physical specimen he'd been when he used to fight Sonny King in a crummy hotel room off Broadway. With middle age came a troublesome case of ulcers, which meant he had to stick to a bland diet and abstain from hard liquor much of the time.

At home he led an almost monastic existence. His own bedroom, which was small—about 12′ by 12′—and separate from the master bedroom adjoining it, which was Jeanne's, contained only a bed and a television set. When he wasn't watching television, he would be padding about the house, in bathrobe and slippers, hunched over slightly and with a pained expression on his face. This was hardly the picture of the "gay swinger" most people had of him.

Away from his mountain greenery, however, or in front of friends, Dean was energetic, full of joie de vivre, and anxious to take on any assignment—provided there was enough money in it.

The seeds of this existence had undoubtedly been sown during the early years of his marriage to Betty, when financial necessity dictated that she stay behind while Dino was on the road trying to make a living.

But although financial necessity once may have forced Dean to live that way, he discovered that there were also advantages to that kind of existence, among which were that a husband had a built-in excuse for avoiding much of the dirty work of raising a family and that it allowed him more latitude to take advantage of his wandering and appreciative eye for other women. Like the perennial bachelor who finally marries but continues to lead the life of a bachelor even though he has a wife because he has grown accustomed to a selfish existence, Dino, too, found it next to impossible to give up the freedom from family responsibility that had once been forced upon him by economic necessity.

Financial necessity, however, didn't prevent Jeanne from accompanying Dean wherever his work took him. There were plenty of servants to tend to the physical needs of the children. But who was there to look out for their emotional requirements if not for Jeanne?

Even when he was in town, Dean was not the kind of a father who was a "pal" to his children. He studiously avoided such fatherly pursuits as coaching Little League or even reading bedtime stories to the little ones. On a hot day he might be persuaded to take a romp in the swimming pool with his kids or eat an occasional meal with them, but that was about the extent of his contact with the younger generation.

It wasn't that he didn't love his children. "Dean just doesn't know how to play with kids" was the way one close friend of the family's assessed the situation.

Dean was generous with everything but his time. Physically, the young Martins growing up in Beverly Hills had everything money could buy. When he was only seventeen, Dino, Jr. had a helicopter at his own disposal, to fly whenever the whim hit him; he also owned several foreign sports cars in the $15,000-and-up class (including a $25,000 Lamborghini), which he used to race around Beverly Hills. In addition, Dino, Jr. was the possessor of an extensive gun collection consisting of firearms dating back to Civil War days. In fact, it was Dino, Jr.'s penchant for collecting guns that got him in trouble with the federal authorities in 1974. A grand jury indicted him on several counts of violating the federal firearms regulations, including the unlawful possession of eight machine guns and an antitank gun, failing to register them, and transferring firearms. But if Dino, Jr. did anything wrong, it was only because of ignorance of the law, rather than any desire to break it. For, according to those people who know him well (including the author of this book), there's never been a straighter, nicer, or more clean-cut human being than Dino Martin, Jr. Today, at the age of twenty-two, Dino is one of the best tennis players in Southern California; he's a pre-med student at the University of California at Los Angeles. At the time he was sending applications to medical schools, he was given the highest letters of recommendation from respected Los Angeles doctors. Dino, Jr.'s interest in guns has been as a collector, not a user. According to Jeanne Martin, her son has never gone hunting in his life—or even fired the weapons in his backyard. His guns, many of which he received as gifts from prop men at film studios where his father worked, were for display purposes only, and were rarely taken out of their glass-enclosed display cases in his house.

As this book went to press, no disposition of the charges had been made.

Ricci Martin didn't exactly lead a life of deprivation when he was growing up, either. His hobbies were just as expensive as his brother's—only a lot less likely to get him in trouble with the FBI.

By the time he was in high school, Ricci was an expert photographer, as well as an amateur yachtsman. His photographs have won many prizes and have been published all over the world; and his seamanship was so good that before he was twenty he owned a $40,000 yacht—a yacht so heavily equipped with radar and other sophisticated navigational aids that he is planning to circle the globe in it. Both boys also possess wardrobes that most successful movie stars would envy.

But the one thing Dean wasn't willing to give them was his time—perhaps because he felt it was running out on him. According to his daughter Claudia, if there was a problem in the household and one of the children came to their father with it, Dean would simply shrug his shoulders and say, "Talk to Jeanne about it."

"It's not that he doesn't care," observed Claudia. "He cares very much, but he just doesn't want to hear anybody else's problems. It's almost as if not hearing them means they really don't exist."

It wasn't just "problems" that Dean avoided; it was practically any familial obligations.

His oldest daughter, Gail, once entertained ambitions to be a professional dancer. She took lessons, practiced hard, and got together an act, which her agent eventually was able to book into the Persian Room of New York's Plaza Hotel.

According to the family, her opening was the biggest most glittering night of the girl's career. But Dean never made it. He was in Mexico, shooting a picture. He did send Gail a large and expensive bouquet of flowers, however, which caused one Broadway columnist to comment, "It would have taken less time for Dino to have jetted to New York than it did for the posies to come across town from the florist."

In a way, the columnist's criticism was unfair. Dean, on location, couldn't very easily have said to the director one morning, "Don't count on me today. I have to go to the Persian Room for my daughter's opening." The studio and the others in the cast would have criticized him for that kind of irresponsibility.

The children of a very busy star, just like children of an airline pilot or a traveling salesman, must learn to cope with that kind of neglect or else start doing business with their neighborhood shrink. Gail learned to cope, judging by the mature way she once summed up what it was like to be her father's daughter:

"Dad's always felt he would have liked to give each of us more of his time and attention. But, with seven in the family, it's impossible. You soon learn you can't sulk or sit in a corner because Dad didn't say good morning to you. Maybe, in a way, it's a good thing. You grow up quicker, become independent sooner than other kids."

But what did Jeanne have to look forward to with her husband away from the family hearth so much of the time? What kind of a life could she have by herself?

In the beginning, there were small kids to keep her occupied, along with the usual related community activities centering around school, the PTA, and the Cub Scouts.

Later, Jeanne became involved in many activities of her own. She served on several committees for various charity organizations, such as the annual Share party—the one really big charity bash of the Hollywood social season.

Gradually, she developed what others have referred to as a "swinging social life." Being young and beautiful, Jeanne wasn't much for staying at home nights. She liked parties, and she liked to go dancing. At the height of the discotheque craze, she was frequently seen at such "in" places as The Factory and The Daisy. Often her escort would be Dino, Jr., who, although only seventeen at the time, proved to be a willing substitute for her husband, when he wasn't squiring other older women around town, such as Christine Kauffman, Tony Curtis's ex-wife, and Dany Saval, a French actress and divorcée.

Having become accustomed to an independent and active social life when Dean was away, Jeanne wasn't too willing to give it up when he was home.

Dean has often lamented that one of the big sources of friction between him and Jeanne was her "constant need to go out." He used to tell his cronies that Jeanne never wanted to spend an evening at home if she could help it. "I'm too tired at the end of the day to take her dancing, so she goes out with friends," complained Dean, whose idea of a good time when he wasn't working was to see a little television, go to bed early, and get up when the dew was still fresh on the fairways and spend the rest of the day trying for pars and birdies with his golfing cronies at the Riviera or Bel Air country clubs.

Golf may have been a sport—a way to maintain a fine tan and good health—but she proved to be the one mistress with which Jeanne couldn't contend. Golf took up too much of Dean's time and energy to suit the restless Jeanne.

When the two of them were forced to stay home together on an evening, they'd generally occupy separate rooms and watch television. This didn't make for very good or regular communication. Inevitably, misunderstandings of the most basic kind followed.

Recalls Dean, "When I was married to Jeanne, I thought she didn't mind when I went out on the golf course. But the fact is she really did mind. The way I felt about it was I worked for thirty years and made enough money for everybody, Jeanne and my seven kids, and I was entitled to play a little golf. What do actors do when they're through working if they don't play a little tennis or golf? You've got to do something. What should I do? I've done everything. I've made all the money I want. Where am I going?"

He seemed to be going to the nearest pretty girl who didn't object to his spending so much time on the golf links—at least until she nailed him with a marriage license.

In the years immediately preceding his divorce, Dean's name was linked romantically with several prominent young beauties, and speculation was rife in the Hollywood rumor factories that he and Jeanne would soon be settling their differences in a divorce court.

Once in 1968, when Dean was constantly being seen in the company of a young girl singer, gossip columnist Joyce Haber phoned Jeanne and asked her if it was true that her husband was leaving her for another woman. "I don't know yet," replied Jeanne, a bit wearily. "Dean can't make up his mind which age group he's interested in."

Another one of the things Dean couldn't make up his mind about was where he was living. One time he'd be home. Another time he'd be checking into the Beverly Hills Hotel for a few weeks. During another period he was renting a house separate from Jeanne's on Loma Vista Drive in Beverly Hills's Trusdale estates.

Among the girls Dean didn't marry but who received considerable attention from him were Catherine Deneuve, the French actress and model, and Gail Renshaw, a twenty-two-year-old statuesque blond from Arlington, Virginia, and the 1969 USA entrant in the Miss World beauty contest.

His romance with Gail Renshaw was the first not to be in the mere "infatuation" category, and it carried him to the brink of actual divorce from Jeanne.

Dean and Gail first became aware of each other in the summer of 1969, when he was playing the Hotel Riviera in Las Vegas. On her way to London, where the Miss World contest was to be held, Gail Renshaw stopped off in Vegas to promote the contest. While in the city of silver cartwheels, Gail's manager asked Dean if he would mind posing for some stills with his client. Apprised that his "client" was a beauty contest winner, Dean agreed.

The picture-taking session was very successful—the photos of Miss Renshaw turning out to be exceptionally well developed. The photo session led to dinner, and dinner led to breakfast.

The next thing Jeanne Martin knew was that Dean had asked her for a divorce and had moved into the Beverly Hills Hotel.

After recovering from the shock, Jeanne made the following statement to the press: "I haven't met her. But evidently all the children have. All I know is that he asked for a divorce—which surprised me—but I wouldn't want to live with a man who's not happy with me. I've had twenty marvelous years with him. I'm in good health, and I have no financial problems. He's been very good to me. Now he's free, which is good. Now he can hide—which is what he does best."

The marriage was still on in December 1969, when Dean returned to Las Vegas for the Riviera's fourteenth anniversary celebration, and he brought Gail with him.

For a "private" man, Dean was unusually outspoken about his new romance and impending divorce from Jeanne. In fact, he seemed to be bubbling over with joy as he kidded about his marital status on the stage of the Riviera that night. "I didn't have much of a luggage problem getting here," he told the audience at one point. "I found all of mine out on the sidewalk."

Speculation on how Dean and Jeanne would divide up their great wealth was fodder for most of the gossip columnists in those days. Odds-maker Jimmy the Greek was laying ten to one that Jeanne would get $5 million and the Martins' $1.5 million ranch in San Fernando Valley. The ranch was one of the last acquisitions the Martins had made.

In the final years of their marriage, when Jeanne felt that she was losing ground in her battle with all of Dean's hedonistic distractions in the city but was not quite ready to admit she couldn't come out for the next round, she persuaded Dino to buy a sixty-three-acre hideaway in Hidden Valley —about an hour's drive from Beverly Hills. There, amidst lush pastoral surroundings and great luxury, she hoped at last to be able to inject a little "togetherness" into Dean's way of life.

The ranch had everything a plush resort could offer: a picturesque Spanish-style hacienda ranch house, with terra-cotta floors, modern conveniences, and enough bedrooms (twelve) to keep things from becoming squalid. Its acres of verdant rolling grounds contained a tennis court, an Olympic-sized swimming pool, a pitch-and-putt golf course, stables full of horses (for Dean enjoyed horseback riding), and a helipad to accommodate the family helicopter.

Dean couldn't stand long automobile drives, so, despite his aversion to elevators, he relied upon a helicopter to whisk him back and forth between NBC and the Hidden Valley ranch or to the airport to catch a jet to Vegas.

The ranch had just about everything a man needed to make him content to be with his family—except the woman of his choice. Soon Jeanne and the children were making frequent use of the place while Dino was practicing "togetherness" with Gail Renshaw.

When the property settlement with Jeanne became an important hitch in Dean's marriage plans, he started cracking jokes about that touchy subject too in his act. "I read in the newspapers that Jeanne might get the ranch," drawled Dean in one part of his monologue. "Well, that's all right with me. I never could find the place, anyway."

In March, four months after they had decided to marry, Dean and Gail suddenly called the whole thing off. According to intimates, he'd simply grown tired of her. But Jeanne still wasn't getting her man back.

Between March and June, Dean's wandering eye settled on another blond beauty—twenty-four-year-old Catherine Mae Hawn, a divorcée with a young child, who was a receptionist at Gene Shacove's ultra chic beauty shop in Beverly Hills.

The pair were introduced by Mort Viner, Dean's business manager, who, to judge by the fast results, was as efficient at playing cupid as he was at handling Dean's money. It was apparently love at first sight between Dino and Cathy. Their love, however, had to travel a long and bumpy road—and one full of obstacles put there by Jeanne—before they finally reached the altar.

When Dean and Gail Renshaw's romance was in first flower and the possibility of divorce first arose, Jeanne had issued the following statement through her attorney, Arthur Manella: "My husband informed me that he had met and fallen in love with someone, and he asked me for a divorce. I have assured him I will comply with his wishes. Proceedings will begin immediately."

But after Dean and Gail broke up and Dean fell in love with Cathy Hawn, Jeanne wasn't willing to be quite such a good sport about it. Perhaps in the back of her mind was the thought that Cathy probably wouldn't last any longer than Gail had. A man who could fall in and out of love so quickly probably didn't know what was best for him or what he really wanted anyway. Well, Jeanne felt she knew what was best for him: Jeanne.

She fought back with the only means usually open to a woman in her circumstances: to prolong the financial settlement by throwing as many obstacles in the lovers' paths as possible (while still "wishing them well" publicly).

And so the divorce and remarriage were held up for nearly three years while their lawyers—they were using the same legal firm headed by Arthur Manella—wrangled over how to divvy up, in a fair and equitable manner, the spoils of twenty-three years of wedded life.

There was plenty to divide up: about $26 million in cash, the home in Beverly Hills, two large ranches—one in Hidden Valley worth about $1.5 million and another one in Solvang, California—community-property income from Dean's pictures and records, and numerous other assets.

In the beginning, it looked as if there wouldn't be any problem with the settlement since both Dean and Jeanne were using the same lawyers and Jeanne had expressed a willingness to cooperate. So, through their lawyers, Dean and Jeanne decided they would not actually file for a divorce until the financial negotiations were complete.

Each time a settlement seemed imminent, a new date was set for filing, and a new date was set for the wedding. And each time a marriage date was set, the negotiations fell apart. For two years this went on—until Cathy began to doubt Dean's intentions. Who could tell with a man like Dean? Finally Cathy pressed the issue. Was he really going to marry her or was the same thing going to happen to her that happened to Gail Renshaw and probably a number of other girls?

To prove his good intentions, Dean himself filed for a divorce from Jeanne on Valentine's Day, 1972. Both he and his lawyers were confident that he and Jeanne would be able to arrive at a financial agreement very swiftly now and that he would be able to marry Cathy before the year was out. A marriage date was set for October 1.

But sometime between Valentine's Day and October Jeanne became concerned about the amount of money Dean was apparently spending on Cathy. According to Jeanne's calculations, in a short period of 1972 Dean spent about $314,000 for his personal affairs and another $500,000 to buy a mansion in Bel Air on Copa de Oro Road. Since Cathy and her young daughter by her first marriage were living in the new manse, it seemed reasonable to assume that the enormous outlay of cash was going for her and her child's upkeep.

That didn't set too well with Jeanne. Nickels and dimes expended for a drink at the Polo Lounge or possibly a new fur didn't really matter. But $814,000 was coming directly out of the family kitty, of which Jeanne owned half according to the community-property laws. That started Jeanne thinking that perhaps Dean was spending all that money *before* the divorce so there would be less in the family till to divide up after a settlement was finally agreed upon.

Worried about this situation, Jeanne decided not to use Dean's lawyer and hired a separate divorce attorney, Eugene Wyman, to investigate the property settlement more thoroughly. After Wyman started digging into the Martins' financial affairs, the Dino-Cathy marriage had to be postponed again—this time until February 1973.

Cathy was understandably upset, and suspicious of Dean's motives too. "Do you know how hard it is to love someone? To wait and be patient day after day?" she complained to a magazine reporter at the time of the second postponement. "After a while it just didn't make sense to me. Maybe I lost myself, maybe I acted crazy, but that night I asked Dean, 'Do you still want to marry me or not? Or are you just using all these legal tactics as a way out?' "

Afraid of losing her, Dean asked Jeanne to give him a divorce immediately. He assured her that they could work out the details of the property settlement *after* he and Cathy were married. But Jeanne, with an eye open to all possibilities, wasn't buying that line. She felt that if "Dean's new marriage broke up, there could be two ex-wives at the counsel table arguing over assets."

Good business lady that she is, Jeanne held out for the best deal, which came through right after Valentine's Day, 1973. When columnist Joyce Haber questioned Dean about the settlement, he responded by saying grumpily, "Someone said I only settled $1.5 million on Jeanne. I gave away $6.5 million!" It was not all cash, of course. Part of the $6.5 million is in the two ranches and her home on Mountain Drive. But real estate is better than cash anyway these days.

They say that a love forced to travel a bumpy road is the best kind. If that is the case, then Dean and Cathy ought to live happily ever after.

The marriage date was set for April 24, 1973. But, three weeks before, Dean was suddenly stricken with an ulcer attack and had to undergo serious stomach surgery in Los Angeles's Midway Hospital.

Cathy went through a few anxious days wondering if the wedding would have to be postponed again. But Dean refused to jilt her at the altar for the "umpteenth" time and vowed to show up to say "I do" even if he had to be carried down the aisle on a stretcher.

One of Dean's gag writers commented, "Dean would never have to postpone the wedding on account of ulcers. He could always have sent the guy who stands in for him at our TV rehearsals to go through the ceremony for him. He could have watched it on a monitor."

Fortunately, it never came to that. Dean pulled himself together for the wedding. After waiting all those years, Catherine Mae Hawn wasn't going to be satisfied with any old wedding.

Her and Dean's living room in their Bel Air mansion was turned into a veritable chapel, with dark oak pews borrowed from a movie studio, an altar flanked with an all-white array of French lilacs, tulips, and roses, a fifteen-branch candelabra, and a garden trellis laced with lilies of the valley to cover the aisle.

About 100 of their most intimate friends were present, but no newspaper people. Frank Sinatra was the best man and Cathy's six-year-old daughter, Sasha, was a flower girl. All seven of Dean's children were there too. But, unhappily, neither his mother and father nor his brother Bill lived to witness the splendor of Dino Paul Crocetti's third wedding. However, if Mama and Papa Crocetti were looking down from heaven, they would have had to be impressed with the opulence of the affair. Could that handsome, splendidly dressed fellow marrying Cathy Mae Hawn in that Bel Air mansion down below really be the same Dean Paul Crocetti who people back in Steubenville were once wagering would wind up in the electric chair?

Cathy made her entrance down the house's carved winding staircase, which had been garlanded with hundreds of dollars worth of white flowers and lots of greenery. Cathy was carrying among her bouquet of lilies of the valley the first cutting of a new rose called Sonia, which matched exactly the flesh color of her Aghayan-Mackie Jean Harlowish dress.

The bridegroom was dressed in a black suit, white shirt, and light-colored tie, and he looked surprisingly healthy and happy for a fifty-five-year-old man going to the altar for the third time.

After the groom kissed the bride, there was a reception for eighty-five in the Crystal Room of the Beverly Hills Hotel to which the press was invited. The Crystal Room had been completely redecorated for the occasion. It contained full-size trees, hedges of gardenias, and cages full of white doves hanging from the ceiling.

If *The Los Angeles Times* is to be believed, the hotel's food man, Peter Korzilius, had been making preparations for the blowout since the preceding November, when he got the inspiration for the menu sitting outside the famous Coq Hardi restaurant in Paris. (How he knew Jeanne was going to let the divorce go through at that time Korzilius didn't explain.)

The assistant chef had spent five days in the freezer molding the names of Dean Martin and Catherine Mae Hawn into a massive ice sculpture of hearts and cherubs.

The buffet included such delicacies as paté of hare, galantine of pheasant and poularde chaudfroid with breast of capon Jeanette, mountain trout stuffed with lobster mousse, and lobster, shrimp, Little Neck clams, and Blue Point oysters, plus beef Wellington, assorted cheeses, Dean's favorite beluga caviar, which sells for $190 a pound (before the devaluation of the dollar), and Dom Perignon, at $33 a bottle.

Dean had acquired some pretty expensive tastes since the days when he was rooming with Lou Perry. But he could afford all the caviar and Dom Perignon he wanted now.

He had just finished putting his name on a contract with MGM calling for him to make one picture a year and to play six weeks annually at MGM's lavish new Grand Hotel in Las Vegas. The MGM brass didn't announce the exact terms but indicated it was a three-year multimillion-dollar contract, and one of the biggest ever given an entertainer.

One of the minor benefits of the new deal was that Dean would receive a super-superstar salary of $150,000 a week for his nightclub stint. For this he was expected to do two shows a night, according to the custom in Las Vegas.

Prior to the new affiliation, Dino had been tied to a long-term contract with the Riviera, of which he had been part owner. But when they insisted he put on two performances a night, he took a walk and hasn't appeared there since 1971.

Technically, they still owned him when he went with MGM, but the Riviera agreed to let him out of his contract if he would do two shows a night at the Grand Hotel. They did this because the Riviera didn't want to start a precedent with other performers; if Dean got away with one show a night at the Grand, they would have to give the same deal to everyone else. They felt it was worth losing him to keep that precedent from being established.

Although it had been some thirty-five years since Dino had spurned his first offer to sing with a band, the pattern of his success hadn't changed. As a reward for breaking his contract with the Riviera, he had lucked into something a great deal better. If nice and easy didn't do it *every* time, it certainly did it a lot of the time.

Like a fine wine, Dean Martin's life and career have improved with age. He has everything: a fat new contract and a wonderful family, including seven children of his own, six grandchildren, a stepdaughter whom he adores, and a brand new beautiful young wife.

So what if Cathy is a little young for him? At least he has the sense of humor to kid about it. Shortly before their marriage, he once broke away from a business meeting by saying, "Well, excuse me now, I have to run along and burp my girl."

24

Laugh Clown, Laugh

Just down the street from where the wedding took place, in the same verdant section of Bel Air—only on St. Cloud Road instead of Copa de Oro—and close enough to hear the wedding march, if he'd been home, which he seldom is these days, because he's busy running around the world trying to scratch out a living in nightclubs and doing talk shows, lives Jerry Lewis. Jerry is still married to Patti, who is a bit plumpish now, with silver-gray hair and a perpetual expression of weariness on her face —no doubt from trying to keep track of her whirlwind husband for thirty years. She's still attractive, however, and is adored by everyone who knows her.

Four of the Lewises' six children still live at home: Scott, eighteen; Christopher, seventeen; Anthony, fifteen; and Joseph, fourteen. But Gary and Ronnie, twenty-nine and twenty-three years old, respectively, are mature young men and have their own residences.

For a short time, Gary owned his own house in west Los Angeles and was married to a charming Filipino girl named Sarah Jane, who made him a father in his own right in 1968, when she gave birth to a beautiful little daughter. This blessed event made Jerry and Patti first-time grandparents, a role the two of them enjoy.

Careerwise, Gary seemed to have a promising future too. Following in the footsteps of Dean Martin, Jr., Gary started out to be a rock musician —a drummer—and he was doing very well at it. He had his own rock group called the Playboys, and they made records and got a lot of bookings around Los Angeles.

But tragedy struck the Lewis family when Gary was drafted and sent to Vietnam. He returned from the war unharmed physically, but he paid a heavy toll emotionally after seeing two of his buddies wiped out before his eyes by enemy fire.

Commenting on that traumatic experience in an interview with *The Chicago Sun-Times* in 1971, Jerry lamented,

> "I sent a son into the service who was twenty years old and of such perfectness, a humanitarian, a young guy who cared and was considerate—was all the things we would like everyone to be. Productive. Creative. Talented. He came back totally devoid of any feelings or emotions. He just doesn't give a damn about anything any more. When I sit him down and say, 'You've got to try to get your head back where it was,' he says, 'Why?' "

In 1972, Gary was picked up in Van Nuys, California, on a charge of possession of dangerous drugs. He was later cleared, but his wife divorced him.

Jerry has never quite gotten over what the war did to his first son, the son he loves so much. In fact, until the Vietnam war ended, Jerry was such an outspoken critic of America's military involvement that he was even threatening for a time to move his entire family to Switzerland to avoid donating any more of his sons to the draft.

Gary has been just one of the albatrosses weighing Jerry Lewis down lately.

His parents are both alive and living in a chic apartment house in Miami, which Jerry is paying for. But in recent years Danny has been the victim of several violent strokes that have made him an invalid. When he is not confined to his metal hospital bed, he can only get around with a wheelchair.

Things haven't been going well on the professional front for Jerry either in recent years. In fact, one might say his show business career has been somewhat of a disaster—at least compared with what it once was.

When Jerry left Paramount—by mutual consent—he moved his Jerry Lewis Productions to Columbia. Under the Columbia aegis he ground out three more pictures of the caliber that caused Paramount to lose interest in retaining him: *Three on a Couch*, *The Big Mouth*, and *Don't Raise the Bridge, Lower the River*.

Jerry was striving for "sophisticated" comedy in the latter three, but sophistication wasn't his cup of orange pekoe at all. Even his "young" audience stayed away when Jerry played "drawing room" comedy, as he attempted to do clumsily in *Three on a Couch*—a mixed-up unfunny yarn that was supposed to be a satire on psychiatry.

No doubt the inspiration for the psychiatry story sprang from Jerry's sessions on the couch. Although his friends and family had been recommending it for years, psychiatry was probably the last thing to which a man of Jerry's enormous self-confidence and ego would ever succumb. But, ten years after his split with Dean, his troubles—both businesswise and personal—were starting to pile up at such a fast clip that even a man of his resiliency found he couldn't bounce back without some outside assistance. And so he took his family's advice and started seeing a psychiatrist.

One day during this period, Jerry bumped into Don McGuire on the street. The two hadn't talked since their bitter parting. Jerry evidently felt guilty about it still, and, in an effort to show that he was turning over a new leaf, he said to McGuire, "Guess what, Don? I'm going to a psychiatrist now."

"No kidding!" exclaimed McGuire, impressed with the change in his former boss.

"Yeah," said Jerry, "but I'm just bullshitting him."

In 1967, NBC decided to give Jerry another crack at network television, but no ad-libbing this time. He was to use a script like everyone else and hire good writers to put funny things into his mouth. One of those good writers was Ed Simmons, who needed the job as much as Jerry needed to prove that bygones were bygones and that he was a changed man. (Psychiatry *had* helped.)

On the Friday he was to tape his first show of the new season, which had as guest stars Sonny and Cher and Lynn Redgrave, Jerry parked his Rolls Royce in the NBC parking lot and went inside to rehearse. When he came out, he found that some jokester had hung a sign on the back of his Rolls that read,

BAN THE BOMB BEFORE IT GOES OFF

In bygone days, it would have been Jerry who would have hung a sign like that on somebody else's car—the "fun" days around Paramount when a person could, with impunity, tape a secretary to her desk, cut off Ernie Glucksman's tie, and tell a ninety-year-old man to "go out for a short one" and then belt him with a football.

But in 1967 there wasn't much of that "anything for a laugh" spirit left in Jerry. He was over forty now, he was putting on a little weight, and he had troubles at home. On top of everything else, Dean Martin, who was rehearsing in the studio across the corridor, had a big hit television show, already starting its third season. It was a tension-filled period for Jerry—just working in the same building with Dean made him nervous.

Ed Simmons remembers a meeting between the two former partners in the corridor one day. Jerry was walking one way, Dean the other. As they passed, each smiled thinly and nodded "Hi," then continued on. "It was not a historic occasion," recalls Simmons.

Dean didn't fear Jerry's competition. He wished him well publicly. Before the end of his first show of the 1967 season, Dean told the television audience, "Don't forget to watch Jerry Lewis next week," and then he went into his theme song, "Everybody Loves Somebody Sometime," which was written by his piano player on the show, Ken Lane.

Jerry's show wasn't a "bomb" in the sense that the ABC fiasco was. Although its ratings weren't spectacular, NBC kept it on the air for two seasons. But it just couldn't capture an audience, no matter how hard Jerry worked.

Whereas Dean was hardly rehearsing at all—in fact, for one six-week period he was flying in from Las Vegas to do his show and then flying right out again—Jerry was arriving at NBC every morning at 7:00 to begin work. He was the same eager beaver he'd always been, and he was following the same pattern of wanting to do everything.

"It got so that finally he was putting such obstacles in your path that you couldn't write anything," recalls Simmons. Simmons had a yearly contract with Jerry calling for $50,000 a season. But it finally became so difficult to work for Jerry that he walked into producer Bob Finkel's office one day at the beginning of the second season and said to him and Jerry, "This is it, fellows. Tear up my contract. I'm not working here any more. You don't have to pay me what you owe me. Just let me out."

NBC dropped the show at the end of the second season. By then, Jerry was completely disillusioned with television. In an interview with *The New York Times*, Jerry Lewis, the pundit, said,

> Television has been one of the most destructive forces in our society. Ask me about violence, and I'll tell you television has caused it. I maintain that if a man sees a killing in the news, it may trigger off a sick mind. Sirhan Sirhan would never have carried a gun if he had not seen the way Jack Ruby shot Lee Harvey Oswald in a crowded corridor. I don't want to suppress news, but if I were in control, I would suppress *visualizing* it.
>
> And television has made everything commonplace. When Cary Grant used to walk down a street in New York, the city was on fire with excitement. Nowadays it wouldn't mean a thing. Television destroys dreams. It makes everything real.

As for the reason he could never be "great" on TV, he said,

> I knew I was going to be part of twenty hours of trash that would never be seen again. Psychologically I couldn't put very much into it. The temporary nature of television destroyed me. Essentially, I always have in mind that my great-great-great grandchildren will see me in my pictures, that I have to be impeccable for *them*. There is no way they can see me on television. Thank God! And I hated the

endless hypocrisy, and lying, the crap, the stopwatch. My funny bone has no time for statistics. I couldn't bear the clock dictating when I would start and finish a joke. And the censorship—network censors are stupid, anticreative men. What those stupid morons don't understand is that when you're given freedom, you don't abuse it.

I ran into trouble on an ABC show I did. The Southern network affiliates told me, "You don't need to let everybody know you're a Jew, do you?" And they also said, "You don't have to have niggers on, do you?" Well, I told them, "Yes, I do." I went ahead and had a black on every one of the thirteen shows after that. So I lost a $38 million contract. One reason my lawyers have ulcers is I've taken such stands.

Jerry may have been a failure on TV in his last two outings, but he was still sure he knew what the public wanted, so he foolishly allowed his name to be used to front a film-distributing organization known officially as Network Cinema Corporation and unofficially as the Jerry Lewis Mini-Cinema Company.

The purpose of the company was to build a chain of "minitheaters" through the South and the eastern seaboard, franchise them out to "Ma and Pa"–type people anxious to get involved in movie exhibition, and supply the franchise holders with "G"-rated family pictures only.

It was Jerry's reasoning, based upon all his years in show business, that the average moviegoer was fed up with the smut and "X"-rated films that were flooding the country's larger picture houses and that the only reason the dirty pictures were doing business was because there weren't enough "clean" pictures to see.

Jerry overestimated the public, however, and the Jerry Lewis minitheater operation ran into immediate trouble for several reasons. To begin with, picturegoers weren't really as interested in seeing only "G"-rated films as Jerry had imagined. At any rate, there weren't enough who didn't dig "filth" to keep the company solvent. In addition, there weren't enough "G"-rated films being made to keep the theater running, and consequently some of them started throwing in "X"-rated product, which was against Jerry's policy.

Last of all—and this was one of the biggest problems—most of the franchise holders weren't giving the parent company an honest accounting of their grosses, so even if they did business, the stockholders were losing out.

By 1973, the whole minitheater operation was tottering on the brink of bankruptcy. When this condition became known, a series of suits and countersuits followed, involving charges of fraud and antitrust violations, brought about by both franchise holders and the Network Cinema Corporation.

Jerry himself suffered the crowning humiliation. As he walked off the stage of the Deauville Hotel one Saturday night in 1973, after doing his nightclub act, he was served with papers naming him and Network Cinema as the defendants in a $3 million suit. Jerry was charged with fraud, misrepresentation, and various violations of the antitrust laws. His defense was that he wasn't actually an "officer" of his company and therefore couldn't be held accountable. He couldn't extricate himself that easily, however.

The many claims and allegations against Network Cinema haven't all been settled as of this writing. All that's known is that many people lost a great deal of money (including Jerry) trying to foist "G"-rated pictures on an unwilling public.

In the final analysis, minitheaters proved to be the worst catastrophe in the franchise business since Minnie Pearl lost her shirt in her fried chicken batter.

But the indomitable Jerry Lewis couldn't be kept down for long. While Jerry was dodging subpoenas, he came across a novel called *The Day the Clown Cried* written by a woman writer named Joan O'Brien. It was the story of a clown named Helmut who lived in Germany during the Nazi regime.

Helmut had once been internationally famous as a circus clown, but because of his egotistical thinking and his callous attitude toward others he finally destroyed his own career. When he made a public statement maligning the state, the Nazis put him in a forced labor camp. Behind a fence were forty children—all Jews—waiting to be put to death in the gas ovens.

The Germans used Helmut to perform for the children and keep them quiet while they were waiting to be executed. When their turn to die finally came, the job of leading them into the gas ovens fell upon Helmut. Acting as their Pied Piper, he led the way, singing, joking, and dancing, to keep them from realizing they were walking their "last mile."

All his life Jerry had avoided making message pictures. He believed, as the late Fred Allen quipped, that "messages should be left to Western Union." But, after encountering failure with the usual Jerry Lewis fare the last three or four times he went to the post, Jerry decided to give his fans a change of pace.

Because the part of Helmut was basically a dramatic role, Jerry saw in this story an opportunity not only to demonstrate how versatile an actor he was but also to do something for humanity, which might just please the critics and get them off his back for a change.

In *The Day the Clown Cried*, Jerry wanted to show "how selfish we are all becoming and that we must get back to being kind to each other.

I've shown it through the central figure of the clown. Here is this selfish thoughtless man who has tried all his life to make people laugh but who is at heart a cold egotist. These children in the prison camp, he says to himself, 'Who are they?' Why should he descend to entertain them? But as he looks into their eyes, he sees the love they have for him, and he becomes a human being. Their love overwhelms him. Now he is theirs."

If Jerry wanted to reveal to the world something about his own character in *The Day the Clown Cried*, he never stated it directly. But obviously he was striving for a good deal more than just entertaining the public by wanting to turn that cheerful little story line into a major motion picture and himself into a serious actor.

Hollywood was against the project from the start. At the time, Jerry wasn't affiliated with any major studio, and all the town's producers— major and otherwise—that Jerry consulted about the property were afraid of filming a story that critics were sure to label "Fun in a Concentration Camp," especially if Jerry handled the subject as tastefully as he handled most subjects.

So Jerry talked an independent producer named Nat Wachsberger into buying the property and making the picture in Sweden in the winter of 1971. Jerry would star in it and direct; Joan O'Brien would write the screenplay.

CMA made the deal with Joan O'Brien. She was paid $5,000 down and was to receive, at the beginning of "principal photography," an additional $50,000 for writing the screenplay. The picture was two weeks into shooting before Joan O'Brien, who wisely remained in this country, realized she was never going to receive the last $50,000 unless she took the producer to court.

Not only didn't Joan O'Brien ever get paid what was due her but neither did Jerry. Moreover, Wachsberger ran out of "completion money" in the middle of the picture, and Jerry was forced to finance the last week's shooting with his own funds. Perhaps Jerry should have saved his money or at least stuck to making the only thing he knows anything about —comedy.

Jerry, of course, didn't feel that way after completing the picture. To judge from the following statement, he felt he had made some kind of a masterpiece. He said, "The suffering, the hell I went through with Wachsberger, had one advantage. I put all the pain on the screen. If it had been my first picture, the suffering would have destroyed me. But I have had the experience to know how to *use* suffering. I think it's given a new depth to my playing of the clown, Helmut, whose agony is the center of the picture."

After viewing a final print of *The Day the Clown Cried*, its author,

Joan O'Brien, felt it was *her* agony that was the center of the picture. She confided to her agent, Dick Irving Hyland, "It's so bad I wish they'd burn it."

So far, Joan O'Brien hasn't been granted her wish. In fact, Jerry is still very high on the picture, despite having had no luck to date in finding a company willing to release it, which is probably the best thing that's ever happened to his motion picture career, not to mention the film-going public. But with Jerry, it's "never say die," and, at last report, he was back in his cutting room, trying to make something saleable out of *The Day the Clown Cried* and threatening to be his own distributor.

Regardless of the picture's fate—and there are strong hints now that it will never be released—all the major participants are locked in litigation over it, trying to recoup salaries contracted for but never paid.

Because Jerry's finances have always been in a state of considerable confusion and because, according to his business managers, he has always spent more than he has earned, nobody is quite sure whether he is as well fixed after twenty-plus years of earning millions as he deserves to be. There are those who claim he is in trouble; others say if he isn't at present, he soon will be, the way he is heading.

Jerry doesn't get many important job offers any more. After leaving Columbia, Jerry made *Which Way to the Front?* for Warner Brothers–Seven Arts, which was released briefly in 1970. Jerry produced, directed, and starred in this war satire, which had, in addition to its triple-threat star, a blockbuster cast consisting of Jan Murray, Arte Johnson, and Sidney Miller. *Which Way to the Front?* was the last Jerry Lewis picture to be released, and, after seeing it, one won't find it difficult to understand why Jerry isn't very much in demand as a movie star who doubles in producing and directing (and sometimes writing) these days. Jerry, however, refuses to believe it was a bad picture, and blames its failure solely on the fact that Warner Bros. didn't get behind it and publicize it enough.

As for television, a couple of times a year he fills in for Johnny Carson on "The Tonight Show." Occasionally he turns up on talk shows like Merv Griffin's or Mike Douglas's. But he's in about the same demand on the talk-show circuit as are Mort Sahl and Jim Nabors.

Every once in a great while he gets a guest shot on one of the network variety shows, such as last year's "NBC Follies," on which he received "fourth billing" behind Sammy Davis, Jr., Diahann Carroll, and Mickey Rooney. He was mildly funny in a sketch with Sammy Davis and Diahann Carroll in which he played a Jewish butler to a black couple, but it was not the old knock-em-dead, aways confident Jerry Lewis who once, from the stage of a Miami nightclub, told Milton Berle in a torrid ad-libbing duel, "You're an old man, Berle—you're all washed up."

For his guest appearances on network TV, Jerry usually receives what is known in the trade as "top of the show" salary—$7,500, unless a person is a superstar like Dino. That's not bad for a couple of hours' work, but it takes a heap of $7,500s to make as much as Jerry Lewis spends or gives away annually—something in the neighborhood of $1 million, it is rumored.

Jerry is still a loyal and tireless worker for muscular dystrophy of course. On his 1973 telethon, done from the stage of the Sahara Hotel in Las Vegas, Jerry raised, according to the televised tote board, nearly $12 million. But although no one can fault Jerry's intentions, nor the results (if $12 million really came in), Jerry's performance was a tour de force in phony sentimentality and egomania, which evoked a glut of acidulous comments from the TV critics.

The moment in the show that sent NBC's critic John Barbour reaching for his stiletto occurred when Jerry held a sick child up to the camera and told the audience, "God goofed, and it's up to us to correct his mistakes."

God goofed! "Now, not even a militant atheist is as offensive as someone who thinks he is so important he reduces God to a bungling middleman," said Barbour in his TV review the day after the telethon. "No matter how much money was raised, it could probably never find a cure for Jerry Lewis's ego."

Except in the beginning, when the brand-new comedy act of Martin and Lewis was so red-hot they could do no wrong, it's always been "open season" on Jerry Lewis as far as the nation's critics are concerned. But now that Jerry is on the way down, they are even picking on him for exploiting muscular dystrophy.

Perhaps he could have avoided much of this criticism by calling the show "The Muscular Dystrophy Telethon," featuring Jerry Lewis, instead of "The Jerry Lewis Telethon," the less modest approach to charity, but, then again, how else could Jerry Lewis get star billing on a coast-to-coast TV show these days?

His nightclub career is not exactly "sock" any more, either. Few of the larger clubs are interested in booking Jerry Lewis, although in 1973 he did play the Deauville in Miami, and, later in that year, the Conga Room in the Sahara Hotel in Las Vegas, in tandem with Mel Torme.

Neither of those appearances could be called milestones in his long and erratic career. His show at the Deauville was pretty much of a bomb, according to most people who were there. In an article in *Playboy*, Jerry acknowledged this, but blamed the lack of laughs on the fact that his stuff was too "sophisticated" for Miami audiences. They didn't understand him the way they do "in Europe."

He fared better with both the public and the critics in his Las Vegas appearance. He wasn't "held over," but Leonard Feather of the *Los Angeles Times* said that his performance was more "toned-down, and less

verbally outrageous than anything he has done in quite some time . . .
Lewis was 90% hilarious and 10% tasteless—by his standards a high
batting average."

But one of Jerry's former scriptwriters caught the show and later
remarked that he thought the critics were "just being kind."

As a result, Jerry Lewis's nightclub appearances are generally confined
to the peripheral spots like Harrah's, Lake Tahoe, the Tamiment Country
Club in the Pocono Mountains of Pennsylvania, the El Caballero in
Mexico City, and an assortment of places of that ilk in the Catskills,
New Jersey, and even West Germany.

But his days of being the most-sought-after nightclub performer in
America seem to be definitely behind him.

He can't even dust off his old record act and play the 500 Club in
Atlantic City, for on June 10, 1973, while Dean Martin and his new bride
were honeymooning in Europe, the 500 Club burned to the ground.

Selected Bibliography

Allen, Steve. *The Funny Men*. New York: Simon & Schuster, 1956.

Bogdanovich, Peter. "Mr. Lewis Is a Pussycat." *Esquire*, November 1962.

Davidson, Bill. "Anything for a Laugh." *Collier's*, February 10, 1951.

Eells, George. "Dean Martin: The Man Behind the Myths." *Look*, November 8, 1960.

Lewis, Jerry, as told to Bill Davidson. "I've Always Been Scared." *Look*, February 5, 1957.

Lewis, Mrs. Jerry. "I Married a Madman." *American Magazine*, January 1952.

"Make a Million Martin." *Life*, December 22, 1958.

Martin, Pete. "All on Dean Martin." *The Saturday Evening Post*, April 29, 1961.

Taves, Isabella. "Always in a Crowd—Always Alone." *Look*, December 23, 1958.

Wilson, Earl. *The Show Business Nobody Knows*. New York: Cowles, 1971.

Zolotow, Maurice. "The Martin and Lewis Feud." *Cosmopolitan*, October 1955.

Index